Thoughts of
a Reformed
Computer Scientist

On the Nature of Real and
Artificial Intelligence

James H. Morris

Disclaimer: Everything here is true, but it may not be entirely factual. In some cases I have combined events, invented dialog, and changed names. Take what I say with a grain of salt.

Table of Contents

Two Appendixes, Documents, and Nerd Zone can be found at jimmorris.org

Prologue: What is Intelligence?

My story is about intelligence—humans', mine, computer scientists', and computers'.

Like many important concepts—kindness, beauty, happiness, love—intelligence is hard to define. At first, I thought intelligence was getting good grades in school. Later, I encountered intelligence tests, which measured it in ways that left out people with emotional intelligence or "street smarts." Then, and rather disappointingly, I noticed that intelligence tests ignore flowers that seduce bees, chimps that collaborate, and computers that play chess, all of which I believe exhibit a sort of intelligence.

As far back as ancient Greece, mathematical proof has been a way to win arguments intelligently after Euclid invented mathematical proofs in geometry. During the Renaissance, Galileo, Newton, and others added empirical observations as another way to argue.

Then Darwin showed us that the rudimentary intelligence of all living things has developed through evolution, which philosopher Daniel Dennett described as "the single best idea anyone has ever had." I'd never thought much about evolution until my teenaged daughter asked me about it. I began reading,[1] and evolution became the intellectual foundation of my belief system.

---

[1] See Dennett, Dawkins, and Ridley in Readings

In the 1820s Charles Babbage, a mathematician at Cambridge University in England, said, "I wish to God these calculations had been executed by steam," yearning to automate his calculations. He tried to build a computer, but nineteenth century technology wasn't up to it.

In 1936, shortly after graduating from Cambridge, Alan Turing renewed Babbage's quest, but before attempting to build anything, he imagined a ridiculously simple machine that wrote symbols on an expandable recording tape using a set of simple rules, such as "If you're in state S (sort of a mood for a machine) and see a 5 on the tape, replace it with a 7, move one symbol to the right, and enter state T." To use such a machine, you would write some initial symbols, the input, on the tape, position the machine at one of the symbols, and start it. If the machine ever halted, the answer, or output, was whatever was left on the tape.

Turing described a series of increasingly elaborate machines that could perform any numerical operation on integers that anyone could think of. Then, he described a universal machine with a more remarkable capability. As input, it could take the symbolic description of the rules for another machine, along with some input for that machine, and do whatever the other machine would have done, leaving the output as before. The set of symbolic rules became known as a program.

So, Turing invented the concept of programming. He then took a time out to crack all of Germany's communication ciphers during World War II before returning to build a practical, electronic machine that could be programmed more conveniently than a Turing machine.

All computers are more elaborate versions of universal Turing machines and continue to evolve to become more natural to program. The term "computer" was originally used to describe "one who calculates" and later referred to women who were hired to do computations, but in 1945, it was officially used to describe the first devices. A computer's storage is called memory, and an early book about computers, written in 1949, is titled *Giant Brains: or Machines That Think*. So, it seems, that from their birth, computers were thought of anthropomorphically.

Turing was fascinated with the possibility of finding programs that could duplicate human intelligence. In 1950 he proposed a pragmatic way to prove a program was intelligent: Could it convince someone it talked to that it was human by chatting via written messages?

Turing was far from the first to be fascinated by artificial humans. They appear in ancient Greek mythology. Far from settling the question, Turing's invention set off speculations about computers becoming as intelligent as humans—or even more so. Some computer scientists began a project they called Artificial Intelligence (AI), writing programs that simulated all manner of human intelligence. Humans' feelings about this enterprise fluctuate like the seasons of the year.

The foremost advocate of AI was Herbert Simon, who led two generations of computer scientists in the quest. Simon was an atheist who believed that everything in nature could be explained by physics. Having decided that intelligence could be manufactured he launched a movement to prove it and laid the following emotional challenge for the rest of us.

> The definition of man's uniqueness has always formed the kernel of his cosmological and ethical systems. With Copernicus and Galileo, he ceased to be the species located at the center of the universe, attended by sun and stars. With Darwin, he ceased to be the species created and specially endowed by God with soul and reason. With Freud, he ceased to be the species whose behavior was—potentially—governable by rational mind. As we begin to produce mechanisms that think and learn, he has ceased to be the species uniquely capable of complex, intelligent manipulation of his environment.

> I am confident that man will, as he has in the past, find a new way of describing his place in the universe—a way that will satisfy his needs for dignity and for purpose. But it will be a way as different from the present one as was the Copernican from the Ptolemaic.[2]

Whatever its practical uses, computer programming has changed humanity's relations to the physical world. We can now control devices with language rather than physical effort. Until now, humans were the only species that used language, but today we have company—if you're willing to consider computers a new species.

---

[2] *Management of human resources: Readings in personnel administration.* - New York u.a.: McGraw-Hill, ISBN 0-07-050003-7. - 1973, p. 197-219

I: AI Spring 1921-1962

Karel Čapek coins the term "robot" in a play that ends with human extinction.

Kurt Gödel proves there is no algorithm capable of determining the truth of assertions about arithmetic.

The movie *Metropolis* introduces the robot, Maria, who, ironically, inspires workers to destroy machines, in the spirit of the Luddites.

Neurologists McCulloch and Pitts exhibit a computational model using conceptual neurons.

Disney's *Pinocchio* reveals a marionette's desire to become a real boy.

Turing's chess program beats a beginner but loses after twenty-nine moves against a computer expert.

Isaac Asimov, in *I, Robot*, introduces three laws of robotics, prioritizing human welfare.

Allen Newell and Herbert Simon write a program that proves theorems in logic.

John McCarthy coins the term Artificial Intelligence.

A nerd's brain is the most sexiest thing on this planet. – Suru

1.   A Nerd is Born

The two-year-old was lying face down on the white tiled bathroom floor, beating his head on it.

"Don't pick him up, Mother," the mother said to the grandmother. "It will only encourage him."

At which point the little boy stood up, walked out to the hallway, where a soft rug covered the floor, and resumed beating his head. The two women laughed, and when they told the story to my Yale-educated grandfather he said, "That's the first sign of intelligence I've seen from that kid!"

My family revered intelligence. *Doesn't yours?* My mother, grandmother, as well as *her* mother and mother-in-law, had all gone to college—a rarity in those days.

My mother, Gretchen Morris, was born in 1916, the second and gentler of two daughters. Though my grandparents were not pleased when she married a Catholic college dropout, they got over it when he fathered their only grandson—me. My father, James H. Morris, Sr., was born in 1911, the fourth of five. His father died when he was two, but thankfully his small but fierce mother was supported by her wealthy in-laws who encouraged proper education.

In 1937 my parents met playing golf. My mother had just won the Women's Golf Championship of Western Pennsylvania and graduated with honors in chemistry from Vassar. My father was selling road equipment for an uncle's company.

When I was two years old, he left for two years of naval duty. World War II sent him off to an island where he lived a sailor's life as depicted in *South Pacific*. At a local saloon, he befriended some cannibalistic Aborigines of the New Hebrides Islands who couldn't understand why the US and Japan were fighting a war when neither needed food or women. My father once remarked that he might have stayed there were it not for us.

I was lovingly raised by my mother. With my father away, my upbringing was her primary project, and her nurturing was backed up by two doting grandmothers and several female cousins. She read to me, sent me outside every day for some exercise, and supervised my education. She wanted me to be intelligent and called me "the brain" at a young age. She was always amused when she asked what I was doing and I would answer, "I'm thinking." She also occasionally said, "I just want you to be *normal*," so much so that I somehow thought that I was weird. In fact, my family and many people I would meet were in the 12 percent of humanity recently called WEIRD: Western, Educated, Industrialized, Rich, and Democratic.[3]

---

[3] See Heinrich in Readings

Paul Simon's Loves *Me Like a Rock* speaks to me when he asserts that his mother's love makes him impervious to the Devil, the US Congress, or any other threat.

An only child, I'd had the exclusive attention of my mother, and when my father returned from war, an Oedipal struggle ensued that lasted until the day I cut my hand on some broken glass while roaming the neighborhood. I came home crying, and my father scooped me up and took me to his navy base dispensary for two stitches and a tetanus shot—administered without warning, to a chorus of laughs, from behind! I liked the attention of the jolly doctors, but more importantly, that was the day I believed my father cared for me. He might be tough, but he took care of me when I needed it. One day, he came home with a gift for me, a machine that printed checks, unneeded at his office. Naturally, I took it apart using whatever tools I could find. That made him angry. *Did he expect a four-year-old to use it to print checks?* My takeaway: *Don't mess with hardware.*

When the war ended in 1945, we moved into our cozy apartment in Pittsburgh, a building called the Gabel, named after my great-grandfather who built it on the family farm in 1900. The backyard of the Gabel was huge. I spent my days wandering around the yard, stopping by the mint patches to pick the leaves that I like to munch on, or running around with my cousins and constant playmates, Barbara and Joanne, who lived in another apartment in the Gabel with my mother's sister and her husband.

My parents sent me to kindergarten a half block from the Gabel to the Ellis School for girls, which allowed about one-quarter boys, but only in kindergarten. I was gentle and well-behaved, and the only time I was sent to the window seat for a time-out, I had been framed by another guy. I was sent to first grade at Mount Mercy, a mostly girls' Catholic school, where I met my nemesis, Tom Feeny. Big, rich, and good-looking, he had established himself as the alpha male by bringing a dollar to school for lunchtime candy, while I only got a dime. I couldn't match him, but maybe I could be smarter in school.

Just as my Catholic education began, I learned that there was no Santa Claus. That inoculated me from the idea of an old man with a white beard who watched and rewarded us. The seven deadly sins—pride, greed, wrath, envy, lust, gluttony, and sloth—just sounded like bad habits. The nuns told us that the Communion wafer we ate was the body of Christ and that we would be transported. I waited but felt no kick.

Third grade was a new school, (the neighborhood parochial school) also run by nuns, but several rungs down the social scale—and 50 percent boys, including Skip Kelly who had been at Mount Mercy with me. Now the pecking order was based on fighting, not wealth, and I was far from the toughest kid. I washed out of the choir but became an enthusiastic altar boy, which, if anything, diminished any sense of religious wonder I might have had.

Here is a class picture with me on the right end of the middle row and Kelly at the left end.

Aside from the three Rs and large doses of religion I learned about hierarchical structure through sentence diagramming. Here is a diagram of the first sentence of the US Constitution.

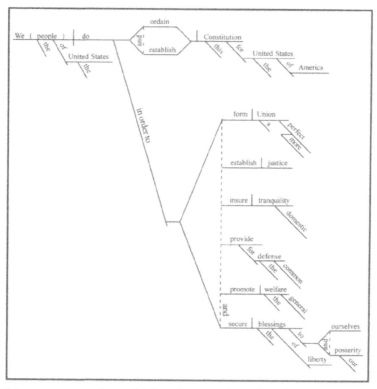

This was a profound idea for grade school: a sentence was a tree structure of words that could be deepened without bound, other than a reader's ability to digest it.

My parents had begun rewarding me with quarters for each A on a report card and encouraged athletics— swimming, softball, and basketball. I sometimes caddied for my mother on their golf outings. Mercifully, she put her clubs in a lightweight bag for me to carry. My father provided me with innumerable toy soldiers, books about West Point, and a few cross-state trips to army-navy games. He was prepping me for a military career. On one of our father-son trips, I heard him tell my mother afterwards that he had been so happily engaged with me that he hadn't had a drink from the bottle of bourbon he had packed in his suitcase.

However, my eyesight problems precluded any of my father's hopes for West Point. I was color blind—something a nun discovered when I drew purple skies in the first grade—and I had an astigmatism with strabismus, which is the failure of the eyes to coordinate for stereoscopic vision. I spent a few years going to weekly sessions in which a doctor had me look into a device showing a bird to my left eye and a cage to my right. Only rarely could I put the bird in the cage. I'd like to think this apparent disability gave me unique perspectives. My right eye, which connected to my left, verbal, and rational brain was the dominant eye. My left eye, which connected to my right, intuitive, and emotional brain was the lazy one. I had two brains pursuing two different lives! If I was going to excel at something, it had to be brains.

On many occasions my parents would tell me, "You've got it made!" I didn't grasp what they meant until I understood that they had lived through prohibition, depression, and war, and they felt that they had created a better world for me.

My father preferred that I go to a Catholic high school but gave way to my mother's desire to send me to Shady Side Academy, the local school for rich boys, where her father had gone. On the school bus the first day, I was happy to see Carl Srodes, a neighborhood friend. We'd met playing basketball at a local playground. He was a very good basketball player.

With its Georgian buildings, Shady Side looked like a small New England college transported to the Fox Chapel suburb of gritty Pittsburgh. When the teacher called the roll on the first day, a noisy kid named Sandy Schumacher didn't stop chattering with his friends. I waited for the teacher to send Sandy to the principal's office, but nothing happened! *Shady Side is like summer camp! Anything goes.*

My father was pleased when I started playing freshman football. He related that his high school team liked to play Shady Side early in their season, so they could steal some equipment. Rich kids were careless with their equipment.

In the pecking order of football teams, the offensive backfield talent comes first, followed by the defensive backfield, where Srodes played. Next came linemen like me and a tall, rangy guy named Gus Schroeder. At the bottom was the team water boy, a slight kid named Jay Carson. Those three became my best friends. Tom Feeny, of course, was far above the entire team because he played in the varsity backfield as a freshman.

My friends thought I was smart and funny, and our small gang grew. We started raising fourteen-year-old hell. My sophomore year, we stayed overnight in a local hotel, trashed the room, stole some stuff, and left without paying. The hotel later sent the bill to my father, who got me to confess, rounded up my friends, and took us to the hotel to return what we had stolen and apologize. Another evening, after a football game, Carson, Srodes, Schroeder, Schumacher, Kelly, and I damaged someone's house trying to crash a teenage party. That someone was an irascible lawyer who called Shady Side's headmaster along with the police. We were nearly kicked out of school but ended up on probation. When my father drove me to the lawyer's house for the obligatory apology he said, "If he offers you a coke, come and get me, and I'll come in for a drink."

I had absorbed two life lessons from my father: *Being a teenage gangster is OK.* He rarely seemed angry with me and told my mother, somewhat proudly, that I was "probably the ringleader." *Take responsibility for my misdeeds*, which was perhaps a Catholic thing.

He had a health scare that same fall, prompting my mother to insist we move to a suburb nearer to his business. It was the first time my parents owned their own house. I began boarding at Shady Side.

***

It was Friday, February 15, 1957. The sun was streaming in through the tall, clear windows of Shady Side's chapel as we were finishing the Protestant service with a hymn when the headmaster announced, "I need to see Jim Morris."

My friends gave me the *look*.

What have I done now? I had really been enjoying my time at Shady Side and didn't want it to end. The short, rotund headmaster escorted me across the lawn towards the red brick main building. *This may be my last day here.*

"Your father was taken sick last night," he said. "Your aunt and uncle are here to take you home."

They were standing in his office. They avoided looking me in the eyes. They led me to the car in silence. It was not until we were driving out of the lush Fox Chapel suburb that I realized, *My father is dead!* I wished one of them had the nerve to tell me. I started to cry, silently. Immediately, I felt guilty and frustrated. He was forty-five. I was fifteen. *I wish we hadn't just quarreled last week.* I felt terrible that it was our last time together. It felt unfinished. My mother imagined that my father would have become my golfing and drinking buddy. That was not to be.

That night I was woken by my mother's crying. I got up to comfort her.

"I just want to be loved," she said, sobbing into my hug.

Holy shit! I'm not prepared for this.

In a matter of days, I went back to school, my mother took over my father's business, and my father went from being my adversary to my role model.

As my classmates began reaching out to me, I became particularly close to my friend Carson. One Sunday afternoon at his house, I was making a phone call, when Carson wordlessly placed a bottle of Ballantine XXX Ale in front of me. My first bottle of beer gave me a feeling of release—of my left brain letting my right brain drive a little. The second bottle sent me over the moon. More powerful than any feeling I'd experienced from the various religious rituals Catholicism had offered.

I became one of the class's leading beer drinkers—along with Carson and Schroeder. Beer was an excellent solution to my problem: how a hardworking, shy kid could be the life of the party (like his father). A potion to turn me into Jackie Gleason! I started smoking cigarettes too. Everyone else was. Tenth grade. Smoking, drinking, and learning how to prove Euclidean geometry theorems in the special advanced math class I had been placed in.

My math teacher drew a triangle on the board.

"Show that if the line AB is equal to AC then the angle at B is the same as the one at C," he challenged us.

"Isn't it obvious?" I asked, beginning to draw on the chalkboard. "Here are some more examples."

"If you measure the lines and angles of each, you will see that it's true for the first three triangles but not for the fourth."

"OK, examples like that are fine in science class, but this is math class, and we must prove things beyond doubt," the teacher said.

Anyone who watches lawyers on TV grasps the difference between something being true, but not being provable beyond a reasonable doubt. A *theorem* in mathematics must be proved beyond any *un*-reasonable doubt. Euclid started with a few theorems called *axioms* that nobody disputed, such as "If two figures are congruent (one can be shifted, rotated, and possibly reflected to coincide with the other) then all their corresponding angles are equal." An early theorem is the SAS rule: *If two sides of a triangle and the angle in between them are equal then the triangles are congruent.*

Once I'd accepted this game, I found it easier than a lot of other math problems, because there were only so many moves possible. If I got stuck I could try reasoning backwards.

A few days later I came up with this proof to satisfy the teacher's challenge.

Statement	Justification
1. Sides BA = AC	Given
2. Angles A = A	Obvious, the "reflexive property"
3. Sides CA = AB	Given
4. Triangle BAC is congruent to CAB (its own reflection!)	SAS Rule using 1, 2, and 3
5. Angles B = C	Corresponding parts of congruent triangles are equal, using 4.

QED[4]

Proving your first theorem is a mathematician's rite of passage, and nerds remember the event, sort of like the first sex act for everyone else.[5] Surveys show that most students hated geometry, and the ones that don't end up being professors.

I was proud of my newfound skill at proving things. Little did I know that a few blocks from my home, someone was creating a thinking machine that could match my talent.

***

In the fall of 1957, a week before my sixteenth birthday, the headlines screamed "Russians in Space!" announcing the success of Sputnik. *I can become a scientist to compensate for*

---

[4] QED stands for the mathematicians triumphant *quod erat demonstrandum* meaning "which was to be shown"

[5] Virgil Gligor, personal communication

failing to go to West Point! I redoubled my efforts in chemistry class and looked forward to physics. Meanwhile, a vocational test suggested I become an accountant, which horrified me.

Equipped with a driver's license, I kicked my social life into high gear.

In preparation for a big Fourth of July picnic at an estate in Fox Chapel, I threw down a few beers before leaving home and had some more on arrival. Lying on the grass, watching fireworks, I started playing with some toes above my head that belonged to Susan Schumacher, Sandy's younger sister. We never spoke, but I turned up at her house a week later, on the pretext of visiting Sandy.

The Schumacher family, like mine, respected intelligence. Unbeknownst to me, Sandy had told Susan I was one of his smartest classmates. Apparently, that had gotten me on her short list. Several people in her family were lawyers and Jesuit priests, and her mother had advised, "Don't marry somebody rich, because they can lose their money. An intelligent person can make money and is entertaining as well." While Sandy and I were talking in the formal but cozy living room, Susan came prancing in wearing a sweater, skirt, and necklace that might have been her mother's.

"I'm being Voguish today!"

I'd never seen such a sophisticated thirteen-year-old!

"Would you like to go see *Vertigo* with me tonight?" I said, casual about it.

"Where is it?"

"At the Silverlake drive-in."

"I'm sorry, I can't go to drive-ins with older boys."

Now she was on my list too.

***

Back at school, I dove into physics, inspired by the physicists who had built the atomic bomb. My first success was figuring out how a radio worked, explaining it to the class, and impressing my teacher. I then pursued the biggest physics theory I could find for my class project—Einstein's theory of relativity. I read several books that explained it to laymen, but I barely understood why an observer of a passing train will see a flashing light differently from a passenger on the train. And general relativity—dropping balls in elevators—was way beyond me.

However, Einstein's theories showed me what separates scientists from most people. Einstein had an amazing intuition but didn't publish anything until he could back it up with math or many experiments. Scientists don't accept intuition as a reliable guide to truth. After all, before Copernicus, reasonable people believed the earth was the center of everything, and before Einstein, even scientists believed Newton's laws were the final word.

I graduated high school, honored as one of the ten smartest students and the winner of the science prize. I sported a "flattop" haircut, a modified version of the GI crew cut. I looked like a geek[6], but my mother approved. Susan was in the graduation audience, and I asked her to come to the graduation dance that night, but she was already going with a younger student. We made eye contact at the dance.

The summer after graduation, I got an unpaid internship at the Pitt's biology department, well worth it, because a nice grad student explained to me how DNA (deoxyribonucleic acid) worked. Coincidentally, DNA strands are sort of like computer programs because they control our biological hardware.

But nobody I knew was talking about computers in 1959, and I was going to be a physicist.

---

[6] Geeks are nerds that focus obsessively on a narrow subject, like computers.

To iterate is human; to recurse, divine.
– Alan Perlis

2. The Giants of Carnegie Mellon

Carnegie Institute of Technology was my safety school, but at my family's behest, I passed on MIT, Caltech, and Yale, for Tech, three blocks from my home and, ultimately, much to our surprise, fully funded thanks to a Westinghouse Electric scholarship.

Introductory Physics was an extra course on my freshman schedule. It covered Newton's theory and involved a little calculus. I saw a beauty in Newton's dependable system, so unlike Einstein's slippery relativity. I finished my first semester with all As, save a B in English. I decided I had what it took to be a scientist and dropped my ROTC class, joined the football team, pledged a fraternity, Delta Upsilon (DU), and continued developing my partying skills. Every now and again, I rented a gorilla costume for social occasions.

When Susan invited me to a dance at her high school—our first date!—I took her to a party at a DU brother's apartment afterwards. Partly to demonstrate that I could find a date. She talked so effortlessly, and in her presence I lost my fear of being judged. At the end of my fraternity pledge training, I asked Susan to be my date for the celebratory grain alcohol punch party. Driving her home in my mother's dark green Mercedes on that snowy night, I collided head on with another car and was arrested for drunken driving. Uncle

Charles, a criminal lawyer, got me out of the arrest, expunging the record. I called Susan the next day to ask how she got home, and she told her mother that I was just inquiring whether she had had a good time. It was my second arrest that year. My reputation as a smart, badass fraternity man was made.

Although Susan was my date to many beer-fueled parties at the DU house, she never drank. Here was a person who, unlike me, could be the life of the party, without drinking. The fact that she was only fifteen made it even more remarkable. She *was* a pistol! And she was smart—just like her brother—but she never tried to prove it.

One night, standing by the DU bar, Susan and I were chatting with a friend.

"Ouch," he said, when he cut his finger on a beer can and it started bleeding.

"Would you like me to give you a transfusion?" I asked, joking.

"What's your blood type?"

"O negative.

"That's mine too!" he exclaimed. "Let's become blood brothers!"

He was serious.

So, I cut *my* finger and we mashed our fingers together. Susan took note of this nonsense, because on our next date (Sadie Hawkins Day, February 29, 1960) she asked me to marry her. I met her requirements: smart, Catholic, Democrat, and blood with a negative Rh factor. (If our Rh factors differed, it would complicate pregnancy.) This time, it was my turn to decline. I was frightened but flattered.

Second semester of my freshman year, I took another extra course on modern mathematics. I learned about *sets*—collections of things with no duplicates and no order, which are written as {dog, horse, 5}. I studied one page of *Modern Mathematics* for what must have been twenty hours before grasping the concepts of a *subset*, a selection of some of a set's members, and a *power set*, the set of all the subsets of a set. The power set of {1,2,3} is {{},{1},{2},{3},{1,2},{1,3},{2,3},{1,2,3}}. This studying episode taught me how to be persistent. *Learning takes time.*

Thanks to the scholarship, I had a guaranteed job at Westinghouse for the summer. On the first day of orientation, twenty other Westinghouse scholars and I sat through a story about George Westinghouse, who invented the fail-safe train brake and alternating electric current. When it was over, an executive sent me off to work at Union Switch and Signal—so that I could learn some electrical engineering.

"That won't do at all." I was brimming with confidence. "I'm going to be a physicist and should go to your research center."

As I was delivering a packet of materials to my new supervisor, I noticed, "This kid thinks we owe him something!" written on one of the papers. Upon arrival to the research center, I was asked a simple empirical question that I was unable to answer. In the following weeks, I noticed that my fellow scholar, who was supposed to be the only student there, had been given real experiments. Meanwhile, I had been asked to repair a radio, during which I learned what 220 volts feels like, reminding me *not to mess with hardware.*

One evening, I met some guys who were playing with the research center's only computer. One was a smooth dude from Yale, the other was a tall, ugly kid also from Tech who gushed, "I love computers!" *What a geek!* I was hooked on physics and still anxious to understand reality on its most profound level.

"Physics won't do that for you," said the young professor.

We were deep in conversation in the wee hours of the morning at a DU party thrown just before the fall semester started, and I was inquiring about the nature of reality.

"Relativity and quantum theory have made reality quite elusive."

Weeks later, he became my professor of thermodynamics, the second course for physics majors, which I found much messier than Newtonian mechanics.

I was ignoring my thermodynamics assignment, sipping beer, and watching TV at the DU house when an older fraternity brother, George Ernst, came in with some enticing news.

"The professor in my class said that anyone who was in the rat race for good grades could write his desired grade on the front of his exam paper—and he'd give that grade to him!"

"That must be a fascinating subject," I said. "Where do I sign up?"

In Introduction to Programming, I found myself in a large lecture hall among hundreds of geeks and standing in front of the room was a strange-looking man without hair, not even eyebrows, who was busy expounding on how to implement something he called "a push-down stack." I didn't get it.

Professor Alan Perlis would assign everyday problems for us to program, like "Find the shortest path between any two buildings at Tech," or "Design a language for describing motel layouts." We were to create our programs in a language called GATE (General Algorithm Translator, Extended). Algorithms, a word we all toss around today thanks to social media, are abstractions of programs. Algorithms don't depend on the syntactic details of any program; therefore, if two programs do things in the same way, then they're expressions of the same algorithm. Put legalistically; you can *copyright* a program, but you can *patent* an algorithm—a different matter—if it's original.

To prepare *input* for a computer, we used a keypunch machine, a sort of typewriter that punches holes in twelve-row, eighty-column card stock. Each column conveyed a letter, number, or punctuation mark, and each card was a line in the program.

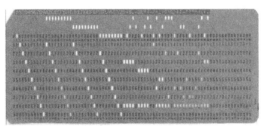

We punched our cards, then carefully arranged the cards of our program in a deck, which we put in a submission drawer. Then we waited many hours for the *output*, which was printed on huge sheets of paper. That's the kind of obstacle we computer pioneers faced. I would sometimes catch Perlis himself racing around in the glass-enclosed computer sanctum, stuffing our cards into the computer.

Because the early computers were funded by the government for important scientific computations related to nuclear reactions, they were large and expensive. The campus's Bendix G-20 cost about $500,000 and weighed a ton. To allow hundreds of students to use it for piddling computations, Perlis needed to batch all our programs together and run them sequentially in between the times the computer was devoted to long important scientific computations.

In time, I learned the first thing every programmer learns — how unforgiving of mistakes computers can be. A missing comma or misspelling prevents the computer from running the program, so you had to submit your amended program and wait for hours again. Even when a program ran, it could still contain other errors, which caused it to give wrong answers. Such errors were called *bugs*, and all programmers confessed to making them. Unlike the computer, most programmers forgave themselves and each other. Misspellings or mixing up tenses were simple bugs, possibly caused by hitting the wrong key, however being vague or inconsistent in your thinking created a more complicated sort of bug, such as a "fence-post error," not realizing a one-hundred-foot fence with posts every ten feet has eleven posts. More generally, what does the phrase "x is between A and B" mean? Can x be A? Can x be B? It shouldn't matter which you prefer, but if you are inconsistent in your choices, you'll make these fence-post errors. If you're working with other programmers, you'd better know which choice they prefer as well. Programmers and digital engineers usually expect that x could be A, but not B. They also like to start counting at zero, not one.

I thought all of this was stupid stuff when compared to the laws of physics, but many of my classmates seemed to think it was fun. No wonder Perlis gave me a C! Even so, I liked him. He was as enthusiastic as he was irreverent, and unlike the professors of other subjects, he had and encouraged, random, swashbuckling ideas. In most universities, computers were a precious resource, sequestered like scientific instruments in departments that could afford them, but Perlis, a graduate of Tech himself who ran the university's computer center, made its computer accessible to everyone.

"Here is an open field that is going to grow, so do whatever you like. It will probably be useful. You don't have to be a genius; just go for it!"

That was his M.O.

I gave computers a second chance when I took a programming course the following fall. Not taught by Perlis, but by a less flamboyant, more comprehensible professor who happened to be doing a PhD under Perlis. Finally, I learned how a computer operated. Any computer is a little world of absolute consistency. Strange but simple. Computers operate on *bits* (binary digits) that are electronic elements that may be charged or uncharged, representing 1 or 0. The name was coined by Claude Shannon, the creator of information theory, which explains how to transmit information efficiently. Each computer has a preferred *register* size for storing bits in its *memory*. The Bendix G-20 preferred 32, so a register could hold $2^{32} = 4,294,967,296$ different configurations because there are two choices (1 or 0) for each bit. [7] The G-20 had 32 thousand registers, named by numerical *addresses*. The usual measure of computer memory is the *byte* (eight bits). So, the G-20 had 4×32,000 = 128,000 bytes of memory, abbreviated to 128K (K for Kilobytes).

A sequence of bits can represent different *types* of information. Most obviously, it can represent an integer. The byte 00000000 represents zero, 00000001 represents one, 00000010 represents two, etc. When you add two binary integers, you use the same rule about "carrying the 1"—just much more often. There is a second type of number representation called *floating-point* (also *real*), which is a binary version of scientific notation. For example, the number of hydrogen atoms in a gram, 6.022141×10^{23}, might be represented by the 32-bit sequence

0 00010111 01011011110001111111101

where the first 0 indicates a positive number, the next eight bits represent 23, and the next 23 represent 6022141. The G-20 had different arithmetic instructions for operating on the two different representations of numbers.

When the people in Douglas Adams's *The Hitchhiker's Guide to the Galaxy* ask the giant computer to tell them the meaning of life, it answers "42." Part of the reason this is funny is because an uninterpreted number is meaningless. If it had been a real computer, it might have said "101010," which is the binary representation of the decimal integer 42.

Bytes can also represent characters. For example, "A" is represented by 01000001, "B" by 01000010. Most importantly,

---

[7] The notation 2^N stands for 2 multiplied by itself N-1 times. By convention, $2^0 = 1$.

a register can be interpreted as an *instruction* to be carried out by the *central processing unit* (CPU), which is the active part of a computer. The bits act as an *imperative* sentence—describing what the computer is supposed to do.

So, if a register in our G-20 holds
10011001000000000000000000000101,
the first 8 bits can be interpreted as the verb, and the next 24, the object. The verb (10011001) is "load the *accumulator*," which is a special register in the CPU that many instructions operate on. The remaining bits (00000000000000000000000101) represent the address of memory register 5. Therefore, the instruction is "Load the accumulator with whatever bits are in register 5." Other useful verbs can store the bits in the accumulator into a memory register, add a number to the accumulator, or subtract a number from the accumulator. This option to interpret bits as data or instructions is fundamental to computers. In fact, a common bug is forgetting which type of information a string of bits is supposed to represent. Even if you know it's a number, you must remember whether it's an integer value, floating-point value, or the address of a register.

I learned that if you start the CPU by telling it to start at address 103, then it will go to the 103rd register and interpret the bits there as an instruction. After performing the instruction, the CPU normally goes on to the next address, 104, and does whatever its instruction is. However, an instruction can prevent that progression to 105 by saying, "Go to address 108," or "If the number in the accumulator is zero, go to address 109, otherwise just continue." With a few pages that contain descriptions of all the available verbs (about 50 for the G-20), which is called the *machine's language*, you can *program* a computer to your heart's content. I found this liberating!

On the Wednesday afternoon before Thanksgiving, I sat down at my desk to get a head start on a programming project to schedule elevators. I got into a flow and finished a draft of the program around eleven o'clock at night. I'd missed dinner, missed meeting up with my returning high school drinking buddies. I didn't care. I was hooked on computer programming.

***

When powered on, a computer must go through a process called *bootstrapping*. Bootstrapping is the idea of "pulling yourself up by your own bootstraps." When you first turn on a computer, you load a tiny program (written as binary numbers) by flipping switches on a control panel. Then, that program loads another, bigger program—perhaps by reading a deck of cards from an attached card reader. This second program might be written in *hexadecimal*, a more convenient way to write binary numbers, four bits at a time, using the digits 0 through 9 and A through F to stand for 10 through 15. The machine loads the cards, and once the first program translates them into real binary, it passes control to the second program, which loads a third program. That program might be an *operating system*. An operating system handled basic tasks like connecting with peripheral devices like keyboards, printers, tape drives, and other storage media. It also took over the job of loading programs and handled exceptional events like a program trying to divide by zero.

Programming a computer in its native language is *tedious*. As if recipes couldn't say, "Bring a large pot of water to a boil," and instead said, "Open the pot cabinet. Take out a two-quart pot. Put it under the spigot. Turn on the cold water. Until the pot is full, wait. Put the pot on the stove . . ."

To overcome the tedium, people started inventing *programming languages.* The first real success was FORTRAN (Formula Translator), invented in 1954 by John Backus of International Business Machines (IBM). FORTRAN allowed scientists to write complex algebraic expressions and define *functions.* Functions are useful because they allow you to package up a program you have written so that you and others can call upon it in larger programs by just using its name.[8]

FORTRAN was designed with physicists in mind. They used computers to simulate atomic or hydrogen bomb explosions to answer questions like whether they would set fire to the world's atmosphere.

Here is a program[9] that computes square roots using an algorithm so old that its invention is claimed by the Chinese, Babylonians, Greeks, Egyptians, and Indians.

```
function SquareRoot(y) {
  let guess = 10
  let oldguess = 0
  while(abs(guess-oldguess)/oldguess>.0001){
    log(guess)
    oldguess = guess
    guess = (guess+y/guess)/2
  }
  return guess}
```

---

[8] See Return Address in Nerd Zone

[9] All the programs in this book are written in JavaScript, a descendant of FORTRAN. The function log displays its parameter and abs is the absolute value of its parameter.

The name `y` is a *parameter* of the function. The names `guess` and `oldguess` are temporary local variables, introduced by the verb `let`. Variables stand for register addresses. An *assignment statement* like `oldguess` = `guess` puts the value (i.e., contents) of `guess` into `oldguess`.[10] The `while {..}` construction is called an *iterative* loop and the part inside the { and } is repeated while the percentage change of `guess` is greater than 0.01%.[11] The value of `guess` at the end is returned as the output of the function call.

If you called `SquareRoot` with `1000`, here are the successive values of the variable that `log` would show.

10, 55, 36.5909, 31.9600, 31.62456

You might use `SquareRoot` in an algebraic expression like

- `B+SquareRoot(B*B—4*A*C)/(2*A)`,

which is the formula used to solve a quadratic equation, as you might remember from algebra class. (Is algebra required anymore?) This instructs the computer to compute `B*B— 4*A*C` and then call `SquareRoot` applied to the result. The code for `SquareRoot` does its job and delivers its answer to code that divides it by `2*A` and subtracts `B`.

Another useful feature of programming languages is the *array* variable, which physicists call a vector. It is a sequence of values described by the expressions V[0], V[1], V[2], ... , V[N-1] where N is the length of the array.

---

[10] FORTRAN began the unfortunate practice of using the equal sign "=" to call for an assignment statement. This has caused confusion ever since.

[11] When the { and } are on separate lines, I place them in an unconventional way to facilitate indentation.

31

If T and P are arrays of characters, here is a function that tests T for having P as a subsequence.

```
function Matches(P, T) {
   let i = 0
   let state = "maybe"
   while (state == "maybe") {
       let j = 0
       state = "maybe_at_i"
       while (state == "maybe_at_i"){
         if (j == P.length) return "yes"
         else if(i+j-1==T.length)
                              return "no"
         else if (P[j] == T[i+j-1]) j=j+1
         else state = "maybe"
         i = i+1
       }
   }
}
```

I used state to express how hopeful the program is feeling. We use == to test values for equality to avoid confusion with assignment statements. P.length is the number of elements in P. The *conditional* command if (B_1) {C_1} else if (B_2) {C_2} ... else {C_N} executes the first C_i for which B_i is true and skips ahead to the end. If none of the first N-1 B_i are true it executes C_N.

Here is another, somewhat silly, function:

```
function Collatz(i) {
   let next = i
   while (next != 1) {
     log(next)
     let t = floor(next/2)
     next = (t*2==next) ? t : 3*next+1
   }
}
```

The character pair != means "not equal". The character *

means multiply. The function `floor` rounds down to the nearest integer, so that `t*2 == next` simply means "is `next` even?" The phrase B ? C : D is a *conditional expression*. If B is true it evaluates to C, otherwise D. This program is interesting only because nobody has proved it always halts and returns **"yes"** since Collatz posed the question in 1927. For example, `Collatz(15)` would log the sequence

15,46,23,70,35,106,53,160,80,40,20,10,5,16,8,4,2,1.

Experts wrote programs called *compilers* to translate these new programming languages into machine language, and academics everywhere started inventing languages and the compilers to implement them. A generation of computer scientists began aspiring to create the Great American Programming Language—the geek equivalent of the Great American Novel.

In 1960 Perlis became a leader in this new endeavor of language design and sat on a committee to create an international programming language, one independent of any particular machine to provide an even playing field for all the emerging computer manufacturers. They succeeded with ALGOL (Algorithmic Language), a coherent and readable language, and Perlis became the president of computing's first academic association, the Association for Computing Machinery (ACM) and the founding editor of its research journal, *Communications of the ACM* (*CACM*), which required submitters of programs to write them in ALGOL.

I began to think to myself, *If this doofus is a big cheese in computing, there can't be much competition.* By comparison, physics was daunting, with people like Einstein and books full of hard-to-comprehend theories. Programming was looking like a good career choice.

In the spring of my sophomore year, I did poorly in a difficult physics course about electricity and magnetism. Perhaps because I took a week off to participate in a big fraternity project building a prize-winning spring carnival booth—a Tech tradition. I finished off the week with a lot of drinking and celebrating, as usual. My physics career dimmed further when I made a dumb mistake in a lab measurement and should have done it over. I didn't bother.

Programming, here I come!

There wasn't a programming or computer science (CS) degree then, so I changed my major from physics to math, which allowed more electives.

Ernst, who had graduated in electrical engineering and entered a special PhD program, continued as my CS guide, and suggested a research seminar taught by his PhD supervisor.

Allen Newell's research goal was understanding human intelligence. In the first session of the seminar, he scribbled scary-looking differential equations on the board representing how breathing and heart rate affect each other. I felt overwhelmed. Then he turned around to us and admitted that he didn't really understand it all, since he was a cognitive psychologist.

I admired Newell's courage and enthusiasm for diving into unfamiliar areas. In 1950 (when I was 9) Newell was a twenty-something who took a research job at the RAND Corporation in Santa Monica, California, a well-funded think tank that tackled military and political problems for the government. He was put in charge of a large computer-supported project to study the country's system to detect approaching enemy aircraft. RAND afforded him an opportunity to meet with computer experts and generals. One expert was Oliver Selfridge who visited RAND to describe a special computer he was working on to recognize written characters. He called its method, pandemonium, because it consisted of twenty-six letter recognizers that "shouted" with volume matching their confidence in their particular letter.

"When I heard Oliver talk, I understood exactly how computers could do arbitrary information processing, symbolic processing, adaptive processing, and so forth. And it was quite clear to me what the path was. It was a conversion experience, and that turned my life. I mean it was a point at which I started working on artificial intelligence," according to an oral history of Allen Newell.

While I was still in high school, Newell had helped launch the field of AI by inventing a new programming language, Information Processing Language (IPL) and using it to demonstrate a program simulating human intelligence. But even here in college, I remained oblivious to his preeminence. He and Perlis were just men avidly pursuing subjects they loved and welcoming students, such as myself, to join in the fun.

For Newell's seminar, I was proud to write a paper reviewing how networks of neurons perform computation. Biologists knew that neurons were located throughout the body and were used to recognize sensations and activate muscles. These neurons connected to other cells and neurons via tendrils called axions and stimulated other neurons by firing electro-chemical impulses along the axions. The strength of the impulse could vary, and a neuron fires when the sum of impulses it receives from incoming axions exceeds its *threshold*. This was also how thinking was done— speculated the scientists.[12] To compile research for my paper, I read a paper by an MIT undergraduate student, Manuel Blum, that showed how these networks of neurons could compute Boolean functions and then read other papers showing how neural nets might recognize certain patterns.

Newell criticized my paper fiercely, saying that neural nets were being oversold. He preferred to describe people's thinking processes at a conceptual level and not relate them to any biological phenomena. His remarks diminished my belief in Newell's congeniality and wounded my undergraduate pride. And there was no going back to physics now.

***

In the summer of 1962 Ernst helped me to learn IPL, which crystallized a new computing technique, *list processing*, where the emphasis was on the processing lists of symbols rather than of numbers. Lists can be extended, have elements deleted, and be rearranged in other ways.[13] Working with it opened the door to solving problems that were more interesting to me, like puzzle solving using the mysterious power of *recursion*. I'd known how to use a loop to iterate through a process, but it took me some time to fully grasp recursion.

---

[12] See Chandra in Readings

[13] See Lists in Nerd Zone

Suppose we want to explore a maze, made of a grid of identical rooms with some missing walls.

Here is an informally written recursive algorithm, named after the mythical Greek who once used it.

Theseus (n):

Mark room n with X.

a. If you can move east to an unmarked room called m, move to it and call Theseus (m).
b. If you can move south to an unmarked room called m, move to it and call Theseus (m).
c. If you can move west to an unmarked room called m, move to it and call Theseus (m).
d. If you can move north to an unmarked room called m, move to it and call Theseus (m).
e. Return.

Theseus explored a maze (looking for the Minotaur) by marking rooms with X and unspooling a ball of string to remember how to get back to the entrance. The program enters the maze at room 1, marks 1, goes to 2 by calling Theseus(2), which marks 2, but is surrounded by walls and marked rooms, so returns to Theseus(1) at line b. As the mythical Theseus returned, he respooled the string that followed him from room 1 to room 2, since he didn't need to revisit room 2 on his way back.

Then Theseus(2) calls Theseus(6), and so on, until calling Theseus(14), where the maze and string look like this:

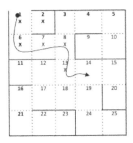

Instead of using a string, the computer keeps a *push-down stack* (a list you shorten from its end) of room numbers with lines of the program to tell it precisely where to return when the algorithm says "Return." Before calling Theseus(6), the computer would add 1c to the stack indicating the line right after the call of Theseus(6). For example, after the call of Theseus(14), the stack contains 1c, 6b, 7b, 8c, and 13b.

After some more exploration the maze looks like this after the call of Theseus(11):

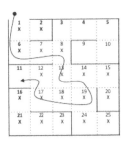

Now the push-down stack contains 1c, 6b, 7b, 8c, 13b, 14c, 19d, 18d, 17e, 12d. After marking 11, Theseus can't explore farther, so it removes 12d from the stack (called *popping* the stack) and starts executing at line 12d. Surrounded by X's, it keeps popping the stack until it finds itself in room 8 and discovers that it can move north to room 3.

Finally, here is the path Theseus follows for its entire tour:

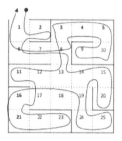

Recursion is also good for playing board games, where two players alternate moving between different board configurations. Suppose we allow each checkers player to look three moves ahead, considering five different moves at each stage. This can be visualized as a *game tree* with four levels of board configurations, where each board results from a move applied to the board below it.

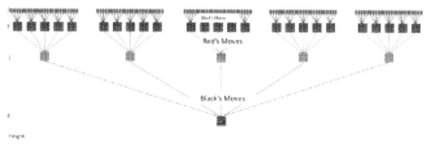

39

Any board's appeal to the black player can be approximated by the formula

(number of black pieces)/(number of red pieces)

where a king counts for two pieces. We use this formula to evaluate the boards across the top of the tree since we can't explore farther.

Each player uses the following recursive function to decide his next move:

```
function Evaluate(height, my_color, board) {
    if (height == 3)
        return
            pieces(board, "black")
            /pieces(board, "red")
    let move
        = plausible_moves(board, my_color, 5)
    let opponent
        = (my_color=="black") ? "red":"black"
    for (n=0; n<5; n++)
        value[n] =
            Evaluate(height+1,opponent,
                     make(move[n], board))
    let best = (my_color == "black")
                    ? maximum(value)
                    : minimum(value)
    return best
}
```

The function plausible_moves returns an array of five moves that might be good for my_color. The for loop evaluates the five moves, calling Evaluate recursively.

Here is a picture of the game tree with some typical values attached.

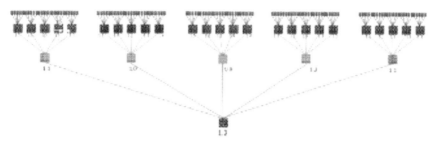

Black should choose the fourth move (reading from left to right) because it has the highest value, 1.2. He may notice that he has a chance to reach a board with a value of 1.4 by trying the second move, but that would depend upon red making a mistake by failing to make the move that yields a value, 1.0.

This kind of thinking is called *game theory*.[14] It was used to analyze the US/USSR nuclear standoff.

***

Before my senior year I retired from our losing football team, which meant I had some free time and found plenty to do as a DU. I was elected the president of the fraternity for a year, in which I spent most of my time drinking, dancing, and participating in mischief. We created an indoor swimming pool that sprung a leak and flooded the basement, greatly angering the university's building and grounds people. A pitcher of beer chucked from our house one night broke a passerby's windshield, and he called the police. Just as we were headed into my senior year, DU was banned from having parties.

---

[14] See von Neumann in Readings

***

In Herbert Simon's autobiography, he wrote, "I advise my graduate students to pick a research problem that is important, but one for which they have a secret weapon that gives some prospect of success. Why a secret weapon? Because if the problem is important, other researchers as intelligent as my students will be trying to solve it; my students are likely to come in first only by having access to some knowledge or research methods the others do not have."

I never took a course from Herbert Simon, professor of business at Tech, but I learned a lot by hearing his seminar discussions with Newell. In my senior year, I attended a memorable lecture of his. He claimed human intelligence was bounded and that economists were wrong to imagine that people could always make good decisions to maximize their wealth. His followers became known as *behavioral economists.* Simon described how Galileo used a new tool, the telescope (his secret weapon) to scan the heavens, and now he and Newell were doing the same—using computer programs (their secret weapon) to crystallize psychological theories.

Simon revolutionized our thinking about thinking. By attracting Allen Newell, Alan Perlis, and other intellectuals to Tech, he remade the university. He was a pervasive force, methodical and crafty in the pursuit of academic success. He sparked a revolution in cognitive psychology and was a founder of the CS and AI research fields.

While Perlis had sold me by telling me programming was fun, Simon told me programming was a weapon I could use in whatever battles I engaged in. Not many people knew how to program in 1962.

Incidentally, when Simon wrote the words "come in first," he revealed an implicit rule of the research game. There is no prize for being the second person to discover and publish a new fact. Researchers often squabble over who discovered something first. Newton claimed to have invented calculus before the German philosopher Gottfried Leibniz. Darwin beat Wallace to the punch in explaining evolution. Alexander Graham Bell and Elisha Gray filed patents for the telephone within hours of each other. Guess who was first.

Simon was dedicated and dogged about his ideas. A secret weapon was not enough. One must also do lots of work, and he opined that ten years of steady effort was necessary to become world class at anything—like Bobby Fischer who had played more chess games by age fourteen than anyone ever had. "My heart is in the work" was a fitting motto for Tech, and I hoped the hours I enjoyed programming might lead me to be great at it.

The program that Newell and Simon claimed demonstrated intelligence proved theorems in propositional logic—the same theorems that Bertrand Russell and Alfred Whitehead had proved in a long treatise called *Principia Mathematica*. Propositional logic is a game like Euclidean geometry, in which you assume some obviously true formal statements and use inference rules to develop other true statements.[15]

Now that I've told you a computer could do exactly what they did, you might say that Russell and Whitehead were not demonstrating intelligence. Although, that might be because you don't believe computers *ever* demonstrate intelligence.

---

[15] See Propositional Calculus in Nerd Zone

The year following Newell and Simon's breakthrough, Dartmouth professor John McCarthy invited a group of engineers and computer enthusiasts to a multi-week conference organized to discuss what he called "Artificial Intelligence." Newell and Simon proudly distributed computer printouts showing Russell's proofs as well as the program that had produced them, and nearly every person at the conference was interested and admitted that this was the most concrete example of AI anyone had ever produced. However, neurologist Marvin Minsky of MIT, sniffed that this wasn't impressive, because Newell and Simon's program didn't learn.

A criticism of AI, that a computer cannot be more intelligent than the person who programmed it, had already been refuted by another attendee at the conference. Arthur Samuel had written a program that learned to play checkers and regularly beat him.

While most of the world was either oblivious or dismissive of AI, Simon was utterly confident that the AI enterprise would ultimately succeed, because he believed in mechanomorphism, the conception that everything, including intelligence, is just a matter of gears and levers.

I never signed on to AI research, which some described as "climbing trees to get to the moon." I admired the work but was not drawn to it. I was more of a Perlis-follower, interested in developing the art of programming.

***

In 1958 Sputnik inspired the Department of Defense (DoD) to create the Defense Advanced Research Projects Agency (DARPA). It was given a big budget and a long leash to compete with Russian research. An enterprising professor from MIT, J. C. R. Licklider, took a job there and began funding professors at three universities, MIT, Stanford, and Tech. Licklider urged them to teach people about computers, and so the three universities each began pursuing the topic of computing—and wrestling with the political question of what disciplines would control it.

The PhD program Ernst entered in 1962 was created by the Newell-Simon-Perlis triumvirate. It was an interdepartmental PhD program (math, electrical engineering, psychology, business) called Systems and Communications Sciences, and was granting PhDs to students before the university administration formally noticed. Tech and Stanford established the first CS departments in 1965, and Tech became Carnegie Mellon University (CMU) in 1967.

Newell and Simon eschewed administration so Perlis (who already ran the computer center and the math department) became the CS department head. A year later, Perlis won the first ever Turing Award—computing's version of a Nobel prize—for his influence in advanced programming techniques and compiler construction. He was a *laissez-faire* manager who promulgated the Reasonable Person Principle that allowed anyone to do anything they thought appropriate until or unless it proved to be unreasonable. In 1967 the three wrote a letter to *Science*, giving their definition of CS. It was CMU's stake in the ground.[16]

---

[16] See Letter to Science in Documents

What is Computer Science?
Science 1967 (157) 1373-4
Allen Newell
Alan J. Perlis
Herbert A. Simon

Professors of computer science are often asked: "Is there such a thing as computer science, and if there is, what is it?" The questions have a simple answer:

Wherever there are phenomena, there can be a science to describe and explain those phenomena. Thus, the simplest (and correct) answer to "What is botany?" is, "Botany is the study of plants." And zoology is the study of animals, astronomy the study of stars, and so on. Phenomena breed sciences.

There are computers. Ergo, computer science is the study of computers. The phenomena surrounding computers are varied, complex, rich.

. . .

Computer scientists will often join hands with colleagues from other disciplines in common endeavor. Mostly, computer scientists will study living computers with the same passion that others have studied plants, stars, glaciers, dyestuffs, and magnetism; and with the same confidence that intelligent, persistent curiosity will yield interesting and perhaps useful knowledge.

Newell, Simon, and Perlis each did their part to transform Tech and put it on the intellectual map. They collaborated without conflict, while representing different poles of attitude. Perlis was encouraging and welcoming. Simon, cold and calculating. Newell was somewhere in the middle, and so was I.

The only private conversation I had with Simon was when he tried to persuade me to enroll in his new psychology PhD program, and I refused.

"Young man, you have Charles River fever!"

MIT, along with Harvard, are in Cambridge on the Charles River, across from Boston, and Simon resented their preeminence and their "automatic presumption of greatness." He told me that my scientific career would be better if I stayed, but I was anxious to finally get out of Pittsburgh.

The only other Pittsburgher who suggested I stay was Feeny, who had just graduated from Yale and was hosting a poker game at his parents' Fox Chapel mansion.

"Pittsburgh is fine for you, Feeny, because you're the big cheese," I said, pointing at him, "But I won't come back until I'm so famous that a brass band welcomes me!"

II: AI Summer 1963-1972

J. C. R. Licklider at DARPA funds MIT, Carnegie Tech, and Stanford to study AI.

Joseph Weizenbaum creates the first chatbot, ELIZA.

The Mac Hack chess program beat a player with a rating of 1510, which is in the top 9 percent of players.

Shakey, the first intelligent robot, is demonstrated.

The fictional robot, Richard Daniel, evades a law limiting robot lives to one hundred years.

Philip K. Dick's novel *Blade Runner* introduces the Voigt-Kampff test of humanity in suspected robots.

A chess program running on a Control Data Corporation 6400 achieves a rating of 1650 using brute force search.

Minsky claims neural nets just need more computing power.

The greatest shortcoming of the human race is
our inability to understand the exponential
function. – Albert Allen Bartlett

3.   Charles River Fever

I went to MIT on a National Defense Fellowship (also inspired by Sputnik) to pursue a PhD. I had applied to the Sloan School of Management, figuring it was MIT's soft underbelly, compared to math or electrical engineering. Even if I could get into those departments, I wanted more flexibility to take computer courses elsewhere. I got an apartment on Boston's Beacon Street and rode a trolley to MIT.

As I strolled along the Charles River, in front of MIT's large domed building and across from Boston, there were sailboats out. I felt I'd arrived at "the hub of the universe," as Bostonians called it.

The center of computer research was Project MAC, housed in an off campus building in Tech Square. MAC (not to be confused with Macintosh) was funded by Licklider to develop two of his favorite ideas: machine-augmented cognition and multi-access computing in which many people could share a single computer simultaneously. They were aspects of a theme he called *man-machine symbiosis*, which suggests that computers should collaborate with humans rather than outthink them.

I made a beeline for MAC upon arrival. I found the famous Marvin Minsky, sitting in front of a big computer. I introduced myself and said I had come from Carnegie Tech, hoping for a warm welcome, even an invitation to become one of his assistants, but he barely looked up. I got a similar brush-off from Oliver Selfridge. Apparently, the presumption of greatness did not apply to me.

There were many other famous people to see at MIT. The septuagenarian Norbert Wiener, author of *Cybernetics*, strolled the stage of a large lecture hall, holding a cigar while he lectured us about the dangers of computing. As an example, he used "The Sorcerer's Apprentice", a two-hundred-year-old poem. He showed a cartoon segment from Disney's *Fantasia*, in which apprentice Mickey Mouse, to save himself work, trains a broom to fetch water. When he can't get the broom to stop, he splits it with an axe, but that backfires by causing brooms to replicate and fetch even more water. As he is drowning in the flood, the wizard returns to make the mess disappear, and Mickey goes back to fetching water himself.

A later book by Wiener[17] contained a more ominous thought:

> The *machine à gouverner* of Père Dubarle is not frightening because of any danger that it may achieve autonomous control over humanity. It is far too crude and imperfect to exhibit a one-thousandth part of the purposive independent behavior of the human being. Its real danger, however, is the quite different one that such machines, though helpless by themselves, may be used by a human being or a block of human beings to increase their control over the rest of the human race or that political leaders may attempt to control their populations.

---

[17] See Wiener, *The Human Use of Human Beings* in Readings

This was the first time I had heard an eminent expert doubt the unalloyed benefits of computers. Nobody at Tech did that. Anyone who demurred from the computer revolution was called a Luddite, after Ned Ludd who smashed a mechanical loom in 1779. Incidentally, those looms forced Andrew Carnegie's father to emigrate from Scotland to Pittsburgh.

In the summer of my first year, I worked at a Texas Instruments metallurgical factory forty miles south of Boston programming a small IBM computer to handle some office tasks. I enjoyed it, but it didn't encourage me to pursue a business career.

Some of my high school friends had gotten married right after college. I began to think it was time for me and realized that I was probably destined to marry someone I already knew. Driving the Mercedes my mother had given me around Massachusetts with more time for fun that summer, I reconnected with former girlfriends.

When I got back to Cambridge in the fall, the management professor who had taught me operations research in my first year invited me to join a team of PhD students he led at MAC. We worked at developing a programming language to support business simulations. The star of our team was David Ness.

Ness had been an undergraduate in the Sloan School and a Rhodes Scholar at Oxford. His time in England inspired him to wear rumpled suits and ties, making him look every bit the professor. In fact, he was already doing a little teaching in the management school. Ness was charismatic and had interesting friends in Cambridge. I appreciated his knowledge of the area and enjoyed his friends. I was happy to become his sidekick.

At about two o'clock in the morning on a summer night in 1965, I was pecking away on a program, when Ness came into my Project MAC office.

"Morris! Ken's?"

Ken's at Copley was a twenty-four-hour restaurant and a regular haunt for the vampire hours we kept.

"Sure," I said as I closed my files and logged off the computer.

We descended from our fifth-floor office and got in my new Triumph TR4. (I'd totaled the Mercedes.) At this time of night, the ride from Tech Square to Copley Square was only ten minutes. The top was down, and the air had cooled from Boston's summer swelter.

We weren't vampires. We were programmers using MAC's wonderful CTSS (Compatible Time-Sharing System). Instead of requiring the frustrating process of submitting cards and waiting hours for results, CTSS allowed me to type in a program at a teletype[18] in my office and have it transmitted to the computer on the ninth floor, which would then store it for me. I could run the program immediately to see the results, tweak the stored version using an editing program, and run it again. Twenty of us at a time could be doing this from different locations in the building, sharing the

---

[18] Teletypes were first used for telegrams but had been repurposed for talking to computers as well.

same IBM 7094, which was fast enough to keep switching among us. It worked like a chess master playing twenty novices, giving the illusion that each of us had its undivided attention. Interactive computing! No more multi-hour waits for results.

A standard IBM 7094 computer had 228K of memory and cost $3.5 million. CTSS's 7094 had two memories of that size, but IBM gave us a big discount. The second memory was used to hold CTSS's operating system, which had to handle swapping processes in and out of the first memory as they took turns.

But there was a catch to CTSS. The IBM 7094 was overcrowded during the day—when all the professors were there—so it seemed sluggish, and you had to be lucky even to get one of the twenty slots. So, Ness and I worked at night. But vampire hours could be hard to maintain. Programming at night was fine. Going to classes in the day was the problem. I tried a system of staying up for twenty-four hours and sleeping for twelve, which looked like rising at eight in the morning on Monday, attending classes all day, staying up programming until eight in the morning on Tuesday, then sleeping until eight in the evening, rising in time for dinner, followed by programming all night, attending classes all day Wednesday, then crashing at eight at night. It meant no programming Wednesday night, but my Thursday and Friday schedules repeated Monday's and Tuesday's. Unfortunately, my circadian rhythms caught up with me, and it led to chaos. I would sleep through Wednesday classes, miss meals, skip showers, and ignore housekeeping tasks. My stuff was so disorganized that it took me months to notice that my apartment had been burglarized.

Aside from CTSS, MAC was a hotbed of computer research. Our little management group was a tiny part. There was a large project called Multics creating a more elaborate time-sharing system with the help of General Electric and AT&T Bell Labs. Minsky ran a large AI enterprise with several computers of its own. One of his followers wrote a chess-playing program, Mac Hack, on a Digital Equipment Corporation (DEC) PDP-6 computer. Mac Hack had a player rating of 1400, something a high school champion might achieve. World champions typically had at least a 2800 score.[19] Mac Hack beat an AI skeptic who claimed that computers would not be able to play high-quality chess. It also beat me. There were professors at MAC studying information theory and hardware design. I first saw what became the internet when Oliver Selfridge demonstrated typing some sentences on a teletype that someone in California was reading.

***

I was taking basic management courses because I wanted to get a Master of Science in management, as a sort of fallback to the PhD. I disliked the required economics courses, but the rest were interesting. As my high school vocational test predicted, I liked the accounting course. It showed me how one used numbers to create a model of reality.

To qualify for my MS degree in management I had to write a thesis. I was going to write on an aspect of the simulation programming language that Ness and I had implemented. I had written papers in college, but presenting something I had done and claiming that it was a big deal paralyzed me. With

---

[19] A 100-point difference between two players means the better one will win two-thirds of the time.

an end-of-summer deadline for submission bearing down on me, one night I said *I'm not going to sleep until I've started writing*. As the sun came up over Cambridge, I wrote a few pages and collapsed. The task was made somewhat easier by using a tool MAC supplied that produced nicely formatted pages from a computer-edited script—a 1965 precursor to MS Word.

The first two years in Boston were my first experience living alone, often dining alone. I got depressed, especially in the dark Boston winter. I was relieved when after a year of programming, playing squash, eating, and drinking together, Ness and I agreed to live together. In the fall, we found an apartment to rent in a nice part of Cambridge. We spent many evenings drinking and imagining the future of computing. One funny (at the time) idea we had was that time-sharing systems could be used for advertising.

We loved working on programs and trying to solve puzzles, such as this one, called the knapsack problem: *Suppose you have a set of items you want to put in a knapsack before taking a hike, each with a numerical usefulness value and a weight. Is there a set of items with a total usefulness of at least U but with weight not exceeding W, the weight you can carry?* Ness and I spent a week writing a recursive program to try every subset of the items. It worked fine for three or four items, but for larger numbers it seemed to get stuck and never print anything.

We kept looking for a bug in the program. Then Ness did a little scribbling and said, "Our algorithm is an exponential process. If there are N items our program will try 2^N different combinations. That number grows explosively. For example, 2^{30} is over a billion. Generously assuming the CTSS computer can handle each case in a millionth of a second, it would take more than a half hour to solve a problem where N is 30. If N is 40 it would take twelve days. Didn't your mother tell you not to mess with exponentials?"

"OK, let's be clever and not generate all possibilities," I said. "First we'll compute the ratio of usefulness to weight of each item and sort them into decreasing order of their ratios. For example, a pocketknife might come first and a big dictionary last. The sorting process runs in quadratic time, proportional to N^2, which grows more slowly than 2^N. Then we pack items from the front of the list because they increase the weight slowly compared to the increase in usefulness. If we exceed the weight limit before reaching the usefulness goal, we'll give up. Otherwise, we'll find a good set of items."

But Ness, becoming a devil's advocate said, "Here's a two-item example for which your algorithm fails. One item has a weight of W and a usefulness of U, making it alone a good answer. The other item has a weight of W+1, making it alone unusable but a very big usefulness of 2U(W+1)/W. Since
$$2U(W+1)/W)/(W+1) = 2U/W < U/W$$
your algorithm will try the heavier one first and give up, even though the second item meets the goal."

"That's a ridiculous example," I said.

"But Morris, if you fix your algorithm to detect that case, I can probably disguise it by devising several items with high ratios whose weights add up to W+1 and whose usefulness adds up to 2U(W+1)/W and another bunch of low-ratio items that add up to W and U. Then you'll still have to try all 2^N combinations to discover the satisfying items."

I gave up. I was embarrassed that I didn't appreciate how hard the problem was. *No matter how good a programmer you are, you must use math!*

Exponential growth is powerful, more powerful than most people understand! Here is a story of the (fictional) Chow family to illustrate.

Ho Chow and his wife Li arrive in San Francisco penniless. With the help of relatives, they find an apartment and begin selling Li's delicious Chinese food from door to door. They make $10,000 a year after paying themselves, so after twenty years of diligent work they amassed $200,000. Ho and Li retire and turn the business over to Ho Junior and his wife. Knowing the ways of America, Junior uses some of the $200,000 to open restaurants called Ho Li Chow (after his parents) and hires some help. Even after paying everyone, Junior and his wife increase their profits by $4,000 every year—$14,000, $18,000, $22,000 . . . as they continue opening restaurants.

After twenty years, Junior Chow showed this chart to his octogenarian parents to illustrate how much better he had done, compared to how they would have, continuing the door-to-door service.

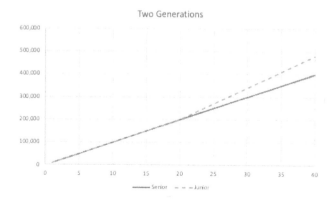

The Junior Chows passed the restaurant chain on to their son Ho Chow III along with the $480,000 nest egg. His parents and grandparents were outraged when Ho III sold the business and invested the $480,000 in the stock market, making about 8 percent per year. After twenty years Ho III, who had never worked and managed to live on 3 percent of his wealth (over $140,000 per year) added 5 percent a year to his holdings.

He had a chart that looked like this:

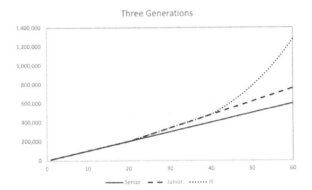

His parents were incredulous at the $1.2 million he had, but Ho III had been to college and explained how compound interest worked. At 5 percent your money will grow exponentially like 1.05^Y and double every fifteen years, while the old business would have taken twenty-five years to double the $480,000. Furthermore, since his wealth was now even larger, he was on course to triple the $480,000 in a few more years. Such is the magic of compound interest. To rub it in, he showed the Junior Chows that if *they* had retired and invested in the stock market when they took over, they would have been better off after their twenty years!

Now the accomplishments of the first two generations look positively puny.

This little story illustrates the biblical Matthew effect: "The rich get richer, and the poor get poorer." If you can depend on your wealth to make more money than you make, retire! Many people think there are only two kinds of growth: *linear*, like the first generation's wealth and *increasing* like the later generations'. However, there are at least three: linear, *quadratic* (like the second generation's) and exponential like all the succeeding generations'.

Exponential processes occur in nature. If you pack a lot of plutonium in a small space, the neutrons released when a plutonium atom happens to split, cause many nearby plutonium atoms to split, and we all know how that ends!

From a distance, an exponential looks like a hockey stick: flat for a time and then more or less straight up, surprising us. Suppose each person with a virus transmits it to two other people a day.

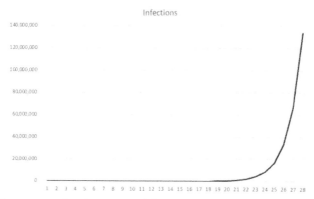

For three weeks few would notice, because there were just a million infected people in the world. But after the fourth week there would be over 134 billion, and everyone would think it started a week before.

59

Richard Hamming, a scientist at Bell Labs, claimed that a person's intelligence grows exponentially. He said, "Knowledge and productivity are like compound interest. Given two people of approximately the same ability and one person who works 10 percent more than the other, the latter will more than twice outproduce the former. [In mathematical terms: $(1.1X)^N$ grows much faster than X^N.] The more you know, the more you learn; the more you learn, the more you can do; the more you can do, the more the opportunity—it is much like compound interest."

Tree structures exhibit exponential growth. You might be impressed to know that I am the thirteenth cousin of Queen Elizabeth until you realize that the family tree growing from our common twelfth great-grandfather has about $3^{14} = 4.8$ million living cousins in it, assuming each of his descendants had about three children.

***

Because feedback was much discussed in *Cybernetics*, I took a course on it that taught engineers how to design electronic circuits that control devices. The basic configuration of a feedback system looks like this:

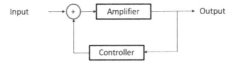

If you tell the controller you would like the sound coming out of the amplifier to be 60 decibels, it will sense the output and, if it is above 60, decrease the power it adds to the input. If it is below 60, it will increase its power contribution. The course did not teach another kind of feedback which simply increases the power regardless of level. That's what happens when a sound from the speakers gets into a microphone connected to the input, causing an ear-splitting screech. But businessmen love that kind of feedback if it generates exponential returns.

The most useful course in my self-designed curriculum was Finite State Machine Theory, an abstract way of looking at digital electrical devices that have a memory. We weren't concerned with the details of the memory, we just said it is in one of its possible *states,* sort of like a person's mood. Instead of looking at the details, we describe a device solely in terms of its stimulus-response behavior. Stimulate it by feeding it an input symbol (e.g., typing a key), and it responds by changing its state and printing an output symbol (e.g., a number or word) associated with the new state. The present state determines what state the device goes into next based on which input symbol it sees. We typically describe a finite state machine by a picture.

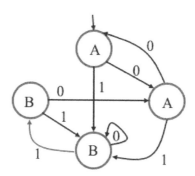

This machine has four states. The symbols inside the circles are what a symbol will print when it's entered, and the labeled arrows describe what state the machine will assume when it sees a 0 or 1. The little arrow coming from no state indicates the starting state. This table shows how it might behave:

stimulus	0	0	1	0	0	1	1	1	0	1
response	A	A	B	B	B	B	B	B	A	B

The course showed me how to analyze finite state machines in various ways. For example, we could ask whether a machine with fewer states could exhibit the same behavior. In this case the two A states can be merged into one because they lead to the same places, whatever the stimulus.

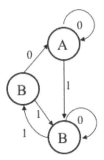

We studied *regular expressions*, a way of describing simple patterns in strings of symbols. Given the alphabet a regular expression, E, can be:
- ε, the empty sequence
- a sequence of characters describing the set with that single sequence
- a sequence of regular expressions $E_1 \ldots E_N$, describing all sequences $e_1 \ldots e_N$ where e_i is in E_i
- $(E_1 \mid E_2 \mid \ldots \mid E_N)$, describing all the sequences in $E_1, E_2, \ldots,$ and E_N
- E^* denoting $\{\varepsilon\} \mid E \mid EE \mid EEE \mid \ldots$

For example, if V is the set of all allowed characters

$$V^* \text{ aagtagt } V^* \text{ tggatg} V^*$$

denotes all sequences with aagtagt followed later by tggatg. We learned how to create finite state machines to recognize the strings that a regular expression describes.

Real machines like computers have trillions of states, but if they have a fixed amount of storage, the theory of finite state machines applies to them.

***

I was introduced to a deeper theory of computing in the Recursive Functions course taught by the math department. It started with the study of Turing machines, which added storage to finite state machines in the form of an extendable erasable tape containing symbols. [20]

Ignoring engineering details, the course dealt with questions of what could and could not be computed in any amount of time. Such questions burst upon mathematics early in the twentieth century. In 1901 Russell uncovered a paradox in math's foundations that is captured in this famous puzzle: "If a barber shaves everyone who doesn't shave themselves, does he shave himself?" If he does, then he doesn't. If he doesn't, then he does. This didn't upset laypeople—since they made nonsensical statements all the time. However, when suitably phrased as a mathematical question, it was a problem for mathematicians.

Thirty years later, Kurt Gödel used the same kind of puzzle to prove that there were statements about numbers that, though true, could not be proved from any set of assumptions formalized as axioms. Mathematicians had been developing

---

[20] See Turing Machines in Nerd Zone

axioms and theorems for the previous twenty-two centuries, aspiring to find a collection of axioms from which every true thing could be proven. Gödel's theorem showed that it was impossible, and the implications are still debated.

Turing's invention of the universal Turing machine was part of his reformulation of Gödel's result. He showed that there are many other things computers couldn't do, like predicting whether a running computer would ever halt.[21] The practical use for a proof that something is impossible is to save people from trying to do it. I was surprised when I witnessed an ambitious young professor of electrical engineering tell his senior colleagues that he was working on a program to predict whether other programs would halt, and all of them nodded sagely.

While some were disappointed by the limitations of computers, many humans, including me, were happy to learn that our intelligence could not be replaced by a computer with an axiomatic system cranking out every true mathematical fact.

***

Of all the management courses I took, Management Information Systems was the most practical for CS. It taught future managers how to best exploit computers in their work. There were many case studies about notable computer projects, one of which automated a warehouse—forty years before Amazon. The most prescient thing I learned in the course was in a paper, written by Harvard Business School professors, Leavitt and Whisler, that predicted that computers would hollow out corporations, eliminating most

---

[21] See Halting Problem in Nerd Zone

of the jobs in the middle between chief executives and janitors. The two foresaw the rise of the corporations that employ relatively few people but generate big profits.

***

Sitting in my MAC office one morning in 1965, I was reading the *Wall Street Journal* and came across a story about autism. I almost jumped out of my chair. *This is who I am!* I'd never heard about autism but recognized in myself many of the characteristics—avoidance of eye contact, ability to concentrate, mathematical prowess, awkwardness in speech, weird perspectives, and bad table manners. (I guess the last is a secondary effect of not noticing looks of disgust in fellow diners.) It also mentioned that autistic people often become accountants and programmers. It was a relief to hear that my weirdness was not willful, that it was a natural tendency. My mother and friends had accepted me so well that I didn't see it as a stigma so much as a quirk.

***

On a visit to Pittsburgh in the fall of 1966, I dropped by Susan's house. In the late afternoon sun, we sat on the living room couch while an energized Susan caught me up. A lot had happened. Susan's mother had sent her to secretarial school in New York, after which she returned to Pittsburgh to a legal secretary job. A year later her father and mother split, and he moved to Los Angeles. She was taking night classes at the Pitt in political science. She had just gotten back from a solo trip to Europe, which she'd paid for with her earnings. She'd been dating around the Ivy League. She seemed much older, a confident woman who was more amused than awed by me.

I'd changed a little too. I was sporting a mustache and John Lennon-style glasses, going for the look of an MIT professor. But I wouldn't be confused for a Beatle.

Also, unbeknownst to me, Susan had kissed her Princeton boyfriend from Baltimore good-bye a few hours before I arrived. Intrigued by this new Susan, I asked her for a date. We went to some of my old haunts on Walnut Street where I told her I was making a lot of money programming and was a "good catch."

We bumped into some of my friends, and I took everyone over to CMU to meet ELIZA a program created by MIT professor Joseph Weizenbaum. ELIZA carried on a dialog with a human over a teletype pretending to be a psychiatrist. You would use the teletype to enter statements like, "I hate my father," and it would type back, "Tell me more about your father." The computer wasn't doing anything remotely intelligent, just choosing certain words from the human's statements and feeding them back in scripted replies, but my friends were mesmerized. So, it passed Turing's test rather easily. ELIZA illustrated an odd but common thing about computers. In and of themselves they are straightforward and boring, but we can't resist attributing human traits to them.

***

Susan and I wrote letters to each other that fall. When I came to Pittsburgh for Christmas, we began dating in earnest. Susan had little interest in computers or what I did with them but liked the idea that I was at MIT, already making money as a programmer, and might be a professor someday.

After a Christmas date I asked, "What would you like to do New Year's Eve?"

"Oh. I'm going to Baltimore."

"Huh? Why?"

"I was invited."

"Well, cancel it."

"Well, are we engaged?"

"No."

She went to Baltimore.

It is a profoundly erroneous truism . . . that we should cultivate the habit of thinking what we are doing. The precise opposite is the case. Civilization advances by extending the number of important operations which we can perform without thinking about them.
– Alfred Whitehead

4. Programming as Mathematics

The seeds of my PhD research were planted when I learned LISP (List Processor), which was the programming language John McCarthy and some MIT students had invented to compete with Newell and Simon's IPL. Like IPL, LISP trafficked with lists of symbols and numbers but was easier to read and use. More importantly, it had a unique, *declarative* approach to programming. Instead of writing an *imperative* program as a series of commands, you write a declarative mathematical statement describing how the computer's output should relate to its input. In terms of programming, it simply means assignment statements, other than `let`, are forbidden.

Factorial is a mathematical *function* described by this sentence:

Factorial(1) = 1, and Factorial(n+1) = (n+1) * Factorial(n)

Theorem: Factorial(n) is the number of ways you can line up n people.

Proof: We use a reasoning method called *induction*.

Base step: n=1. There is just one way to make a line with one person.

Induction Step: Assume an *induction hypothesis* that Factorial(m) describes the way to line up m people for all 1≤m≤n. Consider lining up n+1 people. There are n+1 choices for the first person. Then you follow her with a line of n people, and, by the induction hypothesis, there are Factorial(n) ways to do to that. So, there are (n+1) ✕ Factorial(n) ways to line up n+1 people.

QED.

Induction seems like magic at first.

Mathematicians think functions simply *exist*, independent of how they might be computed. In this case Factorial is an infinite set of pairs starting with <1,1>, <2,2>, <3,6,>, <4,24>, <5,120>, etc.

The LISP program for computing Factorial is this compressed version of the declarative sentence:

```
Factorial(n) = (n=1) ? 1: n*Factorial(n -1)
```

We call this style *declarative* programming. In this language = really means "equal", so we can dispense with == as well as `return`. Notice that we didn't need to say anything about push-down stacks or any other details of how `Factorial` is computed. We don't need to tell the computer how to do it. And, as Whitehead suggests, we don't even need to think about it. Indeed, there are many ways to figure out what `Factorial(5)` is. You might start by replacing it by `5*Factorial(4)`. Then, if you happen to remember that `Factorial(4)` is 24, you can answer 120 immediately. Otherwise, you can rewrite the expression as `5*4*Factorial(3)`. Now you have a choice of whether next to replace `5*4` by 20, work on `Factorial(3)`, or even do both simultaneously.

Most programmers would recoil at the LISP program because they can't use assignment statements, which are intuitive if you understand how computers work. More importantly, as any programmer will tell you, a declarative program often takes much longer to get its answer than an equivalent imperative one.

Here is an *imperative* function to compute Factorial.

```
function Fact(n) {
   let answer = 1
   let k = 2
   while (k ≤ n) {
      answer = answer * k
      k = k+1
   }
   return answer
}
```

Proving that this version computes the number of ways to line up n people would be more difficult. Even if you don't bother proving things about programs, the fact that you *could* suggests that declarative programs are more intellectually manageable than imperative ones. Also, perhaps an AI compiler, given the declarative version, could somehow replace it with this faster imperative version.

Expressing things mathematically allows one to leave out unimportant details. It's a little like saying "Don't marry any Tom, Dick, or Harry," rather than "If it's Tom, reject him. If it's Dick, reject him. If it's Harry, reject him. Otherwise, consider him."

Once you think of functions as objects that exist rather than computing processes, you can imagine passing them as parameters of other functions. For example,

`Sum(n, f) = (n = 0) ? f(0) :f(n)+Sum(n−1, f)`

returns the value of `f(n)+...+f(0)` for any `f` you give it.

I studied McCarthy's paper "A Basis for a Mathematical Theory of Computation" extensively. It illustrated how to prove properties of LISP programs with a technique he called *recursion induction*, which can be used in cases like the one above and many others. While McCarthy presented LISP as a language for describing functions, the more pragmatic students implementing it added a facility for imperative programming, because most people preferred to program that way.

McCarthy had studied logic and based LISP on his imperfect understanding of a mathematical language called the *lambda calculus* (also written λ-calculus), another way of describing computable functions. The λ-calculus was created by Alonzo Church who published his work a few months before Turing and might have scooped him. Had there not been some lobbying by Turing's friends with the journal editor, we might never have heard of Turing. Later, when he became Turing's PhD advisor, he and Turing had a friendly shootout and agreed upon a tie: The λ-calculus could compute anything a Turing machine could but no more.

Before I arrived at MIT, McCarthy had moved to Stanford where he founded an AI research lab in the Palo Alto Hills. I wouldn't meet him for several years.

In 1967, Christopher Strachey, England's leading language designer, sent a protégé, Peter Landin, to MIT. Landin had helped Perlis, McCarthy, and others design ALGOL. While most computer scientists were primarily concerned with the syntax of languages, Strachey and Landin cared about semantics and believed that programming language semantics should be based on mathematical principles. Landin was an expert in the λ-calculus, so when some of my LISP friends were going to his introductory lecture, I eagerly joined them.

Landin paced around in front of us, speaking in a loud, amused, Yorkshire accent. He believed that the λ-calculus could be a universal programming language, a sort of Esperanto, that every other programming language could be reduced to—just as Turing's machine is a model for hardware. He had designed a language called ISWIM (If you See What I Mean) that gave the λ-calculus a more natural syntax, originally designed for Strachey's Cambridge Programming Language (CPL).

ISWIM's most notable feature was treating functions as *first-class objects*, meaning they could be passed around as both parameters and values as they are in the λ-calculus. This can be helpful in writing general programs that work on other programs.

For example, here is a function to create iterators:

```
Iterator(operator, start)=
   let Apply(f)=
      let Loop(i) = (i == 0)
                    ? start
                    : f(i)*Loop(i-1)
      Loop
   Apply
```

Now suppose `product(x,y) = x*y`. Then

```
Iterator(product, 1)(sine)(4)
  =
  let Apply(f)=
     let Loop(i) = (i == 0)
                   ? 1
                   : f(i)*Loop(i-1)
     Loop
  Apply(sine)(4)

  = Loop'(4)
    where Loop'(i) =(i == 0)
                    ? 1
                    : sine(i)*Loop'(i-1)

  = sine(4)*sine(3)*sine(2)*sine(1)*1
```

You could also do this sort of thing in LISP, but a flaw in its implementation made it error prone, so programmers avoided it.

Landin's real talent was demonstrating how any imperative program could be translated into a purely

73

declarative one, eschewing assignment statements, making it clearer and more readable.[22] The majority of the audience was skeptical, but I was entranced with the idea that there could be principles to apply to the unruly field of programming languages.

MAC hired Landin and, shortly after, hired me as his programmer to write an interpreter for ISWIM to run on MAC's computer. At this point, I had stopped taking any courses in management and officially fell under the wing of an electrical engineering professor, Jack Wozencraft. His plan was to start teaching ISWIM to MIT undergraduates in their first programming course, "before they had their minds ruined by FORTRAN."

Landin infected me with his uncompromising approach. I became his disciple in advocating declarative programming, and we became drinking buddies. After a hard day programming and arguing, we'd repair to a saloon; and, around ten o'clock, we'd appear at his Cambridge rental house where his patient wife would make us dinner. Over grilled pork chops, I learned he was a Marxist, the first I had ever known.

Landin returned to England after a year, feeling somewhat uncomfortable with MIT and US politics. He posted anti-Vietnam War messages on his office door. Back in England, he had gone to jail for demonstrating, "when all the best people, like Bertrand Russell, were going to jail," he told me. Students at MIT might have sympathized with Landin, but Wozencraft (his boss) was a West Point graduate.

---

[22] See Declarative Form in Nerd Zone

Years later, in 1975 after Landin and ISWIM had been forgotten at MIT, two professors, invented the language Scheme, which incorporated all ISWIM's features. It corrected the flaw in LISP and allowed functions to be first-class objects. Most importantly, a textbook about programming that used Scheme was written, making it relatively widespread.

As Landin was departing, another Brit visited, joined, and moved into his office on my hallway. Martin Richards[23] was more restrained and more polite, giving every impression of being from the upper classes. He had just finished a PhD at Cambridge and gotten married. His wife, Pat, was a nurse and got a job at Massachusetts General Hospital, despite the immigration meanies.

For his PhD research, Richards had implemented a compiler for CPL. Richards had to write the compiler in machine language, which made the job quite tedious.

At MIT Richards designed a new programming language called BCPL, standing for "Bootstrapping CPL." His goal was to make it extremely easy to *port* BCPL onto whatever computer you happened to have. Computer people use "port" as a verb meaning to move and adapt to a different kind of computer. Once ported, BCPL could be used to implement a CPL compiler on a new computer. In other

---

[23] Photo courtesy of Martin Richards

words, he wanted to make the work he had done in Cambridge easier.

Another notable visitor to MIT during my time was a young Dana Scott[24], from Princeton, and by 1966 already one of the world's foremost logicians. He invented all the finite state machine algorithms I'd learned but was best known for proving the independence of the continuum hypothesis from the axiom of choice—whatever they are. As a sort of hobby, he dabbled in the λ-calculus, so Minsky had invited him to enlighten us about its true nature. Scott left a beautiful package of handwritten notes that I read with great interest. In the introduction to his notes, he mentioned that he would like to find a "semantic model" for the λ-calculus. I had only the dimmest notion of what sort of thing that would be.

Perlis, an MIT graduate student himself, came to give a presentation at MAC on his language Formula ALGOL. It reminded me how invigorating he was, compared to stodgy MIT professors.

However, one MIT professor I chanced to meet was not at all stodgy. One day I had a two-minute elevator encounter with Licklider.

"Are you still at DARPA?" I asked.

---

[24] Photo courtesy of Dana Scott

"Heavens, no! I've been at IBM since 1964, and now I'm back at MIT," he said, looking comfortable as a professor. "I like to repot myself every five years."

That's a new thought!

***

MIT did not have a CS department yet. As a general stopgap they allowed students to create self-defined PhD programs. Since I had already studied topics taught by the mathematics and electrical engineering departments, in addition to all the management courses, I proposed a self-defined CS program supervised by faculty from those three departments. It was approved, and I had a faculty committee to supervise my program. After that, my only hurdle was to pass *ad hoc* oral exams given by the three departments. The math one was easy; I'd taken two courses from the professor who questioned me and gotten As. The electrical engineering one was a little scarier. I struggled through a simple state machine question but passed. I took the management exam for granted—partly because Ness was on the committee—and gave some stupid answers. I would have flunked, but Ness negotiated a face-saving deal in which I would write a paper. In the paper, I observed that platform services that match buyers with sellers can often acquire a monopoly naturally, because each buyer wants to go to the platform with the most sellers and vice versa. I later learned that this phenomenon is called the *network effect*.

After the orals, the final and most important requirements for a scientific PhD are doing research, discovering something new, and writing a dissertation about it. My ambition was to invent a programming language, just as Perlis, Newell,

Simon, McCarthy, Strachey, Landin, and others had done. After years of programming in various languages, I had developed my own ideas for new languages that would make programming easier. However, I didn't have the foggiest notion where to start. In any case, the ambition to design a language was dashed when I discussed plans for a thesis with Wozencraft, who was the best choice for an advisor because he appreciated the λ-calculus and was a full professor[25], not subject to judgments of other faculty.

"What kind of theorems are you going to prove?" he asked.

"Well, I was planning to use all the theorems other people have proved to design a better programming language," I answered.

"Here at MIT, we prove theorems!"

Though his PhD was in electrical engineering he proved theorems about coded information.

"OK," I said. "How do you decide if a theorem is any good?"

"One indication is how hard it is to prove."

I thought this was misguided. CMU students were allowed to create languages for a thesis. Richards had written a compiler for his thesis. Furthermore, Ness's opinion, learned from his study of an opera, *Die Meistersinger*, was that a great thesis should break the conventional rules. But most PhD

---

[25] American Professors come in three flavors: Assistant Professor, Associate Professor, and (full) Professor. Assistants typically have three-year contracts. Associates usually have lifetime tenure. The major privilege of Professors is voting on promoting associates to become full professors.

aspirants eventually learn to do what they're told rather than argue about what makes a good thesis.

Wozencraft, who was new to mathematical logic like me, sent me to Manuel Blum for help. Blum had recently completed an important mathematics PhD thesis, "A Machine-Independent Theory of the Complexity of Recursive Functions," that showed a way to compare the speed of algorithms and opened a whole field of CS.

I found Blum with a posse of graduate students sitting causally in an idle lecture hall.

"What kind of theorems are you proving?"

He greeted me warmly with the typical mathematician's salutation.

I shamefacedly admitted that I was a virgin in the theorem department. I rambled a bit about λ-calculus and changed the subject.

"I liked the paper you and McCulloch wrote about neural computing."

"Oh, yes. I've been fascinated about how the brain works ever since I was a kid in Venezuela, and my father advised me to learn about the brain to get smarter. I started reading books about neurons and how they worked."

"Did it make you smarter?" I joked.

"Not yet."

Humble, but amused.

***

After my New Year's Eve disappointment, Susan and I exchanged multiple visits, travelling between Pittsburgh and Boston.

As always, Carson, my romantic friend, was my coach. In one session I said, "I don't understand love, but I'll just fake it until I do." He was appalled but recommended I send some flowers.

Sitting in my car in front of her house after a date, we engaged in a little kissing and groping.

"I want to cook, clean, and have your babies," Susan announced.

I was a goner, but I didn't acknowledge it.

Instead, I made a last-ditch effort to get her to move to Boston, without success, but when I proposed to her in the late spring, she called her mother, reserved the church, and asked her Uncle Leo, a Jesuit and president of Fordham University, to officiate. Apparently, I had been the only missing piece of her plan.

On my next trip to Pittsburgh we set out to buy an engagement ring. I was equipped with my mother's solitaire diamond ring that my father had purchased from an unknown friend of Uncle Charles's, many years earlier. To my relief, the jeweler certified that it was a real diamond, and Susan agreed.

"I want some blue sapphires to go with it."

"You've been thinking about this?"

"Duh."

The jeweler limited the financial damage somewhat by saying, "Your hand is so delicate. You wouldn't want to overwhelm it with three large stones."

I went back to Cambridge, leaving all the choices about china patterns and wedding gifts to Susan. After all, I was color blind.

One evening after work, Landin and I were drinking in the MIT faculty club.

"Well, I'm getting married in the fall," I said.

"Really?"

Landin was surprised that I had any romantic life.

"Tell me about her. Is she a scientist? A highly paid lawyer? A rich heiress? Where did you meet her?"

"No, she's a legal secretary from Pittsburgh, and I've known her for ten years," I said. "She loves me! We just seem right for each other."

He looked skeptical.

I was disturbed that Landin was unimpressed with my fiancé, but I'd never come close to the kind of woman he suggested. Susan would be a lifeline to my better self.

The week before the wedding, my best man Carson gave me my first marijuana cigarette, just like my first beer ten years earlier. I didn't feel particularly strange, but when I later went over to Susan's house, I was startled by the looks on her face and her mother's. At first I thought I was frightening them, but they were just having prewedding anxiety. Why had I never noticed that before? Maybe it was the pot improving my perception.

Susan and I were married on September 2, 1967. It was a big wedding in a fancy chapel on Pitt's campus. Her brother Sandy gave Susan away and Ness, Ernst, Schroeder, and Susan's younger brother, Chris, were ushers. Srodes was honorary, occupied with a medical internship in North Carolina. The reception was at her mother's house, mostly in the backyard, with dancing in the garage.

After a three-day honeymoon in Québec City, Susan and I moved into a one-bedroom basement apartment near Harvard. I was shocked and dismayed when Susan asked me to wash the windows. It led to our first argument.

She got a secretarial job and started taking night classes at Harvard. We had dinner guests and went to parties—just like real grown-ups. We began seeing a lot of Martin and Pat Richards who lived about ten blocks from us in Cambridge. Susan developed a taste for Bonwit Teller dresses but was otherwise frugal. However, it took me a while to adjust to sharing a checkbook register with someone who didn't balance to the penny.

Many students flounder at the PhD thesis stage and never finish. Those who don't finish are tagged as having an AbD—All but Dissertation—degree. Indeed, I was floundering. Susan's Uncle Leo had warned her that I might only attain an AbD.

When I got back to work, Wozencraft said he had been about to wash me out of the PhD program, but maybe my love life had been interfering with my research. He would give me one more chance. Now a married man, wanting to get on with my life, I started looking for the least embarrassing way to get out of graduate school, and I promised myself, *If I ever get past this obstacle, I'm going to a psychiatrist to find out why I'm struggling so much.* Susan had to get used to my reading and thinking for hours at a time in our small apartment. She began to understand that nerds sometimes ignore the people around them.

I set about looking for something—anything!—original to prove about the λ-calculus. Of course, to prove something new, you had to learn everything that was known in your area—or at least everything your supervisors knew. I went beyond McCarthy's work and began to study the work of other logicians. After much thrashing around, I decided to prove that McCarthy's recursion induction technique could be applied in the more general setting of the λ-calculus. It would not be surprising, but it was original and difficult to prove, satisfying Wozencraft's criteria.

On the way to that theorem, I had to invent an idea, which I called contextual equivalence. Two λ-expressions are contextually equivalent if you could replace one by the other in any larger λ-expression without changing the value of the larger expression. In the context of any programming language, contextual equivalence means that you can't write a program that can tell the difference between the two expressions. For example, "X+Y" doesn't look like "Y+X", but no FORTRAN program would give a different result if one was replaced by the other. A homey version of the idea is, "If it walks like a duck, swims like a duck, and quacks like a duck, it's a duck." This idea was so useful to later students of the λ-calculus that it came to be called "Morris Contextual Equivalence." (Google it.) I later discovered that it was a version of Leibniz's Law, which was stated about a formal logic, so I had been scooped by three hundred years. But in the community of λ-calculus buffs, contextual equivalence was the most useful contribution of my thesis.

Another aspect of the λ-calculus that interested me was *type*, especially the types of functions. We use A×B to name the type of pairs of values with types A and B. We use A→B to name the type of functions from values of type A to values of type B.

For example, the function Sum(n,f), mentioned above, has the type

integer×(integer→integer) →integer

and the function Iterator has the type

(integer×integer→integer)×integer

$$\rightarrow(\text{integer}\rightarrow\text{integer})\rightarrow\text{integer}\rightarrow\text{integer}$$

It is easy for programmers to make mistakes using such complicated functions. So, we would like an interpreter or compiler to check the types in programs. [26]

I proved some more theorems showing how to check the types of λ-expressions, starting with just declarations of the simple types like integer and character. I further proved a variation of a known theorem that any checked λ-expression represented a computation that would always halt. At first, this sounds like a good thing, but it also eliminates useful expressions that may halt in some context.

At about the same time in Belfast, a real logician, J. Roger Hindley, was also studying types and later explained much more about the situation, eclipsing my work on types.

I had proved enough theorems to satisfy Wozencraft by May. Now I had to write the dissertation to explain them. To clear my head between writing sessions, I took up crewel embroidery. One evening, as I was embroidering, and Susan was refinishing a table, she said, "What's wrong with this picture?"

Getting all 130 pages of my dissertation on paper was a tedious process. Susan typed every single one—without the aid of any word processor, because they hadn't been invented. Typing all the mathematics required changing a Selectric typewriter ball innumerable times, but the joint effort on my dissertation earned me a PhD.

My PhD degree is officially from the Sloan School of Management in 1969. However, it says "Computer Science!" I was one of the lucky few to have such a degree then.

---

[26] See Types in Nerd Zone

***

In 1968 a group of academics met under NATO auspices and declared that there was a software crisis. "Software" was another name for programs and, more generally, the field of programming. The group launched the field of software engineering to instill more discipline into the burgeoning practice. A historian of science has described it as "Edsger Dijkstra's quixotic campaign to evict almost all practicing programmers from their jobs and replace them with mathematicians."

But the real crises of 1968 were caused by the Tet Offensive in Vietnam, the withdrawal of Lyndon Johnson from the presidential race, the assassinations of Martin Luther King and Robert Kennedy, and racial unrest, even in Pittsburgh. We were concerned but were too busy with our lives to freak out properly.

It always surprises me how short the moments of triumph, of satisfaction, are. Even the grand prizes, the actual publications, the promotions, and the grants awarded. They satisfy for about five minutes. Then once more our eyes are on the future, hurtling forwards, feeling like we have not yet done enough. – Amber Davis

5. Publishing or Perishing

I'd come from MIT for an interview, wearing a black, chalk-striped banker's suit, white shirt, and tie. I looked like an undertaker talking to a crowd of country clubbers, farmers, and hippies when I entered the lecture hall. I was nervous and feeling out of place as I began to give a talk about my thesis to an audience that included faculty members who would decide whether to offer me a job as an assistant professor in Berkeley's new CS department. Chalk dust was flying as I outlined a bit of mathematics from my PhD thesis, when a dashiki-wearing hippie with long hair, a headband, and a dirty beard raised his hand.

"So, your version of recursion induction works even when you're dealing with partial functions?"

"Yes!"

Yow! Most people have never heard of recursion induction, let alone understand its limitations!

While I was sweating my way through the interview process, Susan was touring around, soaking up the vibe, and deciding that this was where we should live.

"You won't believe this," I said to her when we met at the hotel. "My talk was attended by some street people, and one of them asked a question showing that he really understood mathematics! If even the street people here are so smart, what must the professors be like?"

That evening, a young professor, Butler Lampson, and his wife Lois, drove us across the bay to a San Francisco restaurant where we had dinner with all the professors of the new CS department: Beresford Parlett, the department head and a British math professor, Mike Harrison, and Marty Graham from engineering, and Lampson, who had recently finished a CS PhD. All were accompanied by their wives. Such a gathering for us was a good sign. Susan and I returned to Cambridge with high hopes of a job offer.

I first heard of Don Knuth when Parlett called me. "Don Knuth turned down our offer and decided to go to Stanford, so we're offering you a job as an assistant professor instead."[27]

Knuth was a giant of algorithm design and analysis. He was best known for his multivolume series, *The Art of*

---

[27] Photo courtesy of Jill Knuth

Computer Programming, which attempts to explain virtually all the important algorithms invented to date.

That offer was good enough for me. As Susan and I packed up our life, a headline from the *Cambridge Chronicle* read, "MIT Professor Disrobes at Living Theatre Performance!" The radical Living Theater actors were protesting the Vietnam War and urging audiences to join them in nudity. We couldn't because we were headed to the West Coast.

Our first stop on the way to California was Pittsburgh, where we visited family and friends, but left before Christmas, happy to avoid what we had decided was "a festival of selfishness." We drove southwest to avoid snow, passing through Memphis and Dallas, where the MLK and JFK assassinations had occurred without noticing any memorials. As we approached Tucson on Christmas Eve, we succumbed to the holiday spirit and decided to visit my father's distant cousin for a few days.

I had never met Shiras Morris or his son, Lockwood, who happened to be there for the holiday. And to my surprise, Lockwood was a PhD student in CS at Stanford and enthusiastic about the λ-calculus! I noticed another Morris foible. Shiras, Lockwood, and I were all diffident men married to exuberant and assertive women.

Susan and I arrived in Berkeley a little before New Year's 1969. Marty Graham, who was to become a sort of uncle, had found us an apartment next to the campus where the Lampsons also lived.

Susan and I had forgotten about The Living Theatre until we heard that it was coming to Berkeley. We arrived an hour early to the high school auditorium where the performance was scheduled. It was bedlam, hundreds of naked people cavorting on the stage and in the aisles, and when the actors finally appeared, the audience berated them for not being radical enough. We weren't in Cambridge anymore.

We had assumed Berkeley would be an academic town, like Cambridge. It was not. While people in Harvard Square were usually passing through on their way to somewhere, many people on Berkeley's Telegraph Avenue were simply hanging out. It was our first week there, and we ventured into the bustling Caffe Mediterraneum for dinner.

"Jim! I heard you were coming," said Manuel Blum. "This is my wife, Lenore. Sit down and eat with us."

"Wow!" I said, "I didn't realize you were here. Are you in the CS department?"

"No, I'm in EECS (Electrical Engineering and Computer Science)."

"But you're a math guy. I heard that Knuth told Berkeley he wouldn't come to an engineering department."

"Well, they told me I didn't need to change a thing, so I said, 'OK.'"

"This is my wife, Susan," I said, as we sat down in the Blum's two free seats.

"What do you do Lenore?" Susan asked, as we ordered moussaka and hummus.

"I just finished my math PhD at MIT and have a postdoctoral appointment in Berkeley's math department."

"How did you meet?" asked Susan, gently preempting any descent into nerd-talk.

"We met in Venezuela when I was eleven. My parents had moved there to escape the anti-Communist madness."

As the four of us left the restaurant after dinner, a heavyset woman pulled up her skirt and offered to sell us drugs. The

Blums took it in stride, but I thought, *I see why they call it Berserkley!*

The Blums had a six-year-old son, Avrim, but they didn't subject him to Telegraph that night. They all seemed at home in Berkeley, politically, culturally, and tonsorially.[28]

As I prepared to teach, Susan enrolled at Mills College and started commuting south to the beautiful eucalyptus-shrouded, Oakland campus in our TR4, which had carried us across the country. She joined the married students' club of the all-women's college and soon became its president. She had found her place.

At the same time as I began teaching my first course, Data Structures, student demonstrations demanding a Black Studies department began. Unlike MIT or Tech students, Berkeley students were politically active. There was also a controversy about the fate of a city park. Governor Reagan demanded firmness when demonstrations started and called in the sheriffs. Tear gas attacks on the campus became common. For a few months, helicopters whirred above,

---

[28] Photo courtesy of Lenore and Manuel Blum

patrolling the city, giving us all a sense of dread. The tension reached a peak when a sheriff shot and killed a student. When the university agreed to start a Black Studies department, this created a little hiccup in my life. My assistant professor appointment was held up when the university's available faculty slots, a precious commodity, went to the new department. This was the second sign I'd gotten of my department's precarious status. The first being the ramshackle, wooden, "temporary" building we were housed in, which had been around since 1944. Our department was tiny compared to the huge EECS department that Harrison, Graham, and Lampson had left, but we had the enegy and enthusiasm of pioneers.

PhDs are rarely trained in teaching; but after twenty years as a student, I must have learned something, given the enthusiastic reception the Data Structures students were giving my teaching. However, teaching was not my department's priority. Research was everything at Berkeley.

Parlett emphasized the point by quoting what a math professor said to new assistant professors: "You can piss in the hallways if you prove good theorems." Parlett strongly advised that I immediately publish my thesis in a journal. But I was ambivalent. My thesis got me out of graduate school, but I wasn't proud of it. However, I had just discovered an improvement to McCarthy's recursion induction method that I could describe without needing to explain the λ-calculus. So, I published that finding as my first paper ever, in the *CACM*. Sometime after that, I noticed that Scott had described something similar in the old handwritten notes he had left me at MIT. Nevertheless, I was still proud of my publication.[29]

***

That spring Susan and I were pleased to be invited to dinner at the Lampsons' apartment, which was a floor up from ours with a view of the San Francisco Bay. We admired the new teak dinner table they'd bought in Sa[30]n Francisco. The meal was modest, because the Lampsons were dieting, although they were far more svelte than I was. As we chatted about our lives, Lampson mentioned that he had entered Harvard when he was sixteen.

"Wow, you were almost a prodigy!" I said.

Lampson blushed in anger and exclaimed, "I *was* a prodigy!"

I still don't think starting college at sixteen qualifies, but there is no doubt that Lampson was brilliant. The son of travelling diplomats, he graduated *magna cum laude* in physics at Harvard before switching to computing at Berkeley. In 1969 he was a star of our CS faculty. While still a grad student, he had developed a prototype time-sharing system, and now he was working to build a real system, called CalTSS, to serve the Berkeley campus, which was still mired in the punched-

---

[29] See Truncation Induction in Nerd Zone

[30] Photo courtesy of Butler Lampson

card era. His focus was on one of his research interests—security, keeping users' programs from interfering with the operating system or other users' programs. (Like dope dealers, creators of software systems call their clients "users.")

Lampson's clear, rapid speech inspired someone to coin the term "milliLampson" to describe the speed of a person's speech. The average person speaks at 200 milliLampsons—one fifth as fast as Lampson.

I became a programmer on the CalTSS project: me, a few of the university's staff, and three graduate CS students—Bruce Lindsay, Dave Redell, and Howard Sturgis, an eccentric, old logician with a scraggly beard and pigtails—and a handful of undergraduates, including Paul McJones, Charles Simonyi, and Gene McDaniel. We worked on a Control Data Corporation (CDC) 6400, which had 480K of memory and cost about a million dollars.

Simonyi stood out from the scruffy team. He had flowing black hair and wore spotless white trousers. He spoke with supreme confidence, and I disliked him. I learned that he was born in Hungary, the son of a physicist. As a teen he wanted to be a cosmonaut, but Russians would get priority for those jobs. At seventeen, already a computer whiz, he got a visa for a trip to Denmark and didn't go home. From there, he moved to Berkeley to get a BS degree where he became Lampson's protégé.

Simonyi, Lampson, and the others didn't seem to care whether users of CalTSS could figure it out. I grew to appreciate how nice Project MAC's system was to use and realized that its creators intended it to be a service—not their own personal playpen. Lampson's focus on security was so complete that I facetiously suggested we could guarantee security by making the system impossible to use. To remind them all of the users' prospective, I wrote a short guide. It was called "The Idiot's Guide to CalTSS," which I patterned after *How to Keep Your Volkswagen Alive: A Manual of Step-by-Step Procedures for the Compleat Idiot*, which I admired for making me semi-competent at fixing mine. If anyone noticed the implicit criticism, they ignored it.

My first CalTSS assignment was writing a text editor like one from MAC. As part of it, I was programming a search algorithm that allowed a user to find words in a text.

The straightforward algorithm, shown on page 32, starts matching the pattern against the first character of the text. Whenever a character fails to match, it moves one character forward in the text and tries the whole pattern again.

Consider the pattern WWWB and the text XWWCZWWWWWWWB. When we try the pattern starting at the second character of the text, the third W in the pattern fails to match the C, which is the fourth character in the text. So, the algorithm starts over at the third character of the text, moving its focus back.

For complicated reasons, I didn't want to move backwards in the text, even by one character.[31] Pondering how to avoid backing up, I remembered a fact from MIT's Finite State Machine Theory. Looking for WWWB is like asking if the regular expression

(any character)*WWWB(any character)*

denotes a set containing the text.

---

[31] See Buffering in Nerd Zone

Since any regular expression can be turned into a finite state machine, recognizing the search for a pattern can be done by a machine that never backs up. You just need to do some preliminary work with the pattern to set up the machine. I wrote my search algorithm that way—generating a little machine language program on the fly to do the search, based on the pattern. Here is what the machine looked like.

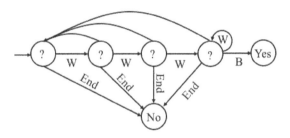

Once you have seen three Ws you can keep moving forward as long as you see Ws, and report Yes if you ever see a B. Report No if you ever see the end of the text. In all other cases return to the beginning of the pattern and move one character forward in the text.

It wasn't until I got back to Berkeley after a few summer weeks visit to Boston that I learned that my clever program had a bug in it that baffled the other programmers. I felt chastened, because they were pissed when they had to program some of it over again, replacing my obscure code. I had made two amateur mistakes. One—I should have tested my program thoroughly before leaving town. Two—I should have obeyed a dictum of Strachey: "It is impossible to foresee the consequences of being clever, so you try to avoid it whenever you can." I should have written the straightforward program. It's always better to do things in the most obvious way feasible, so that other programmers, and even you, can figure out the code later.

***

The following Christmas, my mother came to visit from Pittsburgh and Susan's father came up from Los Angeles. Although Susan and I generally avoided Telegraph Avenue, we took them there. We always enjoyed seeing easterners freak out at the head shops and exuberant activities of dubious legality.

My mother and I often drank and talked all night, and Susan and her father joined right in. Sitting in our small living room, we collectively drank so much vodka and whiskey that we'd run out by Christmas morning, and I was delighted to discover California liquor stores were open on Christmas mornings. The restrictions of Massachusetts and Pennsylvania were a fading memory. It was all casualness and freedom out here. As spring came, Susan and I began smoking pot (supplied by one of my CalTSS friends.) We got to know a neighbor who belonged to the Sexual Freedom League (an official student organization that held weekly orgies), and she told me that three of my CS department colleagues belonged to it.

I learned that the "street person" who had attended my interview talk was Jim Gray, the CS department's first and best graduate student. Gray had been well within the UC Berkeley dress code.

Gray had learned about my ill-fated attempt at back-up-free pattern matching and encouraged me to work more on the algorithm. He told another graduate student at Stanford, Vaughan Pratt, about it. Pratt appeared in my Berkeley office.

"How does it work?"

I pulled out the WWWB example and showed him the finite state machine that did the search.

"How do you construct this machine?" Pratt asked.

"There's a general way to do it for any regular expression, but in this simple case, it comes down to matching the pattern against itself. You can even use the partially constructed machine to do the matching of later characters in the pattern."[32]

Pratt sighed, then spoke.

"You seem to have the right idea. Knuth and I discovered a similar algorithm. While it's obvious that the machine scans the text in time proportional to its length, we noticed that the time to preprocess the pattern can be proportional to the length of the pattern. So, the entire operation is bounded by the *sum* of the lengths of the pattern text rather than the *product*."

"Hmm," I said, "I didn't even think about that."

For short patterns, the difference between the sum and product is not a big deal, but it's significant if one is scanning a chromosome 250 million nucleotides long for a gene with 27,000 nucleotides. Our new algorithm would be about 27,000 times faster.

---

[32] See KMP in Nerd Zone

After I understood that; and, living under the "publish or perish" regime, I wrote a paper titled "A Linear Pattern Matching Algorithm" and submitted it to the *CACM*.

The editor eventually wrote back, "We looked at it for weeks, and when we understood how it worked, we saw how simple it was. Therefore the paper is rejected."

What a jerk!

***

In the 1970s the world's growing community of programmers was divided into three main groups that reminded me of Indian castes. The Brahmins (Hindu priests) worshiped ALGOL, which seemed to be good for scientific computation. ALGOL programmers like Perlis could be oblivious to the grotty details of the computers their programs ran on. However, not many Brahmins worked as programmers and there weren't many ALGOL compilers available. The Shuras (laborers), typically scientists, programmed in FORTRAN which was inelegant but got the job done. Their programs were less readable, and the details of the computers they ran on showed through. Finally, the Dalits (outcastes), like my CalTSS group, programmed in machine code. They built operating systems and compilers and were called "systems programmers." However, the pecking order at a computer center was the reverse of what it was in India. Only the systems programmers were allowed in the inner sanctum where the computer ran.

I decided to port Richards's BCPL compiler to Berkeley's CDC 6400. I thought my colleagues might save some time by avoiding machine language.

Richards designed the process extremely carefully to require the absolute minimum knowledge of the importer:

just BCPL and the machine language of the target computer. His compiler had two phases. In the first phase, it translated BCPL into a machine language called UNCOL (Universal Computer Oriented Language) for an entirely imaginary computer. UNCOL was proposed as an intermediate language for compilers in 1958 but was never fully specified until Richards did so in 1968. Richards gave the UNCOL machine a minimal set of verbs, just enough to support a BCPL compiler, carefully chosen so that each one was easily translated into one or more verbs of most real computers. His version of the second phase translated UNCOL into the language of MIT's IBM 7094 computer.

Since 7094 machine language would be useless to me with Berkeley's CDC 6400 computer, Richards had sent me only the first phase, written in BCPL, as well as its translation into UNCOL. So, I wrote my version of the second phase, a translator from UNCOL into 6400 machine code, to produce a BCPL compiler that worked on a 6400.[33]

BCPL was a great invention because it served the needs of the system programmers. It had a pleasant syntax, inherited from CPL, but allowed them to drive a computer's hardware straightforwardly. It was great for writing operating systems and compilers for other languages.

Now, with my success in porting BCPL to the local computer, the hard part came. I had to convince the Berkeley Dalits to use BCPL. I scheduled a departmental talk called: "BCPL: A Good Programmer's Language." I intended the double meaning: it was a good language for good programmers.

---

[33] See BCPL in Nerd Zone

Most of my intended audience came and several senior faculty members from the department, probably wanting to see what kind of research the new assistant professor—me—had been doing. By this time, I was feeling confident speaking to the folks who had hired me. I wasn't wearing a suit anymore as I breezed through my description of BCPL. The talk later proved successful when some of the programmers on CalTSS started using BCPL.

However, there was an uncomfortable moment.

"What evidence do you have that this language is better than FORTRAN?" asked a newly arrived senior professor.

Velvel Kahan, a mathematician, was skeptical. Tension rippled through the audience.

"Well, it's specially designed for people who program operating systems," I said. "And it has been used by the Bell Labs people to implement UNIX."

"What's UNIX?" he asked.

"UNIX is an operating system."

"Nobody cares about operating systems! Your language doesn't even support scientific computation." The gulf between mathematicians and programmers was apparent.

His specialty! Aha! That's what's bugging him. The audience relaxed a little, realizing he was just riding his own hobby horse. Kahan was hazing me in the way senior professors have always hazed junior professors. Graham, a hardware engineering professor, took offense on my behalf and made his feelings known to Kahan a few days after the talk. The following week Kahan had a chat with me, and, as a sort of apology, told me that "Velvel" means wolf in Yiddish, as if that explained his aggressive manner. He later received a

Turing Award and became known as the father of floating-point, whom every computer manufacturer consulted.

Dick Karp, another new senior professor was also there, but kept quiet. For several years before he had been busy doing research at IBM Yorktown.

Note to self: A better academic career strategy is to work in a corporation's research lab establishing a reputation without the distraction of teaching. Then get a tenured position at a university.

Unlike Kahan, Karp was a humble and shy bachelor. The night Susan and I met him for dinner at the Harrison's house, he revealed that he used to win a lot of chess games in New York's Washington Square, and that he could multiply four-digit numbers in his head, but that he didn't generally reveal these facts, lest people think he was an idiot savant.

His love of mathematics began in his high school geometry class at the legendary Boston Latin School. By the time he'd finished his PhD he had narrowed his interest to practical computing problems that mattered to industry. He took a job at IBM and became world class at finding fast algorithms for such problems after several years. But Karp was bothered by some problems that looked easy but sometimes took exponential time to solve. For example, the knapsack problem that Ness and I tried seems easy because it is easy to decide whether any particular subset of items has usefulness of U without weighing more than W. But the only known, sure-fire way to answer whether there is such a subset can take exponentially long. As far as I'm concerned, if Karp can't find a fast algorithm, nobody can. I felt outclassed by his brilliance and resolved to focus my work on easier problems.

One afternoon, having coffee with Karp and Blum who were entertaining an IBM colleague of Karp's, John Cocke, I considered myself in brilliant company. The three of them were discussing their style of working.

"I'm a plodder and John is a fountain of great ideas who often pesters me to pursue them," said Karp.

"I limit myself to one problem a day," said Blum. "I think about it until I've solved it or get tired. Then I take the rest of the day off."

Steve Cook[34] was an assistant professor of mathematics at Berkeley with a courtesy appointment in CS, a nice, unassuming guy that we would have been happy to have in CS, but math was far more prestigious at Berkeley.

In 1970 Cook wrote a paper that showed that many problems of the type Karp was frustrated by were at least as hard as deciding whether a statement in propositional logic was ever true—a problem nobody had ever found an algorithm for that didn't sometimes take exponential time. (Recall that Russell, followed by Newell and Simon, was able to establish that *some* statements were always true but never

---

[34] Photo courtesy of Stephen Cook

said anything about testing any possible statements.) The paper did not make a big splash, except with Karp. It made Karp feel better that he hadn't found fast algorithms for those problems. And Karp went further and proved that at least twenty-one of those problems, including the knapsack problem, were exactly as hard as the propositional calculus decision problem.[35] Either there is a fast algorithm to solve all of them, or none of them have a fast algorithm.

Karp's theorems triggered a sensation among the algorithm community, and they went on to discover over a thousand equivalent problems. But, to date, no one has found a fast algorithm to do any of them or, conversely, proved that no such algorithm exists. It's become one of the most important problems in applied mathematics. Most experts doubt there is any fast algorithm.

As with Turing's noncomputability discovery, you might think that proving something is impossible is not important, but it prevents many programmers from wasting their time looking for foolproof fast algorithms when they recognize one of those problems.

For their contributions to the theory of algorithms, both Cook and Karp later received Turing Awards, Cook in 1982, and Karp in 1985. For me, all these discouraging theoretical results compared with the rampaging practical success of computers in the world, made me wonder why people worked in theoretical CS rather than simply exploiting computers to revamp the way we work.

---

[35] See Subset Sum in Nerd Zone

In the spring of 1970 I read a paper by John Reynolds in the *CACM*. He described his programming language GEDANKEN, which bore a striking resemblance to Landin's ISWIM. *Here was a kindred spirit.* I invited him to Berkeley to give a presentation. When he arrived, I took him for a drive in the Berkeley Hills to show him a view of the bay and San Francisco.

"I recently filled out a form setting my retirement date to be in 2000," he told me as we sat high in the fog-enshrouded hills. "By then I want to have made a significant intellectual contribution to science."

I admired his purposefulness. I certainly didn't have it.

Susan loved Mills and made some great friends. She graduated in 1970, won the English writing prize, and got a job as assistant to a bank president—not much of an upgrade from her pre-graduation secretarial jobs. It could have been worse. She might have continued to law school and then gotten an *unpaid* job as an assistant to an attorney, as Sandra Day O'Connor had earlier.

When summer arrived, we decided to drive up the coast to Canada in our bug, staying in state parks, under a little tent. We also quit smoking cigarettes. Whenever we wanted a cigarette, we would drink a beer. Eventually, one morning we wound up in a southern Oregon parking lot, nursing hangovers with more beers and sleeping. We turned inland and headed home.

By fall Susan had decided to try journalism and wrote articles for the *San Francisco Bay Guardian*, and the *Berkeley Gazette* covering commercial real estate issues.

Her father died unexpectedly in his Los Angeles apartment on Thanksgiving weekend. We flew down, and I carried out the dismal task of emptying his apartment. Her mother and brothers arrived a day later, and we spent a somber weekend with them. Unlike my father's death, his passing didn't have any noticeable effect on any of our lives. That made me feel sorrier for them because they had lost him so long ago.

***

Working on CalTSS gave me another good idea. At one of the team meetings, a programmer expressed concern that a certain process could see some critical data that belonged to another process. Lampson considered his worry for a minute and then burst into laughter.

"No, you idiot," he said. "As long as the first process can't change the data, the other process will be fine. There's no need for secrecy."

However, it was this exchange between Lampson and the programmer that sparked an idea: there were two independent security issues about communication between processes—authentication and secrecy. Authentication guarantees the identity of the sender of some information.

Secrecy ensures that only the intended receiver can see the information.

These properties could be achieved by a magic envelope that enforced the implications of the sender's and receiver's names. You are not able to write your name in the upper left corner (as sender), unless you have already, personally sealed the contents of the envelope. That ensures the authenticity of the contents. On the other hand, when someone writes your name in the middle of the envelope, only you can open it. When both a sender's name and a receiver's name are present, we have person-to-person secure communication. The receiver knows the contents are authentically from the sender, and the sender is guaranteed that no one other than the receiver will see the contents, at least initially. If there is no receiver address, then anyone can open it, and the sender has made a public declaration of the contents. Anyone can see it and believe the sender made it. On the other hand, if there is no sender's address, the envelope acts as a sort of anonymous suggestion box in which the receiver can see the content but can't be sure who put it in, even if the content contains the name of a sender. There are other magical properties that computers supply automatically, such as envelopes that can be put inside envelopes or copied along with their contents without the copier opening the envelope.

I published a paper for *CACM* about this idea: *Protection in Programming Languages.* I didn't bother inventing a new language, but I added operations to GEDANKEN that allowed a program to use magic envelopes. The operations would enforce the restrictions described above. A programmer could use magic envelopes to ensure that his subprogram could not be interfered with by any other parts of a larger program, even if he didn't know anything about the other parts. To clarify this, I offered some rules for proving that one's program fulfills its role without knowing what its environment was.

The only catch in my idea was that all the programmers of a large system had to be using the same programming language that enforced these security rules in its implementation. Unfortunately, large systems were written in multiple languages.

Lampson liked the paper, but neither of us suspected that such envelopes could be implemented by anybody, in any language, using encryption. Several years later, some clever people figured that out and called it *public key encryption*, which is used everywhere for secure internet communication.

***

One of the best lectures I heard at Berkeley was by a visitor, Alan Kay. He held up a funky cardboard model of something he called a *Dynabook*, which is what we call a laptop today. It was the product of his PhD thesis at the University of Utah. He told us the Dynabook was a tool for education, about which he had many passionate opinions.

"I had the misfortune or the fortune to learn how to read fluently starting about the age of three, so I had read maybe 150 books by the time I hit first grade, and I already knew the teachers were lying to me," he said.

Kay was the first time I sensed any romance about the computing field. Maybe it wasn't all brain-deadening programming and math.

***

In the summer of 1971 Susan and I took a ten-week vacation to Europe. Susan, who had vowed on her first trip to return with a partner, was delighted showing me the highlights. We started in England, where we tracked down an elusive Strachey in Oxford one afternoon. As he was sitting down to some tea, I told him my new opinions about types—that they weren't properly considered mathematical objects. His response was distinctly frosty.

We visited Martin and Pat Richards, who had settled back in England and had a daughter. We then stayed in the Hampstead neighborhood of London with John Reynolds, who was visiting Peter Landin for a term at Queen Mary College. They arranged for me to give a talk there about my thesis. After my talk, we all went out to dinner, and I asked Landin how he was doing at Queen Mary.

"People say I'm having a nervous breakdown," he said. "But I call it not showing up for my lectures."

Landin was in the process of abandoning CS, disillusioned by how theoretical it had become. He devoted the rest of his life to Marxism and LGBT affairs, which had always been important parts of his life. He grew "convinced that computing had been a bad idea, giving support to profit-taking corporate interests and a surveillance state, and that he had wasted his energies in promoting it," according to his obituary in 2009.

Our tour continued to France, where I learned they liked french fries (*Duh.*), and then onto Germany where Susan and

108

I stayed just outside Munich at a boarding school while I attended a two-week, NATO-sponsored CS summer school. Susan's mother joined us, and the two of them, along with the wives of other students, had fun touring the German countryside while we listened to interesting lectures from leading computer scientists.

The school's goal was to create some community among rising, young computer scientists. Luminaries like Reynolds (US), Edsger Dijkstra (Netherlands), and Tony Hoare (UK) were among the teachers. Because one of the organizers had been in the German Army during World War II, there were some who refused to participate. One might have thought Perlis (a descendant of Russian Jews in Pittsburgh) would refuse, but he plunged in with great enthusiasm, bringing his wife and young daughter along.

In those two weeks, Susan and I spent many evenings with the Perlises at their Bavarian hotel—drinking beer and kibitzing. Perlis had just left CMU to start a new department at Yale. One sunny afternoon, we all took a bus tour to see crazy King Ludwig's castle, which Disney had copied for Fantasyland. As we climbed onto the bus, and I passed by Alan Perlis, he said to me, "Morris, you're not ambitious enough." I didn't pause, and he never elaborated.

Edsger Dijkstra was younger than Perlis but was also a star of CS. In 1956 he had invented a shortest path algorithm that bears his name; today it tells Ubers the best routes to take. Every conversation I had with Dijkstra was short and ended with him saying, "Harrumph!" Unlike Perlis, Dijkstra was a grouch who had dismissive things to say about his fellow luminaries. Logicians like Scott were "the attorneys of mathematics." Knuth, "an encyclopedist." And although

Dijkstra didn't say anything rude about Perlis, their lectures seemed like an implicit debate between them, and it was evident that their differing opinions on CS were rooted in their personalities. Dijkstra was a pessimist and dwelt upon human folly, while Perlis was a pragmatic optimist and believed in human progress. I personally found the contradiction between their appearances and personalities to be ironic—Dijkstra looked warm and fuzzy with his beard and glasses, whereas Perlis could pass for an extraterrestrial.

By far the most charismatic was Tony Hoare, a professor from Belfast who later became Sir Charles Antony Richard Hoare, Fellow of the Royal Academy of Science. Hoare was born in Sri Lanka and educated at Oxford where he studied ancient philosophers in the original Greek. Yet somehow, he also learned a lot about mathematics, logic, and programming. Hoare had his first big discovery in 1959, a clever recursive sorting technique called Quicksort. He credited Landin for teaching him about recursion.

In his lectures, Hoare presented a way to prove that programs satisfied their input/output specifications. Unlike McCarthy's methods, Hoare's worked on imperative programs. His system came to be known as Hoare Logic.[36] Hoare's lectures weren't just clear; they were eloquent and dramatic. Hoare was an admirer of Dijkstra, sharing his belief in the importance of programming thoughtfully. The two railed against the attitude of most programmers—that bugs in working programs were just the cost of doing business. Both Dijkstra and Hoare were absolutely opposed to some of Perlis's famously glib epigrams:

---

[36] See Hoare Logic in Nerd Zone

"One man's constant is another man's variable."

"In programming, as in everything else, to be in error is to be reborn."

"There are two ways to write error-free programs; only the third one works."

Their response was "Debugging can show the presences of errors, but never their absence," and suggested that good programmers prove their programs correct.

While I was more comfortable being with Perlis, I focused my research on the goals of Dijkstra and Hoare to make programming more professional. Dijkstra's 1972 Turing Award lecture conveyed a message that programming was a noble undertaking, requiring the genius of a physicist and the discipline of a Jesuit.

Summer school proved worth the time. I returned with perspective on what several leaders were doing and made some friends—just as the NATO organizers had hoped.

***

In the new school year, our department moved from its lowly temporary building into a new building, and I was delighted to have a large office overlooking the Golden Gate Bridge across the bay. I also learned that Berkeley had canceled the CalTSS project, which had lost its promise after Lampson had resigned from Berkeley to start a time-sharing computer company.

That fall I began a mail correspondence with Hoare. First, I shared with him that I found a minor shortcoming in one of the rules of Hoare Logic. He accepted my suggested improvement. Next, I sent him a working paper advocating that programming languages be designed with rules for proving programs correct. He graciously replied, "Welcome to the fellowship of top programming theorists!"

I began to supervise PhD student theses, supporting them with an NSF grant I'd received. The first was Peter Deutsch, who had been programming since he was in short pants. He created an interactive system for proving things about programs. The next was the eccentric Howard Sturgis who had been a brainiac on the CalTSS project. He wanted to describe the good things about CalTSS, but I convinced him to also explain why it failed. In those days, many big software projects often failed, so probing the reasons was important. His thesis title was "A Postmortem for a Time-Sharing System."

The third student was Tomasz Kowaltowski, who had been born in Poland, transported to Russia during World War II, and settled in Brazil afterward. He was dumped into high school and had to learn Portuguese from scratch. We bumped into him in Paris on our summer trip, and I had marveled at the confidence with which he managed French, though he only understood Portuguese. He was already a professor in Sao Paulo and excelled in some of my courses. He worked closely with me on the knotty problem of proving things about list-processing programs that modify the lists in sneaky ways.

To understand the difficulty of analyzing list-modifying programs, think of linked lists as train stations—one for each list element—connected to one-way tracks. If more than one track ends at a station, caution must be exercised to keep trains from colliding. A computer program is like a train traveling from one station to another, but with a magical ability to redirect a segment of track leaving its current station to any other station it knows about. "Colliding" means a program modifying a list another program assumed is unchanging. You can imagine, with a lot of trains racing around, sometimes redirecting their tracks, it might be hard to ensure there are no collisions. To prove that it couldn't happen unexpectedly, you would need to keep track of all the stations that were reached by multiple tracks.

Kowaltowski and I had a plausible approach to proving things, but in 1972 I received an excellent paper from Rod Burstall, a clever Brit, that showed how to prove many things we couldn't. He invented an economical way of describing the state of list structure, which was like drawing a map of the train network that ignored all stations with only one incoming track. Using these descriptions, he was able to prove that programs that rearranged data structures could be proven correct. When I asked him how he conceived his idea, he said it was based on category theory—a branch of mathematics that still eludes me. Burstall was also a serious Buddhist, and he was not alone. I knew other computer guys who loved category theory and were also Buddhists.

I abandoned the problem since I didn't see a way to improve on Burstall, but Kolwaltowski finished a good thesis on the topic.

The fourth PhD student was Reiji Nakajima from Japan. His English was spotty, and one day he revealed that his Japanese wasn't so good either! I introduced him to the λ-calculus, and he went far beyond me into the mathematics. Dana Scott had recently discovered his mathematical model for the λ-calculus, and Nakajima devoured it along with the theories of Reynolds. We pondered the disconcerting fact that Scott's model seemed oblivious to whether the computation corresponding to objects halted or not. He developed an alternate kind of the λ-calculus, which addressed that issue. He became a professor of CS at Kyoto University.

In addition to supervising my PhD students, I had been helping some other students who were struggling. I had a ten-minute conversation with one of Parlett's students who was thinking of dropping out. I repeated an old thought: "Finishing your thesis is the least embarrassing way to get out of graduate school." She finished and ended up as a professor at Harvard.

***

Susan became pregnant in the fall of 1972. Our closest neighbors were the building managers who might have figured it out before us after hearing some morning sickness events. They gently reminded us that the building "didn't allow children," so Susan put her real estate know-how to the task as we began looking for a house for our new family. It was then that I remembered that Steve Cook was once in the same boat—an assistant professor wanting to buy a house, that is. In fact, he had also bought a boat. Not long after his house purchase and his boat purchase, he heard that he failed to get tenure in Berkeley's math department—i.e., he was fired. Something I found alarming because Cook was really good.

Karp later said, "It is to our everlasting shame that we [the computer scientists] were unable to persuade the math department to give Steve Cook tenure." Are the meanies in the math department sad that they'd fired a future Turing Award winner? I doubt it. They probably feel that getting a Turing Award in CS does not make you a mathematician worthy of tenure at Berkeley.

I decided that buying a new house would be bad luck and that trying to get tenure at Berkeley was barking up the wrong tree. I'd already been told to publish more papers. My department was squabbling over the issue of a colleague wanting to hire a young computer scientist he was hoping to marry. The EECS department was threatening to take us over. It was time for me to repot, despite some assurances from the head of EECS that I would make it to tenure.

There was an image of the academic world that was taking shape in my mind. A sea of people, each holding a sign with their own name on it, the way political convention delegates show state's names. The height of one's sign varied depending on their fame, and everyone is striving to make theirs higher. I even felt having a common name was a handicap to fame.

Our daughter was born in May, after an eight-hour labor. My feeling of joy holding her in the delivery room was overwhelming. Something inside me shifted. I said, "She looks just like me!"

"Except for the mustache," the doctor observed.

We named her Jane.

While we were focused on the newest member of our family, the unrest at Berkeley continued. Protests, strikes, clashes, boarded-up buildings, and shootings had been part of the landscape since the free speech movement started in 1965.

Through all of this, Susan and I kept our heads. It seemed that many friends were losing their way. The husband of the Sexual Freedom woman finished his PhD in physics, divorced her, and spent the next several years pursuing conspiracy theories of the JFK assassination instead of physics. Another physicist gave up research and started writing books about religion. Jim Gray tried living on the East Coast and Romania before returning to the Bay Area where he got divorced. In 1969 Ted Kaczynski was a promising assistant professor of mathematics, working at another temporary building next to the CS department's, though I never met him. Inexplicably, he gave up mathematics that year and went on to become the Unabomber.

III: AI Fall 1973-1982

Hubert Dreyfus publishes *What Computers Can't Do* criticizing approaches to AI.

Lack of progress, criticism, and pressure from the US Congress cause both the US and British governments to defund exploratory research in AI.

A program, Chess 4.6, surprised observers by winning the 84th Minnesota Open tournament achieving a rating of 2000.

Star Wars introduces droids C-3PO and R2-D2, whom George Lucas identified as the narrators of the series.

Japan commits $850 million for the Fifth-Generation computer project to build machines to carry on conversations, translate languages, interpret pictures, and reason like human beings.

Tron is a movie in which programs living inside a large system appear anthropomorphically as the programmers who created them.

They may be every bit as intelligent as you say,
but I'd feel a whole lot better about them if just
one of them had run for sheriff once.
— Sam Rayburn

6. Among the Gods

In 1969 the photocopy company Xerox had a monopoly in copiers. Its CEO declared that Xerox would become "the architect of information for the future." In business terms, this came down to introducing technology to offices. To get started, Xerox acquired Scientific Data Systems, a small computer manufacturer in Southern California, and created the Palo Alto Research Center (PARC) in the Stanford Industrial Park, on the south border of Stanford's campus, to develop new computer designs. A physicist, George Pake, was hired to run PARC, and he hired a lot of other physicists. But when it came to computer people, he didn't know where to start.

As I was struggling with the rigors of being an assistant professor at Berkeley, I came across an article in the December 1972 issue of *Rolling Stone*, "SPACEWAR: Fanatic Life and Symbolic Death Among the Computer Bums." SPACEWAR was a graphical computer game played obsessively by programmers on breaks, and the article described what it was like at PARC and Stanford's AI lab, which was directed by McCarthy who just won the 1971 Turing Award.

The computer bums at PARC were former child prodigies with CS PhDs, all under forty. Alan Kay was quoted, "This is really a frightening group, by far the best I know of as far as talent and creativity. The people here all have track records and are used to dealing lightning with both hands." I saw that my former students, Deutsch, and Sturgis, were mentioned, and the article had a picture of Deutsch with the caption "the world's greatest programmer."

On my first trip to PARC, driving down through Palo Alto, I admired the manicured foliage, everything so unlike the funky Berkeley streets. I entered a nondescript office building in the Stanford Industrial Park and was directed to Robert Taylor's office.[37]

Pake had hired Taylor to solve his hiring problem. Taylor had worked for Licklider at DARPA and nurtured the first wave of PhDs in CS at several universities. When Taylor started at PARC in 1970, he recruited many of those fresh PhDs, first and foremost, Butler Lampson, along with Deutsch and Kay. Concerned with my progress at Berkeley, I'd recently asked Lampson to recommend me for a job at CMU. Instead, he invited me for this interview at PARC where Taylor seemed to be the boss.

The handsome, Texan Taylor fixed his pale-blue eyes on me.

---

[37] Photo courtesy of PARC, A Xerox Company

"So why does Butler think you would be good here?"

Feeling on the spot, I said, "Well, we were colleagues at Berkeley, and he must have thought I was OK, and he liked a recent paper I wrote."

"Yeah, he told me about that. What do you know about what we do here?"

"I've heard from Howard Sturgis that you're thinking about a personal computer project."

"That's right, but I have a much larger goal than that. I want this place to become as great as Bell Laboratories"

That's rather ambitious! Bell Labs has Nobel prize winners and invented the transistor.

That's what I thought, but all I said was "Wow!"

"Why did you get into computing, Jim?"

"It seemed like fun, and it's much easier than physics. Do you know Berkeley has guys with PhDs in physics trying to enter our CS programs?"

"What do you like to work on?"

"I've been developing theories about programming languages since MIT, but I also like to just program and get stuff to work—to see it do something useful."

"That's great! What would you like to see happen with computers?"

"I'd like to see computers do good for people and not just serve the military and big corporations."

Oops! Xerox is a big corporation! Shut up!

The interview continued with question after question, probing for meaningful answers. He seemed more interested in what I wanted than what I had done.

After my interview with Taylor, I gave a talk to Lampson and his team about designing a new language. The talk covered my theories about types in programming languages. Unfortunately, I chose an example that involved programs that passed around money. Lampson and his posse jumped all over me, pointing out that any such program could duplicate money the way a Xerox copier could. I kept trying to repair my example. Lampson was laughing with delight, because he knew many people had tried and failed to create internet money. I had stumbled into a puzzle that was not solved until the 2008 invention of Bitcoin.[38]

The next person to interview me was Alan Kay, whose group aimed to introduce kids to computing. Taylor had set up Kay in a separate lab outside his control "so that computing would get more money from management." Unlike Taylor, Kay hired a small group of non-PhD generalists who were dedicated to kids' learning. In our meeting, Kay told me about his Smalltalk language, in which programs were structured into many active *objects* which communicated with each other *via* messages. I wasn't sold on the idea, although it popularized the widely used style called *object-oriented programming*.

Despite my internet money *faux pas*, a few weeks later I got a job offer as a member of the research staff at PARC at twice my Berkeley salary. It wasn't Taylor who called me, but the official boss of the CS lab, whom I hadn't met, Jerry Elkind. While Susan was apprehensive, she agreed it was a better option than my continuing to struggle at Berkeley. Karp was the only person who seemed to want me to stay. "Most Turing Award winners have come from universities," he said. But I followed Licklider's example and repotted myself.

---

[38] See Dingle in Readings

A few months later the three of us moved to Palo Alto into our first house, a $44,000, 1,400 square-foot Eichler with walls that stopped at eight feet and gave way to a foot of glass, making the white walls into faux shoji screens. This design made the modest rooms look a little bigger. Each house on our circle was closed to the street by a car port but wide open to a back yard. There would be no neighborly porch-sitting. Our backyard contained a lemon tree, which Susan adored. Drinking a six-pack of beer in the yard one afternoon we estimated that we could disassemble the entire house in a few days.

Palo Alto was hot and flat. It was in the Santa Clara Valley, south of San Francisco, but it felt like the northern tip of Los Angeles. Susan had loved Berkeley, with its chilly hills reminding her of Pittsburgh, and when she attempted to transplant her real estate career, she found the Palo Alto market to be less congenial. When she drove clients to houses in our VW, with Jane in a baby seat, she was out of place. It wasn't long before she got a Volvo, and we became a two-car family. While she was discovering the stress of working motherhood and watching the Watergate hearings, I continued to focus on my research.

The big change in our life revealed a major tension in our marriage about my priorities. We started going to a counselor—a first for either of us. When I described the atmosphere at PARC he said, "That sounds like being in the NFL."

"Did your parents have a sense of social inferiority?" the counselor asked us during a session.

Susan and I were aghast.

How did he figure that out?

Later I learned that 80 percent of Americans have a sense of social inferiority, so he was just playing the percentages.

We spent several weeks in counseling. It was scary to learn things about myself. I realized that for the five years of our marriage, and before, I had been obsessed with being a brilliant computer scientist. I had to give some of that up and pay attention to the humans in my family. It was painful, but I wanted to change.

In addition, I was experiencing a rather surprising aspect of Palo Alto culture—everyone's hostility to smoking. At first my friends at PARC encouraged me to give it up, but few other places were that gentle. Nobody, except me, tried to smoke indoors at Stanford. Most hosts flatly disallowed it on their property.

Unlike Berkeley, PARC was completely up to date with a fast time-sharing computer. Computers were getting bigger and faster. Semiconductor engineer Gordon Moore observed that electronic elements (transistors, resistors, capacitors, diodes, etc.) that could fit in a single silicon chip had doubled four times in six years, and he speculated that the trend would continue for ten years. People were calling it *Moore's Law*. Moore co-founded Intel, which managed to cram a complete computer CPU onto a single silicon chip, triggering the personal computer era. A few years later, the Santa Clara Valley's name changed to Silicon Valley.

***

Taylor was adopted as an infant and spent his high school years as a competitive athlete and a part-time cowboy, once intentionally antagonizing a brahma bull into throwing him off its back. He entered college at sixteen, served in the navy, got degrees in psychology but passed on getting a PhD, because, in his words, he'd "been to a few county fairs." Eventually he went to work for Licklider at DARPA.

Taylor only authored one paper in his life, but it was a doozy co-authored with Licklider: "The Computer as a Communication Device." It began with a bold claim. "In a few years, men will be able to communicate more effectively through a machine than face to face." It is certainly true for nerds, who already converse without making eye contact or employing body language. Is it true for everyone else?

He followed the Licklider philosophy that computers should be used to augment, rather than replace, human capabilities. At NASA he had funded Douglas Engelbart, the inventor of the mouse pointing device. Engelbart was an idealist with visions of using computers to enhance human collaboration. In 1968 he had given "the mother of all demos," by replacing the teletype with a television screen, keyboard, and mouse, using the setup to show people working together from different locations.[39] He also introduced the ideas we call hypertext and Facetime today. Taylor understood the potential of Engelbart's *workstation* (as he called it) and intended to reengineer it at PARC. He described the proposed workstation as a prototype of Kay's Dynabook, which had also been inspired by Engelbart. Taylor named his workstation the Alto.

Lampson partnered with a talented hardware engineer, Chuck Thacker, to design the Alto workstation. Like Engelbart's setup, it had a *bitmap* display. Until then, computers that used displays could put only characters on them—simply a paperless teletype. The Alto's display was

---

[39] See Engelbart in Readings

called a bitmap display because it showed a rectangle of tiny square dots, called *pixels*, that were determined by a region of the Alto's memory registers containing 606×808 bits, one for each dot. If the bit was 1, the dot was black; if 0, white. (No color or grayscale yet.) It was entirely up to programs what appeared on the display. This flexibility allowed creative programmers to run wild, producing pictures or text in printer's fonts with different width letters.

I volunteered to be one of the first programmers to build basic programs for the Alto, which would help everyone else program it. Gene McDaniel from Berkeley was already implementing the operating system under Lampson's direction. There was a BCPL compiler but nothing else. My first program was Spy, an idea from Knuth, which ran as an independent process that woke up every few milliseconds and noted the location of another process's current instruction. After a few minutes of this, it stopped and displayed a table showing what functions of the other process were busiest. Then the programmer could work to make those parts faster. Today, professional programmers use more comprehensive tools that diagnose many aspects of a systems performance.

Then I wrote a debugger called Swat, which one uses to intervene in a running program to see what is going on. Deutsch gave me the idea to minimize the memory space that Swat took away from the process it was watching (the Swatee) by alternately swapping the entire memory of the computer between two disk images of the memory—one Swat and the other, the Swatee. This meant that Swat had to paw around on the disk to show a programmer the state of a running program and its data. But this arrangement made the Swat quite robust because it could not be sabotaged by the Swatee, no matter how buggy it might be.

I arranged it so that Swat would occasionally display Dijkstra's admonition about debugging not showing the absence of errors—a rueful bow to my apostasy. In the face of reality, I had become a nonconforming Dijkstrarian. I also wrote a scavenger program, which is what Macintoshes today call first aid for disks.

I often sat next to colleagues to help them use my programs. It changed my perspective about programming. It wasn't between me and the computer; it was between me and the other people, the computer acting as the intermediary. I was surprised how frequently the users of my programs would be confused because they had an "incorrect" idea of what my program did. Yet, upon reflection, I would see that their views were justified.

These sorts of encounters remind me of Susan's approach to thermostats. When she's cold, she raises the thermostat to ninety-five degrees. I tell her that the thermostat can only turn the furnace on or off, so it won't get warmer any faster, and she really doesn't want it to keep heating until it's ninety-five. But the heating systems in new cars respond to extreme settings by increasing the fan speed, so they understand Susan. *I should try to understand her too.* Of course, in the future, she'll be able to just say, "Alexa, I'm cold."

As a reward for my effective programming work, Taylor installed one of the first Altos in my office. It was exhilarating, but the fan was a little noisy. I teased him, "You haven't given me one of the first personal computers. You're making me

126

work in a computer room!" Here is a picture of the Alto workstation.

When I showed the Alto in my office to Susan's mother, she thought it was a television on top of an air conditioner. I had to tell her it cost $20,000 to impress her.

The Alto gave rise to a system comprised of printers and file repositories with big magnetic disks, connected by a network. These devices were called *servers* because they responded to orders from workstations. This paradigm was destined to end the dominance of big computers running time-sharing systems.

***

The peripatetic Perlis visited PARC every summer to participate in many research strategy sessions. Taylor probably thought he would be a help in managing all the high-flying computer scientists, many of whom were from CMU. By this time, he was wheelchair bound, but his vibrancy was undiminished. He was no longer pushing his own ideas but had adopted the programming language APL (A Programming Language), invented by Ken Iverson of IBM

Research. Its main data type was the array, usually a matrix or vector familiar to mathematicians. All of APL's operations were applied to all the elements of any array in parallel, which made it good at describing hardware structures. Like declarative programming, APL was an acquired taste, but mind-expanding, which Perlis loved.

Don Knuth called me up and offered to make me a co-author on a paper that he and Pratt were writing about my long-forgotten string-matching algorithm. Knuth generously offered to put my name first on the paper—an important distinction for academics keeping score—but I was more than happy to take my alphabetical place in what is called the Knuth-Morris-Pratt (KMP) algorithm. Knuth had discovered an earlier inventor of our algorithm but submitted the paper anyway, with an appropriate reference. It was published and became widely read, partly because Knuth was already famous.

I took Taylor at his word, that he wanted PARC to be "as great as Bell Labs," so I assumed I had the freedom to pursue my research, not carry out endless programming jobs.

I published "Types are Not Sets," as a sequel to "Protection in Programming Languages." It applied the magic envelope idea to the familiar concept of types. I said that a programmer could define a new type of variables that were understood to be envelopes with his subprogram's name in the sender's return address place. Other parts of the larger program could move the contents around among this new type of variables, and even examine the bits in those variables. But the other parts couldn't store any other type of value in those variables.

Mathematically inclined language theorists asserted that types represented the sets of values a particular variable could assume, independent of the program they came from. I openly asserted that types were more like trademarks, declaring who had produced the values.

Presenting the paper at a Boston conference, I said, "Suppose you are writing a program that, for some reason, deals with students' grades and their temperatures. You declare one variable to have type 'Grade' and another to have type 'Temperature' hoping that you won't mix their values. But both grades and temperatures hold numbers roughly between 0 and 100, so, if the compiler treats types as sets, it would not help keep the variables from getting mixed up."

The paper was well-received. For once, I was presenting an idea that no one else had!

My enthusiasm for the mathematical approach to programming was further eroded at the International Conference on Reliable Software in Los Angeles in 1975. Hoare, representing the Dijkstra school, advocated clear thinking and mathematics. The weakness of his position was shown when an AT&T executive explained how they kept the telephone system functional 99.99 percent of the time: keeping records of problems and discovering causes. An avionics engineer cast doubt on the premise that software was a problem. "You guys may see a crisis, but software has made my job far easier. I used to sweat for weeks designing the feedback circuitry to control the movement of flaps on a wing. Now I just build sensors and actuators and program the rest."

It took a hardware engineer, Fred Brooks, who managed IBM's groundbreaking 360 line of computers, to inject reality into the field. "There is no single development, in either technology or management technique, which by itself promises even one tenfold improvement within a decade in

129

productivity, in reliability, in simplicity . . . There is no Moore's Law for software."[40]

Brooks is also famous for observing that nine women cannot produce a baby in one month. He deserves the Turing Award he received in 1999 "for landmark contributions to computer architecture, operating systems, and software engineering."

A similarly pragmatic engineer was one of the first people Susan and I met at PARC. Chuck Geschke had recently come to PARC with a fresh PhD from CMU. Prior to CMU, he had been training to become a Jesuit, but gave it up to marry Nancy McDonough and father three children. He had to work hard to catch up with the younger PhD students who were mostly experienced programmers. His wife kept him on track. "Look buster, we moved here so you could do this, so buckle down!" He did and also earned much respect for being a wise, dependable colleague.

Susan and I became close friends with the Geschkes, once leaving Jane with them when we took a one-week trip to France. We shared many nights playing bridge. On a ski trip to Lake Tahoe, they put up with my nicotine withdrawal tantrums as I finally gave up smoking permanently. The smoking experience changed my opinion about social

---

[40] See Brooks in Readings

pressure. Without that pressure from the Palo Alto community, I might have been addicted for many more years.

***

When I took Jane to Pittsburgh to visit my mother and relatives, I got some editorial advice on my writing from Carson, who had begun teaching English at a local university. As usual, he was helpful and constructive. "Your mission should be to explain science and technology to people like me."

My mother had a copy of *Powers of the Mind*, a Wall Street writer's story of his tour of the "consciousness circuit." He reported a Harvard cardiologist's endorsement of meditation and pursued the mysterious Carlos Castaneda, who claimed to have trained in shamanism with a group descended from the Toltecs. If a no-nonsense financial guru could take time learning about such things, so could I.

***

As PARC moved into its new, permanent, ziggurat-shaped building, I began to grasp the scope of its efforts. While I was writing basic Alto software and pursuing programming language theories, some people around me were designing breakthrough technology that made them stars inside PARC and famous outside.

One evening at PARC, my colleague Bob Metcalfe was running around the building, stringing yellow coaxial cables along each hallway. He was inventing a new way for computers in the same building to communicate that was different from telephones that used a central switching machine to provide a physical, device-to-device connection. The cable was a sort of thruway that any device could reach via an on ramp. He called it Ethernet because ether was once believed to be the medium radio waves passed through, but, in this case, the cable was the medium. It was like a party line with many, possibly hundreds, of computers connected to one long cable. If two people on a party line heard each other talking they would each wait a while and try again. Since "a while" differs among people, further collisions were usually avoided. The computers did the same thing using a technique called *exponential back-off*. Each computer wanting to talk would wait for a random number of microseconds between 1 and 2^c, where c is the number of times it had collided already. Soon, the interval of time was so huge that the chances of collision were infinitesimal. Telephone engineers believed it would be unreliable. The Ethernet worked just fine.

Unlike most of us, Metcalfe always thought like a businessman. By 1980 he had left PARC to start a company, 3Com—to sell Ethernet systems. To help sell it, he enunciated Metcalfe's Law, which claims that the number of users of a new communication system grows exponentially, because each new user makes the system more attractive to other potential users. Suppose every two users attract one new user each week, perhaps because the newbie wants to talk to at least one of them. So, if there are N users one week, there'll be $N \times 1.5^W$ users W weeks later.[41]

_____

[41] See Metcalfe's Law in Nerd Zone

One of the first people to exploit Ethernet connectivity was Gary Starkweather, who had been an engineering manager for Xerox in Rochester in the 1960s trying to develop a printer that used the Xerox copying technology to print computer output. His bosses regarded this as a distracting hobby and threatened to take his staff away. In 1971 he had managed to transfer to PARC, and the bosses said, "Good riddance." At PARC he teamed up with the CS lab's hardware experts and produced a prototype laser printer, called a Dover, by modifying a large copier the size of a small car. A graphics expert, Bob Sproull, designed a page description language called *Press* for Altos to send printing jobs to a Dover.

With its multiple, variable-letter-width fonts, the Dover was a sensation! It was a cheap, convenient alternative to fiddling with Selectric typewriter balls or going to a printing shop equipped with thousands of expensive metal letters and typesetting machines. Anyone could easily produce a report that looked like it had been printed in a journal.

Susan and a friend used the Alto and the Dover to write a report to their women's club explaining how to fix the budget, and the group followed it as if it had been handed down from on high. Susan was not enthusiastic about technology but learned whatever she needed to—an ideal user to rattle my engineer's mind.

Just as the Xerox copier obsoleted carbon paper, some at Xerox feared that laser printers could obsolete copiers because the original text was no longer on paper, but in a computer. Elkind cleverly mitigated their fears that PARC was inventing the paperless office. He measured the amount of paper PARC used before and after the Dover came online. We started using 30 percent more paper, partly because we would print many drafts of work-in-progress, in addition to running off many final copies for distribution.

Dovers gave rise to manuscript-creating software that allowed you to write "programs" that described fancy pages to be printed. Two of the first of these programs were Scribe, the project of CMU student Brian Reid, and TeX, which Don Knuth created to allow mathematicians to design the appearance of their own publications with all their quirky formulae. An advancement in TeX was a way of describing fonts with mathematically defined curves instead of with pixels, which enabled one to vary the size of any font as well as its style. Knuth once joked that it was a reversal of *Sesame Street*'s pseudo commercial "This program is brought to you by the letter S," because letters were now brought to the computer by programs.

When Reid visited Stanford to present his work on Scribe, Knuth asked "Is Scribe going to be your PhD thesis?"

"Well, the faculty in the CS department are not sure that it's legitimate computer science," Reid replied.

Knuth, who had recently won a Turing Award for his masterly books on algorithms, said "Tell them Don Knuth certifies that it's computer science!" and when Reid graduated, the Stanford CS department hired him.

At the time that TeX and Scribe were debuting, all computers had a *command line interface* in which everything you asked the computer to do was typed on a line. To edit a manuscript you typed commands like, "replace ie by ei on line 6" and, occasionally, "display lines 5 through 10," to see if your commands achieved the desired effect. The actual commands were abbreviated to "r[eplace] ie [by] ei [on the current line]." We used these editors only to create programs or manuscript descriptions. But now that we could see the finished manuscript on the Alto's screen as well as paper, we were itching to edit it directly and bypass Scribe and TeX.

Enter Charles Simonyi, who had followed Lampson to PARC. They programmed the original WYSIWYG (What You See Is What You Get) editor called Bravo. Bravo let you use a mouse to point at some text on the screen and modify it just by typing. In other words, what you were seeing and modifying on the screen was what you would get when you printed it—bypassing Scribe and TeX.

He eventually left PARC for Microsoft where he created Microsoft Word. He became a billionaire, even dated Martha Stewart for a while. He paid twenty million dollars to take a trip to the International Space Station on a Soyuz rocket, fulfilling his teenage dream. He endowed Simonyi Professorship for the Public Understanding of Science at Oxford.

Alan Kay's group eliminated the command-line interface entirely, building on the work of Engelbart and inventing the WIMP (Windows, Icons, Menus, Pointer) interface in which documents, printers, file cabinets, and any other useful devices appeared on the screen as little *icons*. Larry Tesler was the key innovator in Kay's group, coining the phrases WYSIWYG, "user friendly," and "browser." He invented the cut, copy, and paste paradigm we all use. The key insight behind all these innovations was that the user—not the computer—should take the initiative by pointing at what should happen next.

An even more radical approach to the computer interface was advocated by a small group of LISP enthusiasts scattered around PARC led by Warren Teitelman. He called his approach to programming DWIM (Do What I Mean). He built a LISP interactive environment that automatically corrected many of the common mistakes programmers make, somewhat like today's spelling correctors. It was the earliest attempt to employ AI to improve human-computer communication. Most programmers seemed to prefer the "do what I said," relationship with computers they were brought up with. But they were the sort that preferred R2-D2 to C-3PO. They wanted a reliable tool, not a partner.

***

Elkind was our manager, but Taylor ran the day-to-day operations of the CS lab at PARC as if it was his thirty-person academic department. Like professors, we had weekly seminars in which lab members or guests would describe their work. Taylor would preside over these gatherings, which he called "Dealers," because the speaker chosen for the day could make the rules, like a poker dealer. In practice, Taylor made the rules. Dealers were held in the beanbag room, so-called because we all sat on huge beanbags. Thacker would share his plans for new workstations. In my first presentation, I showed the appreciative programmers how to use the Swat debugger. New WIMP interface features were enthusiastically admired.

The smartest person to ever appear in the beanbag room was Taylor's friend from DARPA, Ivan Sutherland. He had opened the field of computer graphics with his MIT PhD thesis "Sketchpad: A man-machine graphical communication system." While a professor at Harvard, he invented what was later called *virtual reality*, aided by the undergraduate Sproull. The idea was to wear a pair of goggles with tiny TVs for each eye and a tracking device that could tell where you were looking. A computer would show you an artificial environment wherever you looked. It was a rudimentary version of the feelies from *Brave New World*. After moving to the University of Utah, Sutherland became the mentor of Kay and Ed Catmull, the founder of Pixar.

The room was hushed as he talked about his struggle to design *self-timed* circuits. It is easier to design and check digital devices that include a centralized clock, making every state transition occur when the clock ticks. This consumes much valuable power and can make operation slower. Today's tiny devices use self-timed circuits.

Another revered visitor was Maurice Wilkes from Cambridge, the second ever Turing Awardee. When I told him I wanted to create a personalized internet newspaper he smiled mischievously and said, "I would love a newspaper that had only the news I wanted to read!" Neither of us realized how dangerous that would be.

While I admired the brilliance of these brilliant people, I was entranced by Taylor's leadership skill. He found herding computer geeks to be easier than herding cattle. Most of us were concerned with who was smarter or who created the coolest artifacts, but Taylor's considerable ego was somewhere else. My counselor imagined that Taylor was like an NFL coach who selected and exploited talent to win championships. He was particularly focused on beating team IBM.

Taylor used to say he managed like Tom Sawyer, who lured his nemesis into whitewashing a fence by pretending to be happy doing it. But that was more Lampson's style. Taylor never tried to design a computer or write a program. He used the technique of Dorothy Gale, from *The Wizard of OZ*. She appeared to be entirely helpless, inspiring the Scarecrow, Tin Woodsman, and Cowardly Lion to overcome their weaknesses and extend themselves to achieve her goal of reaching the Emerald City. We're all living in the Taylor's Emerald City now.

Elkind not Taylor, was the manager of our lab, because Pake believed a PhD was necessary to manage PhDs. His view made sense for physics with its well-established rules for judging research. But CS was a wild frontier. As Landin once said, "Most papers in computer science describe how their author learned something that someone else already knew."

In fact, Taylor had hired Elkind who had a PhD in electrical engineering from MIT. Somehow, Taylor got to stay on as Elkind's assistant. Maybe they had a deal.

Their management styles were different. Taylor catered to the hubris and insecurities of his thirty-something minions. He treated nearly all of us as if we were the most talented, interesting people he knew and seemed to have a deep interest in our every thought and ambition. He was all about relationships. When he wanted something, he offered carrots, not the stick. Elkind was skeptical about everything. He'd had a lot of experience managing technology projects and often challenged our assumptions about technology. He could have been right about some things, but I always felt tense talking to him, trying to explain what I was doing and convince him it was feasible or desirable. He was also more attentive than Taylor to Xerox's business needs and the desires of his bosses.

As much as they were cooperating, it became clear that Elkind would like to have more control of the activities in the lab than he did. When Elkind (not Taylor) decided that someone should oversee our little four-person program verification group, I made it known that I didn't like the idea much, and the other two guys had come as a team and insisted on their independence. The fact they were from Texas made them favorites of Taylor. Elkind's plan died, and Taylor's flat organization chart prevailed.

Shortly after that Elkind accepted a temporary assignment supervising another product-oriented task. A year later, when he planned to return, someone (not me) went to the lab management suggesting we might prefer he didn't. What followed was an awkward meeting several of us had with Elkind.

"Certainly, you can come back," I said to Elkind. "But I'd like you to be more of a cheerleader."

He didn't come back.

With Taylor now firmly in charge of the lab, and his believing I was part of a cabal that ousted Elkind, I felt like a made man.

Now at the helm, Taylor's day-to-day management technique was to sit in his office and wait for any of us to wander in for a confessional. Such as the day I walked in aggrieved.

"Lampson is a prick!" I said closing the door.

"What makes you say that?"

"He insists on winning every argument and will start yelling if he doesn't like the direction it's taking."

"What were you arguing about?"

"The usefulness of declarative programming."

"Was it a Class 1 or a Class 2 argument?" he asked sipping on his Dr. Pepper.

"Remind me what they are again."

"A Class 1 argument is just a pissing match. A Class 2 argument is one in which the opponents can describe the beliefs of each other."

I nodded.

"Did Butler describe your position?"

"Yes, he said that declarative programs were like mathematical statements, but he said "mathematical" waving his arms like it was a cult."

"Could you explain his beliefs?"

"Sure. He thinks programmers can get their programs right without using math, which they probably don't know, anyway. He thinks that math is overkill."

"OK, so it was a fair fight. That's how we get things right around here. Don't you like competition?"

"Not particularly."

"Do you think competing at something can make you better at it?"

"Maybe."

"I love competition. It leads to excellence," he said vehemently.

"OK, I get it, Mr. Darwin!"

Lampson and Taylor had a unique working relationship. Lampson supported Taylor's goals with brilliant engineering and inspiring ideas. But his explosive intelligence could shatter the egos of everyone else. Taylor was able to lubricate interactions so that their mutual agenda thrived.

But Taylor could outdo Lampson's aggressiveness when dealing with people and organizations outside his control, including the rest of Xerox. They were foes to be conquered or outsmarted. Initially, I was misled by the warm and fuzzy way he treated us underlings, but in a company softball game, he wiped out a little physicist guarding second base making me imagine what his youth on Texas sandlots must have been like. He deceived someone so thoroughly in a game of Diplomacy that the someone vowed to never trust him again. He never seemed to get bored with beating me at tennis.

The curious paradox is that when I accept
myself just as I am, then I can change
– Carl Rogers

7. Letting Go

In the summer of 1976, Larry Tesler invited Stanford lecturer Jim Fadiman to give a talk at PARC titled "How to Get What You Want." The beanbag room filled with people who were curious but skeptical. Fadiman began by asking us ridiculous questions.

"How do you know you're a smoker if you're not smoking right now? How do you know you can't fly?"

"No one has ever flown," someone said.

"St. Joseph of Cupertino did so repeatedly," Fadiman said, "In front of witnesses, during the 1600s."

Most of my colleagues shrugged, but I was intrigued by someone who could take on a room of brilliant geeks and show no fear. Fadiman knew little about computers, yet I thought he was the smartest guy in the room. Fadiman had attended Harvard and became a follower of Ram Dass, who was Timothy Leary's partner in the "Turn On, Tune In, Drop Out" movement, which featured the new drug sensation, LSD. While many people "experimented" with LSD, i.e., tried it, Fadiman did real scientific experiments backed by his PhD in psychology at Stanford. He tested how it affected people's perceptions and performance, believing that LSD micro doses contributed to the creativity of Silicon Valley.

Fadiman taught design innovation at Stanford and founded a few hippy-dippy-sounding enterprises in Palo Alto—the Institute of Transpersonal Psychology and the Institute of Noetic Sciences. He wrote several books and a few movies. It turned out that he was at PARC shilling for Omega Seminars, which he delivered for a hefty price out on the coast. Fadiman called his program "EST for *nice* people." The program's attraction was that it would help us get what we wanted—much like the more famous EST (Erhard Seminar Training) program—but by changing our perceptions rather than trampling the competition. Susan had heard of Omega Seminars as well, so the two of us listened to another pitch then signed up and drove down to a small hotel in Carmel-by-the-Sea for a four-day stay.

The first day felt like "Deprogramming for Catholics."

"You don't need guilt," he said to our group of twenty. "When people offer you guilt, say 'No thanks, I'm not having any today.'"

The next day, we dove into some basic facts of psychology—behaviors we learn by positive reinforcement, like driving a car, which can be consciously controlled, say, by learning to drive on the left side and behaviors learned by negative reinforcement, like how avoiding fire cannot be consciously controlled. Fadiman told us that we must avoid the phrases "I have to . . ." and "I can't . . ." and repeated many stories of the legendary Sufi teacher Nasreddin, who once said, "I point the way, but people come and suck on my finger," to warn us against worshiping any guru. On the final day, he explained how our parents' mistakes have hurt us in certain ways. My parents' well-intentioned emphasis on intelligence made me believe I had to be intelligent to be loved, so being in the middle of the pack hurt. As we nodded our heads, Fadiman challenged us to accept the past and move beyond it, especially in raising our own children. Finally, he gave us a simple practice to better our lives. The practice was to recite daily *affirmations*, or statements of facts that we would like to be true.

Affirmations were first used in the early twentieth century by the French psychologist and pharmacist Emile Coue after he noticed the placebo effect when he told his patients how effective a potion was as he gave it to them. His favorite affirmation was: "Every day, in every way, I am getting better and better."

Fadiman's were more definite:

1. I like myself unconditionally.
2. I never devalue myself through destructive self-criticism.
3. I have unconditional warm regard for all people at all times.
4. I am easily able to relax at any time, and every day through every affirmation I become healthier in mind, body, and spirit.
5. I am completely self-determined and allow all others the same right.
6. I am completely responsible for all my responses to all other people and to all events.

At the time, I didn't question where these thoughts came from; Fadiman must have gotten them from his studies of psychology and religion. Affirmations 1, 2, 3, and 5 appear to be applications of Carl Rogers's theory. Affirmation 4 is Coue's, and 6 is from Buddhism.

After reciting those we were to repeat any goals of our own, e.g., "I weigh 170 pounds." Since we were a largely Silicon Valley crowd, he told us that our brains were like blind, deaf computers that couldn't perceive reality and the affirmations were programming our brains to make them come true.

He ended by saying he would consult with any of us for free for the rest of our lives. After a convivial closing dinner, Susan and I drove home with a feeling of lightness and felt better prepared for parenthood. We followed the affirmation regime for several years and it changed our lives for the better. After our weekend of deprogramming and reprogramming, another thing I did to balance the unremitting rationalism of PARC was to read four of Carlos Castaneda's books.[42] I fell in love with them, and when an old fraternity brother, leading the hippy life north of San Francisco, told me the books were a fraud, that Castaneda had made them up from reading about Sufi traditions, I thought, *OK, I'll check out Sufism.*

I'd seen a TV shot of ecstatic Sufis dancing in San Francisco, and Fadiman told me that there were two(!) Sufi groups in Palo Alto. I went to a Sunday meeting, taking three-year-old Jane. We formed a circle and did a sort of Middle Eastern square dance, turning to-and-fro, and chanting something I don't remember. I was amused but didn't return.

Perhaps the upper management of PARC also sensed that we were all too intense because they brought in a noontime yoga teacher. "God! Relax your bodies," she said. "You look like a bunch of insects!" She must have been thinking of

---

[42] See Castaneda in Readings

praying mantises that might appear to be sitting and typing. I felt it gave me energy and returned weekly.

Palo Alto was a hotbed of personal development with EST, Omega, Sufis, counselors, and yoga studios everywhere. Inspired by the noontime yoga, I ventured out and continued my yoga practice at a nearby yoga studio that seemed like a weekly social club.

***

When Gray returned to his beloved Bay Area to a job at IBM's San Jose research center, he and I would meet for the occasional lunch in Palo Alto. He was busy pursuing research on relational databases, a technology later exploited by Oracle. Having settled in San Francisco, he bought a book on sailing, bought a forty-foot ketch, and sailed it away one day consulting his how-to-sail book as he went. He lived on his boat, commuting to San Jose in his old light-blue Porsche. During one of our lunches, he expressed IBM's attitude about personal computers, knowing what he knew about PARC's Alto.

"When the time comes, IBM will introduce a personal computer and win the market," he said. "But it's not time yet."

I once joined him on a sailing trip. We sailed north in the bay and docked for the night near a fleet of mothballed navy ships. The next morning, we continued meandering as we smoked some pot in the glorious sunlight. Gray turned the tiller over to his girlfriend and crawled forward to fiddle with the jib lines. Out of nowhere, a huge oil tanker rushed towards us. Gray crawled back and steered us starboard, barely avoiding it. Up close, an oil tanker looks like a fifteen-story building.

Pecos.

We'll never forget that name. The tanker missed us by twenty feet, leaving us bobbing around like a cork in its wake. I admired and envied Gray, an accomplished computer scientist with a breathtaking zest for life and adventure—a true free spirit. Kind and unique, the ideal Californian. I was wired differently and seemed destined for a more conventional life.

After Jane turned four in 1977, Susan became pregnant again. We decided we needed a bigger house and found a nice colonial house several blocks away. The owner, an elderly widow, seemed like my grandmother when she opened her door with a glass of bourbon in her hand. We bought the house for about $150,000 and were pleased when our Eichler sold for $102,000 after four years. We began to feel like real grown-ups whose lives were coming together.

In the summer, as we were moving into our new house, my mother called and told me she had just been diagnosed with lung cancer. She was sixty-three.

God, you bastard! I thought. *You killed my father, and you just noticed my recovered sense of well-being, so you're throwing another lightning bolt at me.*

Our daughter Rachel was born in the fall. She didn't seem to look like me but proved herself a quick study by commencing to breastfeed minutes after birth.

My mother came to meet Rachel at Christmas. However, prioritizing career over family, I left on a business trip to India on New Year's Eve, which left Susan to cope with both children and my dying mother.

For two weeks, I was Tony Hoare's partner, teaching a computing course at the Tata Institute in Mumbai. They put us up at the famous Taj Mahal Palace hotel, where I noticed a modest chalked sign in the lobby announcing where Prince Aga Khan was holding a reception. There were many wealthy Saudis roaming the hotel. They came for medical care and whiskey. I felt like I was with the Jet Set.

Once outside the Taj, my senses were jolted by the extraordinary—good and bad—smells, Dalits cleaning the ears of others, and children as young as Jane slipping their hand into mine and asking for money. I thought, if these people were American paupers, they might be mugging me.

At the institute, I enjoyed the chance to give lectures to the students who were faculty and graduate students from several Indian universities. One of the students, an experienced engineer, told me a disturbing story.

"We read about an operating system kernel in a long article in the *CACM*," he said as we had lunch between lectures. "We decided to implement it on our university's computer using the specifications from CMU where it was invented. It took a lot of work to complete. When we ran into problems using it, we discovered that it had never really been used by anyone."

"Yes, you're at a disadvantage here, just reading papers about systems that don't tell the whole story. Maybe the referees of papers should use the systems they write about and demand full disclosure," I mused.

Another revealing conversation I had was with a software manager who exposed me to the economic reality of the global programming profession. He asked what kind of research I was doing at PARC.

"Generally, we work on programming environments," I said.

"What are they?"

"Programming languages, debuggers, verifiers, linkers, software libraries—things to make programmers more productive. We also develop theories of how to think about programming."

"Here in India, the most important component of a programming environment is an air conditioner."

"What!" I said, "How does that help?"

"If I want to hire programmers, all I have to do is advertise that they will work in an air-conditioned office. I'll get thousands of applications, some of them very talented. If they can work inside, they are happy to use whatever software tools I offer."

Perlis and much of CS had assumed that programming talent would always be limited and that we should build tools to leverage it. But programmers working for air conditioning had me feeling differently. The world was producing good programmers at a furious rate, and the importance of making the job easier for programmers was vanishing.

Hoare and I often dined together at the elegant Taj. One night, I offered him some friendly advice.

"You and Dijkstra are brilliant computer programmers and engineers, but you're aspiring to be great logicians like Dana Scott," I said over our spicy chicken tikka masala. "The software community needs intelligent, pragmatic leadership. If people like you ascend to abstract mathematics, it suggests writing programs is a lesser activity."

Hoare paused.

"My friend, your standards are too low," he said. "And you're going to end up being a minor functionary at a university."

Yipes! He's pissed off.

I took a weekend trip without Hoare to see the Taj Mahal in Agra. A limo driver at the New Delhi airport talked me out of taking a train to Agra. He honked his horn for the entire two-hour ride, shooing camels, elephants, and walkers from the dirt roads. We made a short lunch stop at a village where I met a pack of barefoot young kids who seemed delighted to see us.

Back in the pristine Palo Alto, I thought of those kids often. *They live in squalid poverty and believe in fantastical gods, but maybe their lives are richer than mine.*

***

Taylor sent me on business trips to CMU so I could visit my mother. I was sad because she seemed to be meekly accepting fate. I tried to teach her to do affirmations. Maybe I should have also suggested pot.

She died in June 1978. In a week, I had her cremated and buried next to my father and sold the small apartment building she had built in the Gabel's yard. I wanted to close the door. My greatest frustration was that, like my father, she seemed to die without having come to grips with what her life was about.

While we were in Pittsburgh for the funeral, Susan and I had both kids baptized at the Episcopal church my mother had been attending. Carson, Schroeder, and Srodes were honorary godparents. Jane had been singing in choir at a Presbyterian church in Palo Alto, so we were becoming a rather ecumenical family.

When I returned to PARC, Taylor suggested I undertake whatever research would fulfill me, and I decided, finally, to design my own programming language—a creative challenge. The world of programming languages for professionals was gravitating to those supported by large institutions like IBM and the DoD, so there wasn't much future in serving professionals. I wanted to design a declarative language, specialized for manipulating text and easy to use for amateur programmers. Taylor assigned a summer research intern to help me.

Eric Schmidt was an unprepossessing young man but had good credentials. The son of an economist, he'd graduated from Princeton, started a PhD at Berkeley, and had already done an internship at Bell Labs. He followed direction easily, was an adequate programmer, and managed upward gracefully. He commuted on a motorcycle from Berkeley where he was the president of the International House living organization.

He reminded me of Susan's younger brother, so I invited him to come to dinner. We became a sort of aunt and uncle to him, and after acquiring a girlfriend, Wendy, he even asked Susan and I to double date.

Schmidt helped me implement my language, Poplar, which blended what I had learned from declarative languages, APL, and SNOBOL (StriNg Oriented and symBOlic Language). Once we had implemented it, people at

PARC tried it on naturally occurring text processing tasks with some success. It was the first time I used a declarative language to accomplish anything. One surprise was that conventional debugging techniques, which involve setting breakpoints on statements, didn't work well with declarative languages because the ordering of statements can be unpredictable. Schmidt and I co-authored a paper, "Experience with an Applicative String Processing Language." After that, I had no idea how to disseminate Poplar to a wider audience. It would have taken a major marketing effort.

Understanding how the average programmer thinks seemed like a good thing to know when designing programming languages, so I initiated a few studies to learn how people program. First, I asked ten different people to write the same program in their favorite language and take notes. I learned that Sproull, writing in the primitive BCPL, was twice as fast as the next best programmer. There was no wasted motion, because he understood his simple tools completely and knew a library program that solved part of the problem. This presaged a future where 90 percent of every programming task is finding and adapting code that other people have written.

Allen Newell regularly visited PARC to work on a book about *human-computer interaction* (HCI).[43] He and Simon had recently won the Turing Award for their contributions to AI, the psychology of human cognition, and list processing, so the book had added impact on academic thinking. I asked Newell for advice about my research on programmers and he

---

[43] See Newell in Readings

described a recent CMU PhD thesis that had suggested a simple description of how people program: Given a problem to solve they do it by hand until they can describe what they do. Then, imagining that they are the processing unit of a computer, they translate their steps into instructions for it. Thus, imperative programming is natural for them. This helps explain why programmers often lapse into using the first person when describing their programs, for example saying, "Then I call the square root function."

Another experiment illustrates how people solve puzzles. In the first, you see four cards with numbers on one side and letters on the other. Which of the card(s) must be turned over to test the claim that a card with an even number has an X on the other side?

In the second puzzle, you see cards with ages on one side and beverages on the other. Which card(s) must be turned over to test the idea that if you are drinking alcohol you must be over 18?

Though the puzzles are equivalent, most people solve the second more readily, saying "16 and Beer," revealing that their social brains are more powerful than their mathematical brains.

So, after fifteen years spent approaching language design as a mathematician, I realized there were other important design principals.

The study of declarative languages was alive and well, however, I was invited to join a group of declarative programming enthusiasts in a conference in Sweden and contributed a paper, "Real Programming in Functional (i.e., declarative) Languages." The introduction summarized my take.

> Functional languages *are* unnatural to use; but so are knives and forks, diplomatic protocols, double-entry bookkeeping, and a host of other things modern civilization has found useful. Any discipline is unnatural, in that it takes a while to master and can break down in extreme situations. That is no reason to reject a particular discipline. The important question is whether functional programming is unnatural the way Haiku is unnatural, or the way Karate is unnatural. Haiku is a rigid form of poetry in which each poem must have precisely three lines and seventeen syllables. As with poetry, writing a purely functional program often gives one a feeling of great esthetic pleasure. It is often enlightening to read or write such a program. These are undoubted benefits, but real programmers are more results-oriented and are not interested in laboring over a program that already works. They will not accept a language discipline unless it can be used to write programs to solve problems the first time — just as Karate is occasionally used to deal with real problems as they present themselves. A person who has learned the discipline of Karate finds it directly applicable even in bar-room brawls where no one else knows Karate. Can the same be said of the

functional programmer in today's computing environments? No.

I wasn't invited to any more declarative programming seances, but I didn't care.

In fact, the whole programming languages thing had lost its allure for me—and potentially others. In the late 1970s, the DoD noticed that it was using 450 programming languages and ran a contest to select a language it would standardize. Many languages entered—though PARC didn't bother submitting anything—but nobody won. The DoD then published a specification and held a tournament to select a designer who best met the spec. The result was a language called Ada. At that point it seemed appropriate for the thousands of aspiring programming language designers to find something else to do.

***

PARC, still loyal to its mission to lead Xerox to the office of the future, proposed that Xerox build and sell a low-cost Alto. The proposal was rejected because of internal corporate competition. Instead, Xerox created a separate organization, the Systems Development Division (SDD), split between Palo Alto and Southern California, to reengineer and market a completely redesigned system called Star.

I began to consult for the SDD engineering director, a former PARC guy. I was astounded at the technical ambition of the engineers, who aimed at a system far more sophisticated than the Alto. It was impressive but looked expensive in terms of computing power. When I questioned them about this, one said, "It's taken Xerox so long to move that the competition can produce something better than the Alto now, so we must leapfrog." I considered transferring to

SDD where the action now seemed to be. But there were two obstacles: the director thought, correctly, that I was an academic with little political savvy, and my salary in research was too high for any value I might have as a manager.

Back at PARC, we were not satisfied with a corporate pat on the head while SDD got to carry the ball forward. Alan Kay was outraged. He went all Howard Roark (from *The Fountainhead*) and threatened to destroy the Alto somehow. We all wanted to impress our friends in universities, so Taylor arranged to give small Alto systems to four universities: MIT, CMU, Stanford, and the University of Rochester, which was where Xerox was headquartered. Each system contained twenty Altos, a file server, and a Dover, connected with an Ethernet.

Stanford and CMU set about building their own versions of the Alto. MIT ignored the Altos in favor of its own project, a computer specialized for LISP. Within a few years workstation startups appeared in each of the cities where those universities resided, except Rochester. Rochester created software to run on Altos, including a SPACEWAR game for the Alto by a PhD student, Rick Rashid. I would see Taylor at PARC on weekend afternoons, playing it with his sons, whom he usually beat.

While Xerox did not embrace the Alto, it did embrace the concept of on-demand printing exemplified by the Dover and set about creating products. So, Taylor spun off a new lab called Imaging Systems, run by Geschke. This lab's job was to support Xerox's laser printing business. Geschke hired John Warnock, a mathematician who could duplicate Knuth's on-the-fly font-generation software.

An early project of Imaging Systems was to produce an improved version of Sproull's Press language for communicating with printers. Warnock, Lampson, and Sproull teamed up to create *Interpress* a much more elaborate language by incorporating a fully programmable page description language.

Chatting with Geschke in his office one day, I asked, "What is Xerox's plan for marketing printers?"

"I think they will first sell big printers to big offices, but I think laser printers will eventually be in schools, storefronts, and even homes, putting all the mom-and-pop print shops out of business."

This was poignant, since his father had once owned a printing shop in Cleveland.

In 1979, as an alternative to SDD's approach, Xerox proposed that Apple manufacture a low-cost workstation. As part of the negotiation, Steve Jobs demanded a demonstration of the Alto. Larry Tesler was the one to give it. Larry relates that as he was demonstrating, "Suddenly Steve jumped up, saying, 'Stop, stop, stop! This stuff is revolutionary! You guys are sitting on a gold mine!'" Steve went back to Apple and began trying to duplicate our software. In fact, we had only shown him a fraction of PARC's innovations. Three months later I was working for Apple.

A few others from PARC became part of Apple's Macintosh team. They all worked at a secretive building fronted by a pirate flag.

I was getting restless at PARC. The excitement of the Alto project was fading, and we were all getting frustrated by Xerox's halting progress. I felt I could predict the way any discussion or argument with my colleagues would go for the first twenty minutes.

***

Susan and I looked forward to Septembers when we would take a trip to the La Jolla Beach and Tennis Club for two weeks. To Pittsburghers, it was the only place in California appreciably more idyllic than Palo Alto. While on the beach that year, I read some books that questioned the benefits of computer technology.[44] Their attitude and the reflection allowed by vacation weeks had me considering career changes. Maybe I could get a job at UC San Diego, which was up the road in La Jolla.

After all, it might be our last September here, because Jane's second grade teacher had objected to our September trip. Rachel, however, was in a nice Montessori preschool where she was described as "the perfect Montessori child," self-directed and persistent. They might not have minded the September absences, but they disapproved of my habit of dropping her off late on my way to work around ten o'clock. When we returned from La Jolla, Susan went to a one-day hypnosis class and enjoyed it so much that I tried it. Sitting in a classroom at a junior college, I raised my hand when the teacher asked who wasn't getting it. She brought me to the front of the room and talked quietly to me, and I suddenly felt transported. I heard people in the class talking about me, but

---

[44] See Vonnegut and Weizenbaum in Readings

158

it was like they were in another dimension. I imagined there was a door to the hypnotic state, ever-present but elusive.

Susan and I took a refresher session of Omega Seminars. In the following week at dinner, I hesitatingly asked her to give up smoking, and she simply did. She also started looking for something more engaging than her part-time job at Stanford's business school alumni magazine where she edited alumni notes. She took a community college course in television production. After appearing on a *National Geographic* TV program about earthquakes, she decided that she belonged in front of the camera, so she marched into a San Francisco TV station and asked for an internship. When that didn't pan out the resilient Susan decided to try radio.

Radio made sense for her. She wrote well and had a sophisticated Manhattan voice, softened by time in Pittsburgh. Also, her mother had worked on the radio at Fordham. It allowed her to express herself orally and intellectually in an artistic way. She went to Stanford's student radio station, KZSU, and learned the rudiments, even how to edit tape with a razor blade. Her first interview was with the author Gore Vidal. Later at home, the four of us listened to the prerecorded interview.

We all heard when Susan asked Gore, "What are you working on now?"

"Trying to get through this interview," the acerbic Gore replied.

You and me both, thought Susan.

When one of us started to say something as the interview played, Susan shouted, "Quiet! I'm listening to this!"

The three of us realized we were going to get less attention from Susan going forward.

159

***

Xerox released SDD's Star System in the spring of 1981. The product was technically spectacular, made from excellent ideas, some so advanced that they are still waiting to be exploited in 2021. At $16,000 per computer, it was also spectacularly expensive. It flopped.

At the same time, Taylor sent me to a two-week Xerox training program called Managing Tasks Through People — in Leesburg, VA. This seemed strange since I managed nobody, but Xerox required Taylor to send people to the program, and he chose me. On the plane going east, I sat next to a pleasant older man in a white shirt and tie. He told me he had gone from being a professor to a university administrator and was happy that he did. I thought that sounded pretty good.

The general theme I absorbed in Leesburg was *You need to change your attitude now. Stop competing with peers and become a skillful coordinator.* We also learned lots of techniques to manage people and situations. For example, in a meeting you will be more effective if you ask others to express thoughts, especially if their thoughts are in accord with yours.

Shortly after I returned, we had a planning retreat for what Taylor called "graybeards," the senior people he trusted. By this time, we had created multiple follow-ons to the Alto computer, and SDD had used PARC's programming language to write an operating system and office software for the planned product. It was time for us to move on to other things, and Taylor was urging that we have a large lab-wide project to integrate and upgrade several programming tools, including an upgraded programming language, a debugger, a new document editor, and systems packager designed by

160

Schmidt and Lampson. The goal was to produce a programming environment that would further enhance programmer productivity. It seemed as much a political project as it was a software project because it sought to harmonize some the work of several previously independent programmers.

After the retreat, I agreed to manage the project, which was called Cedar. Taylor said he would give me a long sabbatical after a year of working on it. Naturally, after my indoctrination at Leesburg and my admiration for Taylor, I tried to pattern my management style after his, arranging coalitions and cheerleading.

The Cedar project moved along successfully, developing new versions of Alto software that were better integrated, running on a much more powerful prototype computer. The team celebrated progress with a big offsite weekend in a house on the Pacific coast, over the objections of Pake, who was worried about Xerox's sharply declining profits.

But after that first year, I got frustrated with my graybeard colleagues. They didn't help the Cedar project much, and I was especially stung by someone's comment at a second retreat that Cedar wasn't going well. Management, I thought, is a little like parenting. You need to understand for yourself what good you are doing and not expect overt appreciation.

My fortieth birthday came that year and we had a party in Palo Alto, inviting four couples: the Geschkes and Warnocks from PARC, our next-door neighbors, and some friends from Atherton, a swank suburb to the north. It was not a great party because few of them knew each other. Unlike Susan, I hadn't created a network of friends in my eight years in Palo Alto.

I was happy to start a nine-month sabbatical, leaving Cedar to develop for four more years, demonstrating truly innovative software tools. I got Newell to invite me to visit CMU, and Susan and I decided to spend the sabbatical in Pittsburgh partly so that our daughters could get to know Susan's mother and attend Ellis School.

***

Shortly after I arrived in Pittsburgh, Xerox's CEO announced that it was giving up on its office of the future fantasy because Canon was threatening its bread-and-butter copier business.

Many accounts of Xerox's folly have been written, castigating its management short-sightedness for not exploiting the wonders PARC created, leaving Apple and others to do it. However, it wasn't all upper management's fault. For all our brilliance, the PARC and SDD people were mostly creatures of DARPA, part of the DoD, famous for $400 toilet seats. We mistakenly assumed Xerox could sell a complete revolutionary office system to an inherently cautious office market. The largest sale of a Star system was to a US Navy laboratory with deep pockets.

The second problem was more fundamental.[45] Xerox had climbed to the top of a metaphorical mountain (the office copier market) and wanted to ascend an even higher one (computerization of the front office), but to get there it would have to descend into the valley of declining profit where its stockholders and customers would abandon it, saying "You're not really a computer company." Only a company like Apple, with much less to lose, could attempt the ascent, starting with a cheap toy, the Macintosh.

---

[45] See Christensen in Readings

After watching the failure of the Star product, I realized how naïve we had been. With much effort over several years, we had created a new programming language to build the product and a new operating system to support it—both of which were arguably better than the industry's state-of-the-art products—yet our excellent tools made no difference when the business case for the product was so far off. We laughed at Jobs and his Macintosh team for using machine language and a rudimentary operating system not realizing that he was producing the right product for the time.

Despite Xerox's business failure, the CS accomplishments of the PARC group were significant. Three of them later won Turing Awards: Lampson (1992), Kay (2003), and Thacker (2009).

IV: AI Winter 1983-1989

Geoffrey Hinton and others invent deep neural learning, an effective way for neural nets to learn.

Industry begins writing computer programs that capture human expertise at specific tasks. Digital Equipment estimates saving $25 million a year.

Cray Blitz achieves a chess rating of 2200, which only the top 1 percent of chess players achieve.

CMU's HiTech wins the 1985 North American Computer Chess Championship.

The Terminator describes a cyborg, an amalgam robot/human assassin sent back in time from 2029 to 1984.

Japan's Fifth Generation project ends in failure.

Jack Schwartz, a successor to Licklider at DARPA, dismissed expert systems as "clever programming" and cut all funding to AI.

The movie *Robocop* suggests police should be cyborgs because ethics cannot be automated.

Manage others the way you would like to be managed.– Brian Tracy

8. Running a Project

We rented our Palo Alto house to Bob Sproull and his wife, Lee, who were taking sabbaticals from CMU. He had moved to CMU four years earlier when Lee got a professorship there. He had been so vital to the Alto project that Taylor let him take one to Pittsburgh, which he kindly lent to me, so I wouldn't get homesick.

When we arrived in Pittsburgh, we moved into a rental house on a swanky street near CMU. Richard Mellon Scaife lived across the street, and I eagerly awaited Halloween when I could accompany my kids to his mansion, ring the doorbell, and say, "Trick or T-bill!" There was a Presbyterian church down the street with a minister so charismatic that I reconsidered my agnosticism, and we joined the congregation. I was still open to having a transformative religious experience.

I ran into Feeny in the local shopping district. He seemed happy to see me and said he would try to arrange a brass band to welcome me.

Susan and I hosted a September soiree for all our high school friends, most of whom still lived in Pittsburgh. Unlike SV gatherings, almost everyone here was completely confident they belonged and happy to be with each other. Carson was now an English professor, had stopped drinking, had started writing poetry, and was getting a divorce. Schroeder was running his family manufacturing business. Srodes was a highly respected oncologist. I was amused to hear that one of Susan's friends, who was trying to describe me to her husband, started by saying, "Do you remember the movie *Animal House?*"

Rachel and Jane started at Ellis School, Rachel in kindergarten and Jane in fourth grade. Rachel didn't like the atmosphere, so unlike her Montessori experience, but Jane made some smart friends and began to thrive. While Susan searched for ways to get back into radio, I audited a CMU course on the history of technology. It made a compelling case that human needs and economics drive the development of technology, that scientists and engineers don't determine its course.

"Dr. Morris, do you believe in Artificial Intelligence?" the professor asked in the middle of a class.

I'd never considered that question explicitly.

"No," I said. "I'd still like to believe there is some magic to life."

The students were a little surprised to hear a CS professor say that. It was heresy in Simon's university.

The CS department at CMU had grown in size and stature. It was already preeminent in two branches of CS—engineering and AI. Allen Newell, despite misgivings about neural networks, brought a young enthusiast, Geoffrey Hinton, to the faculty. Hinton recalls, "Newell had great personal integrity. He was in favor of hiring me even though I was strongly opposed to his view of AI. We taught a course together and had good discussions about several issues." While at CMU, Hinton developed a technique called *deep neural learning*, a systematic way of adjusting the connection strengths in a neural net, responding to positive or negative outcomes. Neural nets were still not successful compared to other AI techniques, but he persisted for the next thirty years. They also hired Raj Reddy, a young professor from Stanford. Reddy didn't endorse the speech recognition theories of Jim and Janet Baker but brought them to CMU as graduate students to pursue their approach. They eventually produced the world's best dictation software, DragonDictate. Reddy also had a habit of adopting any passionate person whose career was in jeopardy. He hired Brian Reid who had initially been rejected from the PhD program as well as a pioneer of robot cars who had been denied tenure in another department. He hired the eccentric roboticist Hans Moravec despite his refusal to teach or attend meetings.

But CMU had lost several good mathematics professors to MIT, Stanford, and Yale. Now, in 1983, the department head, Nico Habermann (a student of Dijkstra) had been on a mission to build up the mathematics group. He hired young mathematicians, luring them with the promise that the department would support their research without requiring them to get grants. To cap off his efforts, Habermann hired Dana Scott, who came from Oxford, with the promise that Scott could hire some junior faculty.

The introduction of the IBM personal computer (PC) confirmed that a paradigm shift in computing was starting and urged by Newell—who always thought big—the university was on a quest to find an industry partner to provide this new way of computing for the whole campus. The president of CMU, Richard Cyert, negotiated a headline-grabbing $15 million contract with IBM to develop the system, announcing that every student would have a personal computer—a first for any university.

Before Sproull left for Palo Alto, he called me to have lunch saying, "there's someone I want you to meet."

When I sat down at the Carnegie Museum's bustling restaurant a block from the campus, Sproull was chatting with a guy about my age.

"This is Doug Van Houweling, the vice-provost of computing, better known as the computing czar," Sproull said. "He's the one who put together the IBM deal."

"Really? Congratulations!" I was impressed. "That is a big deal."

"Thanks," the grinning Van Houweling said. "We're all pretty excited about it."

"What's going to happen now?" I asked, genuinely curious.

"Well, the contract goes into effect in January, and we're going to stand up a new organization of about twenty-five people to develop the campus system that we'll call Andrew after Carnegie and Mellon."

"Is IBM going to run it?" I asked.

"No, CMU will have control and will make all the technical decisions," Van Houweling said. "IBM, unlike the Digital Equipment Corporation (DEC), is willing to step back and learn from what we do. IBM is going to assign ten good engineers to help. But they won't be in charge."

"You've been a DEC shop for years, so I'm surprised you didn't go with them," I said to Van Houweling.

"I think Cyert wanted IBM. He might have brought me here from Cornell because I'd developed a good relationship with Big Blue. We've spent over a year working on this deal, wearing out several IBMers. The current one, Keith Slack, is a great guy. We sat down one night and outlined the whole deal, and it pretty much flew."

"My student James Gosling has already accepted a job with IBM," Sproull interjected. "And he'll be assigned to Andrew. Do you know about Gosling, Jim?"

"No."

"He's the most prolific hacker of all the grad students," Sproull said. "He's already known throughout the UNIX community for his implementation of the Emacs text editor. Emacs is not as fancy as PARC's Bravo. It doesn't use a mouse or have multiple fonts, but it's programmable, so programmers love it."

"There's already a good business manager in place," Van Houweling added. "And we have a wing of the business school available for occupancy."

"But the purpose of this lunch," Doug said, putting his hand on my arm, "is to see if you're interested in running the Andrew project."

Wow, I wasn't expecting this!

"It's an idea," I said, trying to be casual about it. "But I'm here from Xerox PARC on a sabbatical, and I'm hoping to do a little research. It's my reward for running a project. And I need the break."

"Allen Newell told us about that," Van Houweling said. "He said you were doing a good job, and Sproull here agrees."

"Ha! Now I see what's happening! You asked Sproull to run Andrew, and he's leaving town to escape."

"Not true," they said in unison.

"OK, I'll think about it," still casual. "Especially if Sproull promises to help when he's back."

When I told Susan about the offer that night, she was excited but apprehensive.

"How much will they pay? Will you get a faculty position? Are you really that tired of PARC?"

A few days later, I met Keith Slack on his weekly visit to CMU, and he confirmed what Van Houweling said about IBM's attitude as we sat outside enjoying the warmth of the late summer. Next, I went to Newell who told me that the CS department would appoint me a full professor.

"This idea is appealing," I said. But I'm reluctant to get in bed with IBM. Working for Taylor and Xerox makes helping IBM sort of taboo."

"The thing about taboos is that, when you actually break one, it's quite enjoyable."

That's a new thought!

Newell then sent me to talk to Reddy, whom I knew only by reputation.

Raj Reddy had come from an Indian village, where he went barefoot for his first ten years. His parents were not rich, but Reddy showed such a passion for learning that an uncle paid for engineering education in Australia, which he followed up with a PhD from Stanford under John McCarthy.

When I entered his large office, he sat down beside me on the couch and put his hand on my shoulder. It put me completely at ease.

"What do you do around here?" I asked.

"I started working on speech recognition for my PhD and have been doing it ever since," he said. "Now we're expanding into Robotics. Newell and Simon know that game-playing is the easy part of AI. True intelligence requires acting in one's physical environment to control one's fate. Hans Moravec has pointed out that the talents robots need—vision, hearing, speech, and manipulation—are much harder for computers than mental tasks like playing chess. AI is good at all the things we learn in school but terrible at what infants learn in their first few years! The Robotics Institute that Westinghouse helped us start will tackle these things."

"That's very ambitious!" I said.

"I have some other dreams too. I'd like to have computers capture the ancient texts from India and China to make them accessible to the world. What do you want to do?"

"As you probably know, I'm considering this new campus computing project with IBM. I've been at PARC for many years, but maybe it's time for change. I'd welcome the opportunity to make some of the PARC ideas flourish here, because Xerox is abandoning them."

"We love all PARC's technology, especially the printer," said Reddy enthusiastically spreading his arms. "Do you know we have a project here that builds on the Alto?"

"Yes, Rick Rashid and some people from here visited PARC last year."

"Anyway, if you come here, I'll be happy to help you do whatever you choose to pursue."

While Perlis, Newell, and Simon were father figures for me, Reddy felt like an older brother. I told Van Houweling I was almost sold, and he set up an appointment with President Cyert, someone else I'd never met, though I'd been hearing that he was a strategic genius intent on transforming CMU from a regional to a national university.

"Doug says you're interested, and I'd like you to accept the job. How much do you want?"

Cyert was a diminutive, intense man that got right to the point.

"Well, at Xerox this kind of project manager gets paid about $80,000."

"We can do that."

That did it. By this time Susan was sold too, and the kids were getting along with their grandmother. So, we broke the news to them that we were moving to Pittsburgh.

When I went back to PARC by myself for a good-bye visit in mid-October, I discovered that our group was dissolving. Kay had left to become the chief scientist at the game-maker Atari. Tesler and a young programming prodigy, Bruce Horn, had departed for Apple to help them create the Macintosh. Metcalfe had left to found 3Com. Geschke and Warnock had founded Adobe Systems to create PostScript, a successor to Interpress, for connecting computers to printers. Several PARC engineers followed, often because they wanted to work under Geschke. Taylor, Lampson, Thacker, and the other remaining graybeards were lobbying Sam Fuller, the VP of research at DEC, to start a Palo Alto research lab for them.

Schmidt had turned down Taylor's job offer and went to SUN Microsystems, which sold the SUN (Stanford University Network) workstation, inspired by the Alto. He took me to lunch with a few of the founders—Bill Joy and Andy Bechtolsheim, the brains behind SUN—to recruit me. But I felt committed to CMU. I recommended that they all go to Fadiman's Omega Seminar. Fadiman had bragged about a venture capitalist (VC) who always sent his start-up teams to Omega and then turned them loose to innovate.

Back in Pittsburgh, a group of striking steel workers disrupted the Sunday service at our new church. They were trying to embarrass a US Steel executive who belonged to the congregation. Susan ran back to our house to get a tape recorder, interviewed some of the workers, and it turned into the first story she aired on National Public Radio (NPR). After that, she started working at Duquesne University's large radio station, WDUQ, and continued to get stories about Pittsburgh on NPR every few months.

***

The stakeholders in the Andrew project had a variety of goals. The IBM chief scientist wanted "to open up a window" through which IBM might learn. The product managers wanted advanced software. Cyert wanted to enhance CMU's national standing. The CS department wanted a demonstration of its research. But I had yet to hear what the CMU students wanted.

After accepting the director's job, I wanted to put my own stake in the ground, so shortly before Thanksgiving I wrote a memo titled "Quality Communication through Time and Space"[46] to set my agenda for the project. It was my version of the Licklider-Taylor manifesto, supplemented with all my reading of futurists[47]. Here is the introduction:

> Many years ago, in freshman English at Carnegie Tech, I read a provocative essay by Jacques Barzun about how a university should allocate its limited capital funds: first to dormitories, then

---

[46] See Documents

[47] See Toffler in Readings

173

to libraries, finally to classrooms. His point was that students first and foremost learn from each other, and bringing them all together was the most important role of the university. Libraries win out over classrooms because, given an inquiring student, the accumulated knowledge of the years will always outweigh whatever wisdom and knowledge transmitted in the lecture halls and classrooms.

To update Barzun to the computer age and our current agenda:

Through Space: The primary goal should be to broaden, deepen, and improve the communication among students. The rest of the campus community will also participate in this improvement; but the system should not be looked upon simply to amplify the messages of the faculty.

Through Time: The secondary goal should be to improve access to the accumulated knowledge of the community and the world as represented by the libraries and other information sources.

The third goal should be facilitating the traditional teacher-student relationship by rechanneling basic knowledge and assignments through a computer system. This will allow the precious commodity, face-to-face communication to be devoted to inspiration and encouragement.

I didn't get much reaction to my memo but was pleased to hear it quoted by a professor who arrived at CMU five years later. It must have become part of the culture.

In December, I attended the CS department's traditional Black Friday meeting to review grad students. The entire faculty, sixty strong, filled the large room in a congenial mood. When I saw Scott, Newell, Habermann, Reddy, and Mary Shaw (one of the few women PhDs in CS) I felt I was among great colleagues. When the grad students attempted to influence us by delivering cases of beer at lunchtime, I knew I was in the right place.

I officially started as a professor of CS and director of Andrew in January of 1983, and my first task was to hire about fifteen programmers. It promised to be easy. The CS department was pumping out PhDs at a rate of about ten per year, and they all admired Gosling, who was already on board. Working for me should look like a great post-doctoral job. Not to mention, I was paying IBM-level salaries, which were fifty percent higher than an assistant professor's salary.

There were a handful of IBMers already signed up. Mike Conner, an affable Texan, was the associate director. Don Smith was a tall mature networking expert from North Carolina. Mike West, Larry Raper, and Tom Peters (a Dijkstra look-alike) filled out the IBM group. And it was no surprise when I heard from Gray who had left IBM for Tandem Computers.

"Congratulations, Jim. Do you know why IBM is doing this?"

"Not really."

"Well . . . the CEO gave a lot of money to his alma mater, and they spent it all on DEC equipment. He asked his staff to explain why and discovered that universities don't like IBM much. So, he said, 'Fix it.' That's why they're playing so nice to CMU. But watch out for shifting winds."

"OK, I will."

"By the way, you should try to get my friend John Howard from IBM San Jose to join you. There's nothing he likes better than getting down to coding."

On my next trip to Palo Alto, Sproull and I persuaded Howard to join us as an IBMer. Then, once back in Pittsburgh,

I began the interviewing process in earnest. Following the academic department model, like Taylor would have, I had the entire team make a consensus hiring decision for every job candidate. One of the lessons I learned from the Xerox training was that hiring requires consensus, because everyone must live with the result.

The first hire was Fred Hansen, a dour PhD from Stanford I knew, whom the group approved. Satya (officially Mahadev Satyanarayanan) was a new CS PhD, and when I called him to offer a job, he questioned me carefully. "Will I have an office? Who will I report to? Will you nurture my career?" Taken aback, I just said, "Trust me," and he did.

The ten-office corridor in the business school grew overcrowded as the new hires and IBMers arrived. I made lemonade of this lemon by making every IBMer share an office with a CMU person. I shared an office with Mike Conner, and I hoped tactics like this would mitigate the cultural disparity.

I found myself imitating Taylor as a leader. As in, I established project goals and then left it to the staff to find the means. I gave them my computer-as-communication-medium manifesto. I showed them a video of the Alto's features. Whether they followed or deviated from the way I would have done things, I kept silent or expressed amazement. I wanted them to know that their accomplishments would be their own.

In my first month on the job, Steve Jobs arrived to sell Macintoshes. In his hotel room, wearing his hooded sweatshirt, he excitedly showed Van Houweling and me the yet-to-be-released Mac. His demonstration was editing text and drawing pictures. Most people might have been

176

astounded by this, but I was a PARC person who viewed the Mac as a crippled Alto in a plastic box. I asked about networking.

"Networking would let Big Brother into our lives," Jobs said dismissively.

I had no answer to that, but Engelbart, upon hearing Jobs's opinion had said, "That's like having an office with no door, windows, or telephone."

Afterwards, I said to Van Houweling, "I hope that thing doesn't get in the way of our plans."

"Yeah, CMU should avoid Macs," he said. "When we began the negotiations with IBM, they really wanted us to use the PC. But Newell and the CS people were Alto lovers and argued that PCs were not powerful enough. IBM reluctantly agreed that we would aim at a workstation that they'll be selling in a few years. So, endorsing the puny Mac would make them cry foul."

Therefore, our next task was to choose the sort of workstation we would use to develop software as we waited for IBM's workstation. The Alto was out of the question, and Xerox would not allow a bunch of hackers to get inside its Star System. The CS department advocated our building on their system, which was built on the PERQ (a CMU spinoff product) and ran an operating system created by the young professor, Rick Rashid. Bill Joy visited to pitch SUN UNIX workstations and spent a long night with Gosling running benchmark programs to show that its performance was superior to any other hardware that ran UNIX. Gosling loved the SUN, as did the other UNIX hackers from CS.

Still, Gosling and I drove over to the PERQ company to discuss its possibilities. On the way back he shared his real feelings.

"The PERQ is a dog. It overheats so badly that we could use them as space heaters in our offices. The students working on the CS system are demoralized about the whole thing."

My next conversation was with Rashid.

"My operating system is actually much better than UNIX for workstations," he said. "I built it to be small and decomposable."

"I think operating systems are like underwear," I said. "Unless they are terrible or amazing, they don't matter. Our project is going to use commercially available software whenever possible." With that declaration I dismissed not just Rashid but the whole operating systems research community.

In the end, Van Houweling and I persuaded IBM to swallow the bitter pill of buying us twenty SUN workstations to develop our software with the promise that we would use their workstation as soon as it became available.

***

I had yet to do any teaching or research at CS, and my office was in another building, so I went to meetings in CS to get acclimated. The first meeting I attended was at Newell's house. The faculty fretted about DARPA's cutback in AI funding. It was the beginning of an "AI Winter," a period of disenchantment following too much hype, and we learned that Newell was considering taking a leave to work at DARPA to turn them around. I wasn't worried about my funding but realized how dependent the CS department was on DARPA, which supplied about 60 percent of its budget.

This was not a normal academic department. CMU CS was a think tank that did a little teaching on the side.

At the same meeting I said that we might consider hiring a visiting professor whom I had hired for Andrew. He was an expert in parallel computing and had written some well-received books.

"He seems like a reasonable guy," I said.

"We don't want reasonable people," Simon thundered. "We want people who disrupt and redirect their fields!"

At another meeting, Simon and Reddy espoused the goal of creating a factory that had zero workers. I had a gut reaction and said it was a horrible idea and even cited Gandhi's belief that work could be ennobling. My opinion fell on deaf ears, despite Raj's Indian heritage. They were all intent on AI, whatever the consequences. The room we met in had a portrait of Andrew Carnegie whose ruthless pursuit of manufacturing efficiency was legend.

My appointment as a full professor still had to be vetted by a series of faculty committees. I was content to think the fix was in because they needed me for the Andrew project and Newell was behind me, so when I had to write a "statement of purpose" essay for the committees to read, I sort of phoned it in. The review of my publications surprised any skeptics with its strength, and my papers about programming languages, as well as the KMP paper, impressed them. Not to mention that Hoare (who had won the Turing Award in 1980), Reynolds, and others gave me glowing recommendations. And it didn't hurt that I'd beaten all but one of the brilliant CS graduate students in their fall programming contest.

***

Susan and I were both happy to be back in Pittsburgh, and we bought a six-bedroom colonial house in the Squirrel Hill neighborhood. Susan's family had lived across the street from it, and she had always admired it. Also, it had been built by my childhood pediatrician, so I felt a connection. We had to perform about $100,000 of renovations that year to avoid capital gains from the sale of our Palo Alto house for about $400,000. Here I had thought I was a computer scientist, but I had really been a real estate speculator, using my PARC salary to help fund the Bay Area's housing bubble.

We joined a local tennis and drinking club, and I bought a real-looking gorilla costume for special occasions.

The following summer, we rented a house in Palo Alto for a month. During the first week, the beautiful blue skies enraged me. *Why, oh why, did I ever leave this place?*

My California colleagues were thriving post-PARC. Geschke was the chief operating officer at Adobe. Schmidt was working sixty-hour weeks at SUN. He said, "Jim, you were a great mentor to me, and I'll always appreciate it, but now I've moved on to more powerful mentors." DEC had hired Taylor and company, and they moved into a four-story building in downtown Palo Alto. I wished them well but was happy to be off on a new project of my own.

***

Returning to Pittsburgh, I divided the Andrew project into two efforts. The first was the network and its services, which we called VICE for "Vast Interconnected Communications Environment," and came down to deciding how information was to be stored and transmitted among workstations. I appointed John Howard, to be the VICE team's manager. I

180

chose not to follow Taylor's no-hierarchy policy. The second effort was going to develop user software for the workstation, and I appointed the recently returned (as promised!) Sproull to be the manager. This move cost money, because Sproull had just resigned from CMU to form a consulting company with his friend Ivan Sutherland. The bond between the two was so strong that the Sutherlands had moved to Pittsburgh along with the Sproulls. It was Sutherland who demanded we pay genius rates. This effort was called VIRTUE for "Virtue Is Reached Through UNIX and Emacs" (a recursive acronym!). Insanely clever acronym creation is a geek pastime.

Naturally, Gosling got the first delivered SUN. His SUN workstation arrived with 1,000K of memory and a bitmap display and cost $10,000. This capable computer came to be called the "3M machine," one megabyte of memory (i.e.1,000 kilobytes), a 1-million-pixel display, and able to execute 1 million instructions per second. The price of the new IBM PC with only 64K memory and a character-only display was $3,000. IBM had researched the student market. If that was all students were willing to pay, we would have a problem someday.

Gosling seemed able to create a program to do anything you asked almost overnight. After I showed him the Alto video, he calmly began duplicating its examples as if they were mere student exercises. In just weeks, he had invented a windows-based user interface for UNIX that DEC and SUN copied a few years later.

To stoke enthusiasm for everyone working on Andrew, I started an *ad hoc* awards program—an IBM practice. When someone accomplished something, I'd give them a $500 bonus and an object to signify their achievement. Gosling received the first for his impressive window manager. I presented him with a window squeegee with a small plate attached to it bearing his name. I gave the second award to Fred Hansen who managed to connect our IBM mainframe to the Ethernet. It was a difficult job because IBM did not believe in high-speed local networks, and it was reflected in their computers. It was a funnel, symbolizing how he had to squeeze the bits through the machine's slow teletype interface. Hansen wore the funnel on his head for the rest of the staff meeting. While money is invisible, the growing group of award winners would keep the objects they received on their desk.

Gosling, however, took the displaying of objects a bit too far, enough to cause a crisis on the campus when he installed a few yard-art pink flamingos outside his second-floor office. We had moved into a new building, funded by the overhead on IBM's contract, overlooking a busy street. The black glass building, built specifically for the computer center, looked like Darth Vader. Gosling wanted to give it some color. When an article in the local paper described his prank, the architects of the building complained about the visual rebuke, and Van Houweling told me to take the flamingos away.

"We'd better not do that," I said. "It was Gosling's idea. If this becomes a *cause célèbre* you'll start to see unauthorized plastic animals popping up all over campus."

He relented, and the pink flamingo became the Andrew project's inanimate mascot.

For his next act, Gosling created a mouse-driven WYSIWYG editor that matched the Alto version. With this early progress in 1983, I was able to give a dazzling live demo to a room full of university faculty that showed the computer screen on a rear projection TV. For those of them not familiar with the Alto, this bordered on magic.

When Sproull's attention faded away, in part to spend more time with his consulting company and his new infant daughter who liked to howl with laughter when parked on the floor in VIRTUE group meetings, I appointed David Rosenthal, an excitable, British UNIX hacker to lead the VIRTUE group. Unlike the solitary hacker Gosling, he recognized that software had become a community enterprise. One day we were faced with a need to reformat a lot of text. He said, "I think we should use sed (a programmable UNIX editor) to do this." He'd never used it, but he found the online documentation, read it for a few minutes, and got sed working to solve the problem. He would spend hours reading posts on a UNIX computer forum, keeping up with new developments, which seemed to occur every week.

While the VIRTUE team was busy creating eye-popping demos, Howard's VICE team was embarking on the creation of a networked system that would allow everyone on campus to share files easily. They were experienced with time-sharing systems in which all users of a computer could access its files directly. Each time-shared computer could support a community of about one hundred users. Larger communities needed to split up and then share files by moving copies around among their respective computers. File sharing among different computers was a cumbersome process subject to confusion about versions of evolving files. Version control is a problem whenever people collaborate editing documents. Elaborate systems have been created to cope with it.

"Wouldn't it be cool if everyone at CMU (about eight-thousand people) could have the illusion they were sharing one huge UNIX time-sharing system!" Satya suggested.

To achieve the illusion, programmers used a well-known technique called *caching,* in which your individual workstation with its small disk would seem to hold all the files at CMU.[48] Even though the shuffling of files between a central repository and the workstations was barely perceptible, it took a lot of work and ended up being the most significant innovation of our system.

***

Early in the Andrew project, I hired Fadiman to come to Pittsburgh and work his four-day magic on my team and their spouses. I thought that Fadiman might mellow out some of them, and that it would provide a common experience for us, away from the computers.

Bob Sidebotham was a part of the VICE team and a classic geek—intensely thoughtful. He was distinguished for being the most irascible and argumentative person in the project. And he was a confirmed bachelor.

"What is this crap?" Sidebotham asked during the first session. He continued to be his disruptive self, suggesting that Fadiman was wasting our time. On the third day, Sidebotham

---

[48] See VICE in Nerd Zone

came in and shared with the group. "I had a wonderful time last night on a date. We had ice cream, and I tasted it intensely for the first time!" He ended up marrying the date and was later described as either "Bob before Omega" or "Bob after Omega."

By 1984 the Andrew project was humming along, and we were hoping to deploy the first version to the campus within a year.

MIT and Brown University had also launched campus computing projects that resembled ours. MIT's was called Project Athena and was funded by both IBM and DEC. Brown's smaller project was called The Scholar's Workstation and was focused on Apple's Macintosh, which was released in January 1984. The first Mac had 128K of memory, cost $2,500, and was introduced to the public by a (now famous) Super Bowl commercial implying that the IBM was Big Brother. Apple's market was higher education, specifically the Ivy League. Steve Jobs personally delivered a Macintosh to Brooke Shields, a Princeton student, following her breakout as a teen movie star.

In October of 1984, a young David Sanger from the *New York Times* visited the Andrew project. We gave him an open-kimono demo and awaited his story that would tell the world how cool our system was going to be. Although we weren't sure if he grasped it. The *Times* story, "Computer Work Bends College Secrecy Rules" criticized CMU and IBM for making a business deal in which IBM would own all our software. Meanwhile, Sanger assured readers that MIT and Brown were still pure. His article never even described anything about Andrew. CMU felt any publicity was good, but IBM was pissed. As was I, so I wrote a letter to the *Times* saying that nobody at CMU was keeping secrets and complaining that we had been sandbagged.

With the announcement of the Macintosh, a battle about what computers CMU students would use while waiting for our system broke out. Van Houweling's ambitious boss mischievously became a Macintosh advocate and enjoyed butting heads with IBM whenever possible. The tension between them grew until Van Houweling took a job as the University of Michigan's computer czar, coincidently also called "Big Blue," where he went on to create and lead the Internet2 consortium, leading the way to a much higher bandwidth internet. After his move, I felt my air cover disappearing, and I missed him as a friend.

I sought advice from the acknowledged master of CMU politics.

"The network, not the computer, is the important thing to get right," Newell told me, as I sat in his office. "The devices people use will change, but the network architecture will last. Computing devices and their interfaces will proliferate and evolve from workstations, to desktops, to laptops, and heavens knows what else."

His perspective became my guide, and I was able to cease fretting about the student computer for a while. Newell was always generous with this kind of help. He was steadfast in his research and refused to hold any administrative position. But, like my childhood hero, the Lone Ranger, when something important was happening or needed to happen, he would ride into town, devote himself tirelessly to make things work out, then ride out. In this case, he came to all a two-day Andrew retreat and helped drive a consensus to deploy our system as soon as possible. That year, he helped others at

CMU launch a large, DoD-funded operation bigger than Andrew, The Software Engineering Institute (SEI). Newell was not involved in software engineering but recognized its importance. He remarked, "Its goal is to implement systems with large numbers of average-intelligence programmers." He helped a successful pitch to the National Science Foundation (NSF) to create the Pittsburgh Supercomputer Center to help the CMU and Pitt physicists.

IBM had informally promised to pay for wiring the whole campus for high-speed computer communication, but they wanted us to use their technology, called token ring. As with computers, CMU was sure it wanted to use something else— Ethernet. But no IBMer liked to be seen advocating for someone buying non-IBM technology, and we didn't have Van Houweling to charm IBM anymore. The impasse was holding up Andrew's network strategy, which was being developed by John Leong.

John Leong had been raised in Mozambique, lived through its Marxist-driven civil war, went to an English prep school, and migrated to Canada with his Chinese parents. Like Taylor, he'd been to a few county fairs and had learned to suss out the culture and thrive wherever he went. He was able to break the impasse by discovering a PARC spin-off selling a converter that allowed the Ethernet protocol to run on the IBM token ring cables. That allowed IBM to save face while paying for the wiring.

That same year, Gosling resigned from IBM and went to SUN. Susan and I rented him a second house we owned in Palo Alto, and his SUN friends, as a sort of welcome, filled the front yard with pink flamingos.

It fell to Andy Palay, a CMU PhD in AI, who was calm and patient, to take over Gosling's inscrutable code. He struggled to understand what it was doing and eventually gave up and rewrote the WYSIWYG text editor, and in doing so, established a way to embed any kind of displayable object, even animated ones, in a document. He used it to enhance the editor to allow others to embed pictures, drawings, tables, and equations in documents. Then, the talented Tom Neuendorffer created a playable piano picture you could insert in a document. This was a real innovation—beyond what the Alto or the Macintosh could do. Microsoft later incorporated the editor's features into Microsoft Word, and when Apple sued Microsoft years later for intellectual property theft, Microsoft cited the VIRTUE software as prior art which they had copied. Microsoft won.

I was becoming aware of how obtuse programmers could be. Their need to be ruthlessly consistent could make them blind to users' needs. Here is a typical conversation between me and a programmer.

Me: "Your spell checker in the editor has a bug."

Programmer: "Really?"

"Yes. I misspelled 'their', but it didn't catch it."

"What did you write?"

"t-h-e-r-e."

"But that's spelled correctly.

"Not when I wrote 'They saw t-h-e-r-e grandmother.'"

"But 't-h-e-r-e' is in the dictionary."

"I know that, but it's incorrect in that sentence."

"My program just checks for whether a word is in the dictionary."

"That's a bug."

"No it isn't."

"Well, it doesn't do everything I want it to do."

"Get over it."

I hired a rare English professor who could program, Chris Neuwirth, to write documentation telling Andrew users how to use its novel tools. When she tried to use the VIRTUE interface, she found it confusing. Naturally, because it had been written by geeks. I thought it would help our cause if she could describe some of her difficulties to the team.

"Where should I begin?" she said. "The window manager is crazy. The only way I get a new window is to type control-N and it goes and splits a randomly chosen window in two. The fonts look terrible. The text editor is OK, but when I print a document, it messes up all the page breaks. I can't enter anything in the last row of a table . . ."

I could see the thought balloons popping up above the programmers' heads.

Who is this woman?

Where did she come from?

Get her out of here!

I had to—gently—interrupt her growing list.

"Chris, how many items do you have there?"

"Fifty-six."

"Chris, you get three wishes today." A veteran programmer stood up. "Just tell us the three most important ones we should fix."

She picked the window manager and two printing glitches but continued to fume.

Her point was validated by Steve Jobs when he visited and tried our system. "OK, I get it," he said. "This is kind of funky." I didn't know it at the time, but a "funky" user interface was grounds for immediate termination at Apple. Most computer company founders were engineers, thinking everyone could deal with confusing, counterintuitive technology. But Jobs was a user with the power to fire engineers.

I might have been similarly blind to users if not for Susan. She used technology in her radio work and appreciated the Alto printing system but had little patience with confusing technology. I learned a lot of lessons helping Susan use poorly designed technology.

We made the first release of Andrew to the CMU campus in 1985. Since we were still waiting—it had been three years! —for the arrival of an IBM workstation, we had to install forty SUN workstations in clusters and some faculty offices.

Now that everything was set up and running, it seemed like a good time for IBM and CMU to declare victory. A day of celebration was staged, full of speeches given by top executives at both IBM and CMU. Cyert was the headliner. At the end he introduced me as "the brains behind Andrew." I gave a short speech acknowledging the many people who had contributed, including Van Houweling, who I still missed.

Andrew now needed design talent, so when I heard that a talented PhD student, Nathaniel Borenstein, was struggling to get a thesis started, I reached out to him. After a few discussions, we agreed that context-based help—popping up in a dialog box germane to what a user was doing—was an idea worth exploring. In 1985 most systems just put a standard user manual online and left it to the user to find the relevant chapter. Borenstein designed and implemented a rudimentary help system on a UNIX time-sharing computer and performed controlled experiments that compared users' success with it and with the standard online manual. He wrote an excellent thesis, demonstrating his understanding of human needs.

He was a unique character. He read at a high school level at age three and spent his actual high school days smoking pot. He became the first US student ever to be awarded money damages for the violation of his freedom of speech. Borenstein accepted my job offer at the ITC without hesitation and set about leading a four-person group to produce a superb email application using the facilities of VICE and VIRTUE. A key to his success was his ability to collaborate with all his colleagues. His application integrated with the fancy document editor, so that one could send email messages with embedded graphics to other users of the system. The rest of the world's email was far behind, allowing only a single font in messages and unreliable delivery. It became a capstone of our whole project. He went on to invent the standard for the way multimedia objects are encoded for transport over the internet.

He was sympathetic to users but was still a programmer who used the Emacs text editor rather than the mouse-driven editor we had created. He could edit his programs faster with Emacs. Another discovery I found disturbing was that an experiment by the English department showed that normal people writing a business letter got it done faster using a simple editor rather than on a Macintosh's WYSIWYG editor. There was a consolation, however. The business letters written with the Macintosh were judged better by English teachers. The writers were happy to spend more time on them. One subject commented, "I'm drawn to the Mac! It makes it fun to write."

These phenomena presaged the coming cleavage between the programmers and everybody else. As normal people became PC users, professional programmers stuck to their UNIX terminals and command line interfaces where they remain today.

Observations like this made me question my choice to hire only CS PhDs and software engineers who generally lacked understanding of users. Engineers, nearly always men, seem to think everyone should put up with their hyperrational views. Empowering women on design teams might have improved perspective, but they were rare. Lenore Blum was one of the first to do anything about the dearth of women computer scientists. She became the head of Mills's math department and started a computer science department there.

Another opening to more women came from social sciences. So, it was natural that when I heard that Newell was calling all the faculty from CS and the social sciences together to discuss combining CS and psychology in a research program in HCI, I was an enthusiastic participant. But nothing came of the discussions, because Newell and everyone else went back to their ongoing research.

***

The computer center staff began a transition from supporting DEC time-sharing systems to Andrew. Some of my staff wanted to take over the operation themselves, but I discouraged them. I wanted to create a new vision to keep up the innovation.

To build further on Andrew's success, we applied for and won a three-year $3 million contract from the NSF to support paperless proposal processing. I assigned a few programmers from Borenstein's mail group and two new outside hires to the job.

The work was going well, but I started having encounters with Gordon Bell, NSF's director for CS funding and formerly the hardware genius behind DEC. He had also been a visiting professor at CMU, but his heart was with his alma mater MIT and DEC. He was skeptical that we could improve NSF's proposal processing. He also did not approve of the deal between CMU and IBM, which gave him a mischievous idea.

"Nothing personal, but I'm going to pull your funding unless you put the WYSIWYG editor software in the public domain," Bell told me over the phone.

"I would like to do that, Gordon, but IBM owns it."

"Not my problem."

I spent the next year persuading IBM to release the software. Like Taylor giving Altos to universities, I wanted to see our software baby flourish in the world and believed IBM would never sell it themselves. The IBM manager capable of permitting it saw no upside for his career. If it became popular, he would become known as the guy who gave away a treasure. When he finally agreed, I was exhausted.

I was not good at managing upward and was sick of begging people to do the right thing when it didn't serve their personal agenda. Senior people in both organizations often responded to my requests with, "Why should I do that?" which would leave me enraged. *Why do people place their self-interest above worthy goals?* I was naïve.

In 1986 IBM finally announced its workstation called the RT. CMU acquired 250 RTs to deploy on campus. IBM also offered it to other universities as a package deal with Andrew, but not one adopted it. An RT cost $8,000, which is far more than students would pay themselves. We learned from industry reviews that, as a generic UNIX workstation, the RT was considered inferior to products from SUN and others.

Nevertheless, Andrew was off and running with improved features—like Andrew Mail—debuting every year. The user interface remained funky, but CMU was full of geeks who were unbothered by funky software. Andrew had established CMU as the university with the most advanced campus computing service in the mid-'80s and was CMU's computer system for many years before it was overtaken by software from Microsoft, Apple, and then Google.

To spur our sponsors to support more innovation I wrote a new vision statement, "Thoughts on an Information Utility,"[49] an upgrade to my 1982 vision. Here is its summary:

> The speed and volume of information is increasing drastically. Technologies such as lasers, fiber-optics, and satellites are being exploited to produce an information flood. . . . Communication is becoming more personalized. The Xerox copier gave everyone the ability to become their own publisher. Electronic mail gives computer users the ability to create their own wire services. Although the computer appeared as new technology at the same time as television, it has had much less direct impact on society. With the proliferation of personal computers, it is possible for computers to play a more explicit role . . .

> Our economic growth is increasingly dependent on information processing; over half the GNP involves information processing. Information processing is applicable to virtually every field and is unique in that it can be used to facilitate its own development.

---

[49] See Thoughts on an Information Utility in Documents

There can be a significant technological multiplier effect on investments in it. A better communications infrastructure is needed. . . . [C]omputers can facilitate productivity, but their ability to do so in isolation is limited. In business, it is obvious that linking one's computer to the company databases is an important first step. . . . [S]ophisticated production techniques, like "just in time" production control, require one to have strong communication links with suppliers. . . . We need to think in terms of nation-wide, heterogeneous communication systems that accommodate diversity in information representation and transmission. . . . The ARPANet has been an indispensable tool for the CS community; indeed, it helped create it. Its expansion to other research communities as NSFNet has begun. Any information utility must begin with such a network as its base. . .

Unlike conventional research and development, the work to build an information infrastructure will benefit this country directly and will be less exploitable by foreign competitors. A system built into the existing telecommunications and computing culture of the academic and scientific community cannot be easily translated to another place. [This was false!]

Like the early automobile industry, the personal computer industry cannot grow significantly without infrastructure. . . . The current market for personal computers is based upon software that enhances the productivity of individuals in isolation, e.g. word-processing, data management, and spreadsheets. . . . their potential to sell computers will not be dramatic . . . When people can use computers to find large amounts of information, relevant to their interests, a true mass market for computers will develop.

> In 1980 no IBM PCs existed; now there are over five million. Approximately six million personal computers of all types were sold in 1985. . . . there are now unexploited opportunities associated with the new, widespread ownership of computers. National bulletin boards are flourishing. The DARPA and UNIX network communities deal with a flood of messages. . . . A recent news story tells how someone used the Source electronic forum to collect material for a book and to enlist the help of hundreds of contributors and reviewers.

In retrospect, these words seem to be a plea to make the internet a public resource rather than a private club. I had lifted the word "utility" from the ruminations of the Multics designers in the late 1960s. Today it's called the cloud.

The IBM people read visions and thought them "interesting," but didn't offer any encouragement.

By 1987 I was exhausted by the politics, so I declared victory for myself and requested a one-year leave of absence from the project. Alfred Spector, an aggressive young CS professor who had helped with VICE, took over my position, and I had time to teach a class for the first time at CMU.

My first course was about programming languages and the λ–calculus. The students, all undergraduates, were confused about what it had to do with their careers, and I couldn't blame them. Still, after a year, I decided not to return to the ITC. I could see that pursuing important new goals would involve convincing the staff, the university, and the funders to change course. I was reminded of Marty Graham's comment about academic administration at Berkeley. "'I can't afford to enjoy this any longer,' said the fox who was fucking the skunk."

As word circulated of my resignation, I received job offers from Schmidt at SUN and Van Houweling at Michigan. Taylor got Sam Fuller to visit me in Pittsburgh to discuss starting a DEC lab there.

I even had an interview with Steve Jobs who had founded a new company, NeXT Inc., after being forced out of Apple. Jobs had been hanging out at CMU and had adopted many advanced but untried technologies for NeXT's workstation.

I asked, "Why are using Rashid's Mach operating system?"

"I really don't care about the underlying software, but I really wanted to hire Avie Tevanian (one of Mach's designers)," Jobs said.

Fifteen minutes into our discussion, Jobs and I both knew it was not going to work for us. He seemed arrogant, and I seemed stubborn.

Susan wanted to stay in Pittsburgh. She had gotten interested in investing after the year in which our broker made large commissions while we lost money. As usual she went all in, founding an investment club, writing a column for a Pittsburgh newspaper, and dispensing advice on the radio, sponsored by a local investment firm. I, too, was content to stay. I was thinking about starting my own company.

The entire evolutionary record on our planet illustrates a progressive tendency toward intelligence. – Carl Sagan

9. The Evolution of Intelligence

When Jane was studying biology in high school, a minister at our church told her that evolution was bunk, so she asked me what I thought. I thought he was an idiot and said so. One of his bogus arguments was that scientists argued about evolution. To me, that meant there was something interesting about evolution, so I decided to learn about it. I began reading.[50] I soon appreciated that belief in evolution could replace belief in God. The threat to God by the scientific revolution of Newton had been blunted by William Paley, who wrote that if a pocket watch is found on a heath, it is most reasonable to assume that someone dropped it and that it was made by at least one watchmaker, not by natural forces.[51]

---

[50] See Dawkins, Dennett, and Ridley in Readings

[51] Willian Paley, *Natural Theology, or Evidences of the Existence and Attributes of the Deity collected from the Appearances of Nature*, published in 1802.

198

Darwin   Mendel   Watson & Crick

The general idea of evolution was two-millennia old when the English naturalist Charles Darwin presented a convincing case that the watchmaker was not some sort of superhuman designer, but a blind process of random variation guided by competition among specimens. The hardest pill to swallow was that this watchmaker had no goal whatsoever so that nature, including humans, was not predestined, in any sense.

Darwin's theory was embellished by the Czech monk Gregor Mendel whose experiments with plants showed that the variation was often a choice between fixed alternatives possessed by ancestors. Those alternatives are called *genes*.

In 1953 Watson and Crick explained how DNA represented genes. Each cell of any living specimen holds chromosomes, chains of *nucleotide* molecules called DNA. In any specimen, the chains are identical because they are copied when cells divide. A *gene* is a specific sequence of (typically about twenty-seven thousand) nucleotides located in a particular region of a chromosome. Each gene induces some trait of its host specimen. The offspring of sexually reproducing specimens will contain new versions of chromosomes by mixing and matching genes from its parents.

We think of fitness as a person's well-being, but biologists have a special way of measuring the *fitness* of a gene. It is measured by how much it replicates through the generations of its hosts. If tall people have more children than short people, then the tall gene for height will fill the slot for height more often in the chromosomes of the next generation. And shorter people, along with their short gene, might become extinct after several generations.

Evolution seems less unlikely if you appreciate the power exponential growth. Assuming each woman has an average of two children, after N generations, about 2^N of her descendants are competing to reproduce. Among that huge number of people, some very fit ones should emerge.

Intelligence is a component of fitness. Specifically, it is an invisible process that mediates between our senses and our actions. It helps us predict the consequences of what we might do, given what we see. If I compare my fitness with Feeny's, he wins on size, strength, coordination, and handsomeness, but I have the edge in intelligence. On a football team, I should draw up the plays for Feeny to execute.

Darwin hoped that his theory was compatible with altruism. Unless you could expect reciprocation, why should you sacrifice your own fitness for someone else? He suggested, "If one man in a tribe . . . [helped others], the tribe would increase in number, spread, and supplant other tribes. In a tribe thus rendered more numerous there would always be a rather better chance of the birth of other superior and inventive members." Scientists have been arguing about his idea ever since.[52] I hope that Darwin was right, so I won't feel foolish for being altruistic. When a teacher asked my grade school class what sort of animal each of us would like to be, I

---

[52] See Altruism in Nerd Zone

passed on lions and tigers and said, "a penguin," because I'd heard they had no natural enemies. As a teenager I had disliked a friend's attitude who insisted that being generous was stupid. Our disagreement was age-old. He was reflecting the beliefs of Social Darwinists who had interpreted Darwin's "survival of the fittest," along with Adam Smith's "invisible hand" of markets, to justify greed and imperialism.

I was heartened about altruism after I read Richard Dawkins's cunningly titled book, *The Selfish Gene.* He urged looking at evolution from a gene's point of view. Speaking anthropomorphically, he claimed that genes made creatures altruistic, inducing them to sacrifice their fitness for the sake of the many family members who shared their genes. In other words, the selfishness of the genes who wanted to replicate themselves overcame the selfishness of the creature because it would result in more copies of those genes in the next generation. To make the argument without anthropomorphism: genes that induce altruism produce more replicas than genes that induce selfishness. Put bluntly, we are the instruments of our genes.

I found this viewpoint helpful in trying to understand people and human progress. Instead of asking who succeeds, we ask why a certain gene survives through the generations. Such questions create revealing puzzles. Aside from altruism there are many traits that seem to mitigate against fitness: homosexuality, color blindness, baldness, to name a few.

You might be skeptical of genes' centrality because they aren't capable of replicating without hosts. But consider which lasts longer. A gene (like brown eyes) can last virtually forever unchanged while you (the human with brown eyes) will be lucky to be around for one hundred years. The gene that supports photosynthesis is 3.4 billion years old, close to immortal. We specimens are disposable vessels.

Humanity has followed a path that is arguably better for genes than people. Childless adults are happier than parents, according to surveys—something I remembered when a daughter was struggling to have a child. I thought she might have a happier life without children. Why do people have kids? Their genes make them do it.

At the end of his book Dawkins speculated about something other than genes that might replicate themselves:

> We need a name for the new replicator, a noun that conveys the idea of a unit of cultural transmission, or a unit of *imitation*. 'Mimeme' comes from a suitable Greek root, but I want a monosyllable that sounds a bit like 'gene'. I hope my classicist friends will forgive me if I abbreviate mimeme to *meme*. If it is any consolation, it could alternatively be thought of as being related to 'memory', or to the French word *même*. It should be pronounced to rhyme with 'cream.'
>
> Examples of memes are tunes, ideas, catch-phrases, clothes fashions, ways of making pots or of building arches. Just as genes propagate themselves in the gene pool by leaping from body to body via sperms or eggs, memes propagate themselves in the meme pool by leaping from brain to brain via a process which, in the broad sense, can be called imitation. If a scientist hears, or reads about, a good idea, he passes it on to his colleagues and students. He mentions it in his articles and his lectures. If the idea

catches on, it can be said to propagate itself, spreading from brain to brain."

Dawkins's offhand idea of the meme has been embraced by many intellectuals who see it as a building block of intelligence and cultural evolution.[53] The word "meme" has also popularized by the internet to describe any idea bouncing around it.

Following the reasoning about genes, a meme that helps its hosts to thrive will be replicated more often. However, like selfish genes, memes just want to be replicated by any means possible and helping the specimens that carry them is not the only strategy. While genes use sex to induce people to replicate them, memes use novelty. "Man bites dog" replicates better than "Dog bites man." Jokes are memes. Unfortunately, false memes can out-replicate true ones because they have built-in novelty.

Memes are sometimes packaged as entertainment. "Life is but a dream," is a Buddhist meme that appears everywhere. Shakespeare said it. The nursery rhyme "Row, Row, Row Your Boat" ends with it. It's the title of Beyonce's autobiographical film.

Memes first replicated themselves through imitation. Monkey troops discover tricks that are imitated and survive the discoverers. Nobody knows why humans developed language, but it was a game changer. Language allowed memes to replicate faster and farther than monkey tricks. Writing, printing, recording, visual media, and the internet offered increasingly powerful replication methods for memes, making them even more accurate and widespread. It

---

[53] See Blackmore in Readings

took millions of years to develop genes for legs, arms, and brains, while the memes that underpin our civilization—agriculture, religion, money—started just ten thousand years ago, long after the genetic hardware was in place.

People transmit memes without owning them. I'm sure Licklider didn't remember saying to me, "I like to repot myself every five years," but it became my motto. My father sometimes said, "Money is the root of all evil," but pursued money all the same. I had forgotten the meme "Finishing your thesis is the least embarrassing way to get out of graduate school," until the recipient reminded me.

When Jehovah's Witnesses knock on your door, they are working for their memes. "Do unto others as you would have them do unto you," is a meme nearly every religion propagates, along with memes about what happens after death. Religions, in fact, are systems of cooperating memes, sometimes called *polymemes*, that have thrived throughout human history. Religious institutions confer benefits on their adherents but are also selfish organizations that want to grow. The cost to the followers can be substantial. Dawkins is a militant atheist—based on his estimates of the costs.

Jared Diamond never says "meme" in *Guns, Germs, and Steel*, but it explains how Eurasian civilizations were able to conquer the American Indians, Australian Aborigines, and Africans by using memes for guns and steel, along with the gene for smallpox.

The book was prompted by a question his New Guinian guide, a hunter-gatherer, asked him: "Why is it that you white people developed so much cargo and brought it to New Guinea, but we black people had little cargo of our own?" Diamond observes that he—or any other modern man—is not as fit, either physically or mentally, as his guide. Consider a contest in which Diamond tries to survive alone in the jungle and his guide tries to survive in a modern city. Diamond would die quickly while his guide would just look around and conclude he was living among lunatics.

The intelligence of an individual, like Diamond or me or you, is backed by the intelligence of our tribe. Similarly, any practical robot depends heavily on the internet. Google distills the internet's information into a sort of "intelligence" with its method of prioritizing pages. A market is another excellent way to distill the intelligence of a community through competition. For example, prediction markets like the Iowa Electronic Markets are far better at predicting political outcomes than polls and pundits, including the expert Nate Silver who sums up all the polls.

One of our earliest polymemes was agriculture, which enhanced our genes' fitness greatly. However, it *decreased* the average human's quality of life. Diamond cites anthropological investigations that show that farmers were smaller, had more disease, and worked constantly when compared to hunter-gatherers who were larger, healthier, and averaged only two days of work per week.[54] (Maybe observations like this inspired my father's impulse to stay in the South Pacific.) The major effect of agriculture was to increase the human population while making it less equal. *Why did people farm?* The same reason they have kids. More people means more copies of genes.

Modern humans are buffeted between genes and memes. For the first two hundred thousand years of human existence,

---

[54] See Suzman in Readings

the genes drove. Now memes try to displace them, as in the battle against racism. I wonder if the authors of the book of Genesis were thinking like Diamond when they told the story of Adam and Eve, who ate from the tree of knowledge, prompting God to expel them from the Garden of Eden (which sounds like a pre-agricultural place). Perhaps God was angry that He was being displaced by intelligence.

The history of technology is rife with easily identifiable memes. Replication occurs when the designer of a device understands the usage of the meme in other devices and incorporates it in a new one. The punched cards we used to write programs are descendants of cards used in the Jacquard loom, invented in 1804. Spoken languages evolve. Programming languages are a small ecosystem easily studied. Functions, addresses, and recursion appear in nearly every programming language.

Technology, especially software, evolves as people keep tweaking each other's designs. A year before Richards sent me BCPL, Ken Thompson and Dennis Ritchie at Bell Labs grabbed the BCPL compiler files from MAC's file repository and installed BCPL on their computer before calling up Richards and thanking him. Then they designed two languages patterned after BCPL named "B" and "C", perhaps after its first two letters. They used C to implement UNIX (for which they received a joint Turing Award in 1983). Because C retained BCPL's portability—one might even say virality—C and UNIX spread to every kind of computer there was. C has many descendants: C++ (Bell Labs), Objective C (at Apple), C# (at Microsoft), C0 (at CMU), and Go (at Google). Nobody ever used BCPL to implement its father, Strachey's CPL, which quietly passed away. But since his friends felt that CPL stood for "Christopher's Programming Language", his initial, at least, survives.

Despite its early demise, CPL rescued an important meme from obscurity: the address of a computer's register. Until then, programming languages had been coy about the existence of addresses causing confusion among programmers and many obscure bugs.[55] CPL, and then BCPL, made addresses explicit by interpreting @x as the address of the variable x, x as the contents at that address, and rv x is the contents at the address that is stored at that address. Thus rv @x = x.[56]

Of course, algorithms, like the ancient square root program, are particularly handy memes that can be activated without human involvement. They are easy to replicate by copying; it requires a human to install an algorithm in a new larger program.

Unlike genes, there is no current theory of how memes are held in our brains or bodies. Dawkins was just spit balling when he described memes, and until the intellectual equivalents of Watson and Crick come along, "meme" is just a placeholder. We guess that memes might somehow be represented by neurons in humans, but in computers they are obviously represented by programs.

---

[55] See Address Confusion in Nerd Zone

[56] rv is short for "right hand value," the interpretation of a variable on the right hand of an assignment statement, in contrast to the "left hand value," the interpretation of a variable on the left hand of an assignment statement. The C language uses the prefix * instead of rv.

Some carry the idea that humans are merely a means to an end for memes much further. In 1988 my Sunday newspaper reviewed Hans Moravec's book *Mind Children*[57], which made a rash prediction: robots would, at some time, exceed humans' intelligence becoming the most intelligent species on Earth. He seemed completely at peace with this idea, thinking of the robots as our descendants, of which we should be proud.

It extends Moore's Law, based on the observations shown as dots. It doesn't explain how it might happen. It just shows the number of calculations per second a device can do for $1,000 of the purchase price. He estimates the natural intelligence of creatures by counting their neurons and estimating the speed of calculations they can do. It even suggests a computer might someday exceed the collective intelligence of the whole human race.

---

[57] See Moravec in Readings.

Moravec's picture below embodies his argument that computer technology might someday achieve superhuman intelligence.

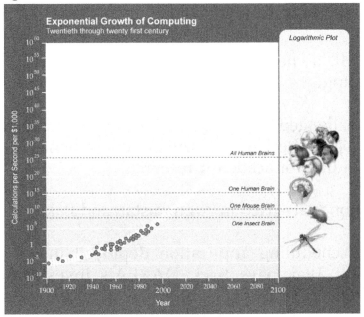

I was chagrined that such a madman was on the same faculty as I.

V: AI Spring 1990-1997

The market for industrial AI reached over $1 billion dollars.

CMU's chess program, HiTech achieves a 2530 rating.

Challenged by Japan's Fifth-Generation computer project, the US and British governments restore funding for academic research.

Drones are used in Afghanistan and Pakistan.

A scheduling application deployed in the first Gulf War pays back DARPA's investment of thirty years in AI research.

A CMU semi-autonomous car drove coast-to-coast across the United States with computer-controlled steering for 2,797 miles.

IBM's Deep Blue computer beats world chess champion Garry Kasparov.

We must design for the way people behave, not for how we would wish them to behave.
– Donald A. Norman

10. Human Computer Interaction

With the CS department at CMU flourishing, Newell spent a few years using his exquisite political skills to convince the university to elevate CS to become its own college. In 1988 the School of Computer Science (SCS) had been founded, which encompassed the CS department, the Robotics Institute, the Andrew Project, and the Language Technology Center, which pursued the translation of natural languages. Habermann became the first SCS dean.

In 1989, Spector, who was then the director of the Andrew project, left CMU and started a company called Transarc, which was partly owned by IBM, to enhance and market VICE, which he renamed the Andrew File System (AFS). He took half of the project with him. I was surprised but not dismayed. As I said, I was contemplating new paths for myself.

As Newell might have predicted, AFS became the most long-lasting contribution of Andrew and is still used in many places beyond CMU today. In 2016 AFS won a national award for its lasting influence.

"We're going to start a research lab at SUN," said Schmidt over the phone one afternoon. "Are you interested in running it?" He had just been named chief technology officer at SUN.

"Not unless you want to locate it in Pittsburgh," I said. "But I'm flattered to be asked."

Eventually Schmidt acquired the Sproull-Sutherland firm, partly because Ivan's brother, Bert Sutherland, was already the director of SUN's small Mountain View research group. Sproull started a second lab in Burlington, MA. Ivan Sutherland was his usual self, avoiding formal management duties. He had won the Turing Award in 1988 for inventing computer graphics, twenty-five years before. Maybe it took that long because he was not a schmoozer. Sproull was his interface to humanity.

Meanwhile, Gosling, who had been in SUN's research group since leaving IBM, had invented the Java programming language, which is a successful descendant of the ALGOL and BCPL family trees. SUN chose to distribute Java widely at no charge. It was a decision encouraged by SUN co-founder Bill Joy who said, "If you give away source code, innovation will occur . . . [but] the innovation will occur elsewhere . . . no matter how many people you hire. So, the only way to get close to the state of the art is to give the people who are going to be doing the innovative things the means to do it. . . . Open source is tapping the energy that's out there."

Joy's idea is a special case of the fact that the best results for genes, memes, and technology occur through evolution in the largest populations. Another example: the largest gene pool other than the entire human race's is the African one, which seems to produce the best athletes. Note that "best" here means the best of the best. The average representatives of the various-sized pools are roughly the same.[58]

***

At an interdepartmental dinner one night, I sat next to Pete Lucas.

"I manage the psych department's computers," he said to me. "Andrew could threaten my job!"

"Yes," I said, seeing his point of view. "I hadn't appreciated that many departments, including CS, have staff people who are protecting their turf. But it drives me nuts that so many people resist using just Andrew Mail, which would smooth out campus communication."

"Well, Andrew is a little funky for the psych faculty, and they seem to be gravitating to Macintoshes, so I'm probably safe for a while."

Lucas laughed.

"What could we do to make it less funky?"

I was serious.

---

[58] See "The Distribution Functions of the Sample Maximum as a Function of Sample Size,"
https://www.sjsu.edu/faculty/watkins/samplemax4.htm

"Well . . ." he said, thinking about my question for a moment. "I like it as a programming tool, but the people in psych just want something to run their statistics on. Did you do any studies of the CMU population before designing Andrew?"

"Nope."

"The market for PCs will stagnate if its vendors don't start doing that."

By the time we had dessert and coffee, I discovered that Lucas had many intriguing ideas.

In the coming months, the two of us would continue to meet and chat at university activities related to computing. Eventually, this led to a friendship and a shared understanding that the computer industry desperately needed designers who understood human capabilities.

One day at lunch, Lucas revealed to me his specific career ambition—to become what he called a post-industrial designer. He wanted a career like that of Raymond Loewy, who was the father of industrial design in the 1930s and designed some of the icons of our time, such as the Coke bottle. So, I introduced Lucas to my friend Joe Ballay, an old fraternity brother, who was the founder of CMU's design department, a part of the fine arts college.

While engineers say they "design," Designers (with a capital D) have a far more elevated notion of their practice. They are "architects of everything," conceiving of master plans and supervising specialists to carry them out. Like actual architects, Designers see engineers as tools, and the engineers reciprocate by regarding Designers as dilettantes.

The three of us began discussing ideas when we were not engaged in our academic responsibilities. One of which was a device in one box that could be a printer, scanner, copier, and fax machine—a new idea in 1990.

Our first official meeting was with some of Ballay's friends from the Design firm Fitch Richardson Smith who were interested in CMU technology.

Lucas introduced himself as, "a psychologist and a fan of industrial Design."

"I'm a recovering computer scientist," I said.

A few weeks later, the three of us paid them a return visit to their Columbus, Ohio Design studio, which opened my eyes to how diverse and exciting Design consulting could be. Driving back to Pittsburgh through the rolling Ohio hills that night, Lucas, Ballay, and I decided to start a company. Lucas proposed calling the company MAYA Design as a tribute to Loewy's motto, "Most Advanced Yet Acceptable," and that was fine with Ballay and me.

Since we didn't yet have a client to Design something for, we needed an example of our talents to show prospective clients. Remembering an idea that had kicked around PARC, I dreamt up an information storage system that could scan paper documents, extract all the words in the text, and store the image of the document in a database indexed by all those words. It eliminated all the usual copying, filing, distributing, and losing that goes on in an office. To process a document, users would type enough words into a computer to identify it. They could read or modify it on a computer or print it. It was sort of a paper-based Google. Ballay made a little model of our scan-print-fax device, and we called it the Hyperfax machine. We traveled around showing the model and telling our story. After a trip to Palo Alto, Taylor jawboned Fuller (now his DEC boss) into giving us a multiyear contract to pursue it. It was then that Lucas said, "I don't know about the potential of Hyperfax, but this is a wonderful way to launch my dream consulting company." After some negotiation with DEC, MAYA was up and running in 1990.

Lucas resigned from CMU, Ballay came on as a consultant, and I took a leave to become president of the company. When I was back on campus for a small meeting about some faculty issue, Newell remarked facetiously. "Your new company had better work out for you." This was the only time I recall Newell being irritated at me. Perhaps he was miffed that I was pursuing something like his HCI agenda outside of CMU.

I placed a short text request for job applicants on an internet discussion group called "comp.misc." It wasn't long until I received a fusillade of reprimands from the discussants reminding me that the internet was "not for commercial use." None of us knew, but Al Gore would change that in a few years.

***

I was busy with MAYA but was still engaged with CMU. When Perlis died in 1990, I initiated a campaign to raise a few million dollars to create an endowed chair in his name. Reddy was the first donor, pledging $10,000, and I felt I had to match it. He was also an admirer of Perlis. SCS hosted a large twenty-fifth departmental anniversary celebration where I delivered a heartfelt speech about Perlis with his family in attendance while someone distributed donation envelopes on the dinner tables. It took a few years to amass the required millions.

In 1991, Habermann announced he was taking a leave to work at the NSF for a few years. Newell held a meeting to choose an interim dean of SCS to serve while the university searched for a permanent one. As usual, none of the senior faculty in the room wanted the job. I refused because I was committed to MAYA. We spent an hour discussing alternatives. Finally, Reddy reluctantly agreed to do it.

While Reddy was acting dean, the search continued for a permanent dean. I was a candidate. Lucas told me that I didn't want to be a dean. He thought it was a terrible job. Newell's opinion was different.

"Deans can do great things," he said. "At Stanford, Fred Terman helped create Silicon Valley." He further advised. "If you take this job, resolve to cut back on your personal research. Nico persisted doing research two or three days a week and CS suffered."

As part of the process, I was interviewed by Robert Mehrabian, the president of CMU. After some preliminary chit chat, I impolitically said, "I've been looking at the amount of overhead the university is paid on CS's research projects, and I believe it would pay for space in downtown Tokyo for the whole college." At the time, Tokyo had a real estate bubble.

"You have no right to any of that money!" Mehrabian exploded.

I was abruptly escorted from his office.

This only contributed to my reputation for "telling it like it is," or in the less flattering words of Gray, "Morris often says what everyone in the room is thinking but would prefer that nobody actually say it."

Reddy became the permanent, effective, dean of SCS, and I continued at MAYA.

***

Late one night, Lucas was driving the rental car on Boston's Route 128 during one of our many visits to DEC. I was sitting shotgun and gazing at some stars, which got me thinking.

"Even though computer displays have millions of multicolored pixels, they don't use them to display search results efficiently," I said. "The Macintosh desktop metaphor still shows just about twenty items the way a teletype would. You can move them around with the mouse. Big deal! There must be a way to get more information out of all those pixels. For example, each document matching a search word could appear as a pixel on the screen. Then, to get a sense of what sort of answers came back for, say, 'bridge,' I could issue commands such as, 'Everyone talking about the card game called bridge turn green and cluster on the left. If you're about a structure over rivers, move to the right. If you're about a dental appliance turn blue.'"

We laughed about the idea, but a week later Lucas took this idea and created a magic screen interface for Hyperfax that he called "One Hundred Points of Light," a sly reference to George H. W. Bush's "One thousand points of light." This magic screen showed a hundred small documents, and you could move whole batches of them by typing search commands that would arrange or rearrange the documents into meaningful piles instead of folders. As with real desks, these piles were organized with the most recent items on top, but they got smaller as if in a 3D space. When we showed it to people from DEC, the charm of the idea was compelling. We published a paper about the idea and patented it.

Lucas's idea appeared in a prescient book, *Mirror Worlds: or the Day Software Puts the Universe in a Shoebox . . . How It Will*

218

Happen and What It Will Mean, by a computer scientist.[59] He described how the internet would swallow all the world's information. A review said, "These representations are called Mirror Worlds, and according to Gelernter they will soon be available to everyone. Mirror Worlds are high-tech voodoo dolls: by interacting with the images, you interact with reality. Indeed, Mirror Worlds will revolutionize the use of computers, transforming them from (mere) handy tools to crystal balls which will allow us to see the world more vividly and see *into* it more deeply."

In 1993 the book attracted the attention of the Unabomber who wrote to him, saying his predictions "are inevitable only because techno-nerds like you make them inevitable. If there were no computer scientists there would be no progress in computer science" (contradicting what I'd learned in my CMU class). Two months later he mailed Gelernter a bomb which severely injured him. Despite his madness, Kaczynski had a purpose for his crimes as he explained in a thirty-five-thousand-word manifesto he forced the *New York Times* to publish. He hated the industrial world and sought to halt its progress. He saw computers as just the latest instrument for dehumanizing civilization.

Now that I was running a company that Designed user interfaces, it was time for me to attend national HCI conferences where computer types mingled with psychologists and Designers, just as at MAYA. At my first one, I was bowled over by how much bigger and more entertaining it was compared to CS conferences, especially because 50 percent of the participants were women. The

---

[59] See Gelernter in Readings

219

crowd included computer types, psychologists, and Designers.

Lucas and I made occasional trips to SV—looking for business. We would visit people I knew, tell them about our business, and ask about problems we might help with. Geschke's company, Adobe, was flourishing. Steve Jobs had used their printing software to implement his desktop publishing system linking Macs with a small printer from Canon, Xerox's nemesis. I pitched an idea to Geschke—that MAYA could help Adobe design a universal exchange standard for editable documents allowing users to share documents without bothering to print.

"Sorry, Jim. We're already working on that," he said. "And we don't want you suing us down the road over any intellectual property ideas."

Their idea became the Portable Document Format, PDF.

Back in Pittsburgh, at MAYA, we created a working Hyperfax system for our little ten-person office. Every paper document that entered the office was immediately scanned into a computer and filed by date in a central storage place. Everybody in the office could call up documents on their magic desktop and arrange them in ways suitable to their needs. A surprising benefit was the storage of the original paper documents in single chronological file. They never got lost sitting on someone's desk.

I was in love with the Hyperfax idea. I traveled around DEC to give demos to groups that I hoped would make it a product. I went to conferences to give talks with the title "Fax Will Beat Email." When Borenstein was in one of the audiences, he expressed his doubt about the idea, as he expected computer technology to quickly make most business communication electronic. It didn't change my mind.

Despite our efforts, DEC never developed an interest in building a Hyperfax system. They weren't in the office support business and had been cozying up to Microsoft who was. Furthermore, Wang, another Boston company, was already selling a paper-friendly product with limited success, so DEC would have to sell something demonstrably better. Fuller was open to MAYA itself selling Hyperfax, but there was no way we could engineer a real product with our current staff, much less sell it. Lucas didn't want to, anyway, because he wanted to remain a consultant.

Although MAYA was picking up a few new clients—like IBM's Lotus organization—and generating nice profits, we weren't going to change the world. I was frustrated. It had been two years and owning my own company was turning out to be less fun than I had expected. Attempts to hire experienced software engineers failed. There was no way we could compete with SV, so MAYA was forced to make do with recent graduates of CMU's undergraduate program. Smart, but oblivious to the working world. On the inside, Lucas and I had grown irritable with each other over our stylistic differences. He clung to his Design ideas too tenaciously. I was too skeptical of everybody's ideas. *Oh God, was I turning into Elkind?*

***

In the summer of 1992, Allen Newell was dying of cancer. He was one of the most revered professors at CMU at only sixty-three. I suddenly wished that I had gotten more of his time.

"You know, I am really sorry this is happening."

"Not nearly as sorry as I am!"

Newell, forever the sunniest person I've ever known.

CMU's CS department had depended upon Newell for his superb leadership for so long that now its future seemed uncertain. Reddy asked me to come back, and I agreed. I wanted to help the institution that had done so much for me. I wanted to honor Newell and Perlis's memory. I suggested Reddy make me the head of the CS department. He agreed. I withdrew from MAYA and sold my share to Lucas for $1 million. We continued to have occasional contact.

At the memorial service, Simon began what I expected to be a eulogy to Newell by saying, "Allen's first priority was to do science, so I think that's what I'll do today." Then he launched into a lecture explaining some aspect of their theory of cognition.

After the service, I wrote and disseminated a page of principles I'd learned by following Newell's actions and sensing his beliefs over many years at both CMU and PARC. I wanted to perpetuate his influence, but I might have also mixed in some of Fadiman's affirmations. I wanted to assume what I could of his leadership skills.

I was happy to see the page pasted on some office doors:

Allen Newell's Precepts
Jim Morris

- **Do what you love, love what you do.**
  His incredible energy and enthusiasm sprung from this.

- **Help others to find a similar state, no matter how different their choices might be.**
  Since he was happy and secure in the rightness of what he was doing, Allen was open-minded about what other people did and often could help them make good choices.

- **Don't worry about how intrinsically smart you are or anyone else is.**
  I never saw him feel threatened by another person's brilliance or offended by their lack of it. He only judged performance.

- **Be intellectually tough—uniformly on everyone**.
  Allen was intellectually the toughest critic I ever had. At first, I didn't think this fit with his supportive attitude. But then I realized that it wasn't personal; he applied tough standards to himself and everyone else.

- **Be careful about what you commit to do, and then really do it.**
  He agreed to do only some of the things I asked him, but he would always help with something he believed was important. When he did, there was no doubt about his level of effort.

My dreams of being a top computer scientist faded, and I was on track to becoming a university "functionary" — exactly as Hoare had predicted back in 1978. So, I resolved to be more than a functionary by doing innovative things for the department and university. However, I did not aspire to be a new "giant." The founders Newell, Perlis, and Simon were irreplaceable. I saw myself rebuilding the CS department's confidence by recruiting and nurturing future giants and leaders.

One of my first tasks as the new department head of CS was to manage a ticklish situation with Scott. Scott had created a principles of programming languages (POP) research group by hiring Reynolds and three younger computer scientists. They were more fanatical about the λ-calculus than I had ever been. I saw them caught in an intellectual whirlpool while the rest of us were riding the tidal wave of computer applications. Scott had clashed with Habermann over resource issues and resigned from CMU to take a professorship at an Austrian university that promised to treat him better. But Austria had not worked out well, and now he wanted to come back to CMU.

Scott was an academic nomad, going from Berkeley, to Princeton, to Oxford, to CMU, to Austria. He was often frustrated by his institutions because he thought his mathematical talent extended to administration. Habermann was returning from his NSF stint that fall. As a courtesy, I called him.

"Nico, Dana wants to come back," I said. "We're not under any obligation, but should we invite him back?"

"OK," he said, "but don't promise him any more lavish support."

I had my OK.

Shortly after Habermann returned to Pittsburgh, my Sunday morning yoga class at a health club was interrupted by a phone call from Susan.

"Nico Habermann died this morning from a freak heart arrhythmia!"

The CS faculty was shaken, untethered by the two deaths that had eliminated our perennial leadership. An alumnus remarked, "Our giants are gone." Simon remained but was mostly engaged with the psychology department.

My first goal was to realize Newell's dream of an HCI program. My model was MAYA, and my ally was a student of Newell's, Bonnie John, who was an assistant professor of CS. The engineers in CS thought that HCI was a soft subject, so they were soon shocked to discover that its approach was more scientific than theirs.

John would attend oral exams of finishing PhD students. If they said, "I implemented this programming language and people really like it," she would ask, "How many people have used it? Did you compare their performance using other languages? Were these results statistically significant?" She was just like my old tormentor Kahan.

The engineers would start to mutter. "Who invited her? What does she know?"

An HCI program would legitimize John's work by providing a context along with sympathetic faculty. She then would have a chance for tenure as a psychologist in a CS department. She was already amassing an excellent publication record, mostly at the national HCI conference.

John and I began hosting a series of meetings with potentially interested faculty to discuss research agendas and the kind of work PhD students might do in HCI. We arranged for a highly regarded social psychologist, Bob Kraut, to come for a job interview. Kraut was at Bellcore (a rebranded Bell Labs) where Borenstein was working for him, so he had a sense of CMU geek culture. But his presentation was mostly social psychology explaining why many cherished computer innovations failed. The CS faculty weren't used to such skepticism.

"He may be an excellent social scientist, but we can't evaluate him because he's not a computer scientist," Jeannette Wing, a young language theoretician, shared with me. I began to see that CS was crystalizing around a narrow set of topics new PhDs like Jeannette had learned, and that the Newell-Simon-Perlis era of "anything goes" was ending.

I got another inkling of the mismatch between CS and psychology when Al Corbett, who was seeking to transfer to CS from the psych department, gave an interview talk. He mentioned a study which showed that people learning LISP had a hard time balancing parentheses. The programmers in the audience regarded this as drivel, obvious but irrelevant.

As it became clear the CS department was inhospitable to psychologists, John and I gave up trying to launch a simple research program and—with Reddy's support—launched a new department of the CS college that we called the HCI Institute (HCII). It took nearly a year. John transferred from CS, and we hired Kraut. Brad Myers, who had published more papers at the HCI conference than anyone else, was having a tenure struggle, so we asked him on. He transferred from CS. Two postdocs[60] from psychology, Corbett and Ken Koedinger, joined us to work on cognitive theories of learning. They had produced a successful computer program to teach algebra.

While the MAYA model depended on Designers, Designers don't typically fit well in a research university— Designers lack deep engineering knowledge and don't do scientific experiments.

So, I was delighted when John said, "Now we need some Designers." It was then that I learned that she had studied in Stanford's mechanical engineering department, which housed industrial Designers, along with our mutual friend Fadiman. We invited the head of CMU's Design department to be an affiliate and lend us teachers. We also recruited Chris Neuwirth and a few other social scientists from the humanities college to affiliate.

I first encountered Randy Pausch as a voluble CMU graduate student, arguing with people in the hallways about technology. I had forgotten about him as he completed a PhD in operating systems under Spector and got a job at the University of Virginia until I saw him at an HCI conference, again in a hallway regaling a group about his recent invention. Later that day, he wowed the crowd with a

[60] "Postdoc" stands for post-doctoral fellow, a title given to people with doctorates hired temporarily by a university department.

presentation about his course, Virtual Reality on Five Dollars a Day, explaining how he cobbled together enough equipment to support twenty students. He had the kind of bubbling enthusiasm Perlis had, which most recent PhDs lacked. I decided the HCII had to have him. I had to struggle to get him a tenured position, because he was so charismatic that some professors were suspicious.

Upon arrival, Pausch launched a course called Building Virtual Worlds in which he encouraged undergraduates of all stripes to apply for the course but required a personal interview. Once in the course, small teams created short virtual reality experiences. Demonstrations of their work became a standing-room-only annual event, attended regularly by the university's president—far better attended than football games.

After a few years in the HCII, Pausch created a whole new organization, the Entertainment Technology Center, to pursue his goals. He joined with a CMU professor of drama, and they designed an MS program in consultation with Disney Imagineering, Pixar, Electronic Arts, and other computer gaming and entertainment companies. They started students off with improv lessons to teach them to collaborate creatively. Aside from placing students at these companies, the center has engendered many startups that create games and virtual reality experiences. Some examples: training for firefighters, augmented reality piano learning, a kiosk to alleviate children's anxieties when visiting the doctor, animatronic robots, and a service that allows you to see possible interior designs within a home.

The group of computer scientists, psychologists, and Designers that John and I collected during the first few years made the HCII into a powerful organization, dominating the HCI conferences with the number of accepted papers and always winning best paper awards. HCII continued to produce a stream of MS graduates who became leaders in industry and PhD graduates who launched HCI activities at Berkeley, Stanford, MIT, and other universities, and I came to view HCI—not CS!—as the fundamental science of computing, fulfilling the sentiment of the 1967 Newell-Perlis-Simon letter to *Science*. I might rename HCI to Intelligence-Physics Interaction because the computer is a physical object supporting the communication of human intelligence with all physical objects using language.

Newell's approach to HCI was a bit narrower, rooted in the field of human factors that emerged in World War II when an apocryphal bomber cockpit had two similar adjacent buttons. One dropped the bombs. The other ejected the pilot. After multiple disasters, psychologists were then brought in to advise about the design of cockpits to eliminate the reliance upon memory. Until then, engineers assumed training would prevent human mistakes.

Programming languages were part of this broader HCI because they helped humans communicate their desires as completely and clearly as possible to a computer. For example, programmers can add redundancy to their programs by including comments to help any readers. Type declarations are a more effective way to add redundancy because they describe the interpretation of variables and can be checked by a computer.

Many of us thought we should make the languages like mathematics, but not all humans are mathematicians. Proving things about a program's behavior is difficult. You must formulate a description of what the program is supposed to accomplish and then prove it. Getting a computer to prove it is not always possible—as shown by Gödel and Turing.

I was surprised to read the following verdict on all the mathematical attempts to improve reliability written by Tony Hoare:

> Ten years ago [in 1985], researchers into formal methods (and I was the most mistaken among them) predicted that the programming world would embrace with gratitude every assistance promised by formalization to solve the problems of reliability that arise when programs get large and more safety-critical. Programs have now got very large and very critical—well beyond the scale which can be comfortably tackled by formal methods. There have been many problems and failures, but these have nearly always been attributable to inadequate analysis of requirements or inadequate management control. It has turned out that the world just does not suffer significantly from the kind of problem that our research was originally intended to solve.

Newell once made the sensible suggestion that programming languages should be designed by HCI experts who understood the capabilities of normal humans. But strangely, his language, IPL, was one of the least human-friendly languages ever invented. It looked worse than machine language and didn't even allow mnemonic names, insisting that each name be a letter followed by numbers. When Ernst chided Newell about this shortcoming, he said "K198 is plenty mnemonic to me. It holds the subgoals that the program is working on." Newell could program without the creature comforts most programmers needed and was creating IPL just for himself and Simon.

The emphasis on programming languages ignores the fact that human-computer interaction is a two-way affair. When we test and debug a program, it is often telling us that we asked it to do the wrong thing. Often the problem is in our understanding of the universe, not in our failure to say what we want. Suppose we launch a programmed robotic rocket to the moon with instructions to bring back some valuable minerals, but the robot tells us that the moon is made of green cheese. Would we call that a program bug?

Programs become reliable only through extensive usage. Suppose you are offered a product that was used only by a little old lady and only on Sundays. You would buy it if it were hardware but refuse it if it were software. Why? If it's hardware, the product used by a little old lady once a week has a lot of life left in it. But if it's software, it probably hasn't been used enough. In fact, *maintenance* is known to be the most expensive aspect of software. It involves tracking and responding to users' complaints. Software companies offer to maintain a product at 25 percent of the purchase price per year, meaning it's half the cost if you use it for four years.

The best executive is the one who has sense enough to pick good men to do what he wants done, and self-restraint to keep from meddling while they do it.– Theodore Roosevelt

11. Sustaining the CS Department

With the HCII cruising after its launch, I engaged with the job of being the CS department head, which was more like being a parent than other management jobs I'd had. I did a little teaching in undergraduate programming classes—to set an example. It was 1992, and many of the algorithms and math techniques had been discovered long after I'd left school. I enjoyed learning each of them to prepare my classes.

In my first class, a kid looked at the example I was presenting, pointed out that it was flawed, and then explained to me (and the class!) the right way to do it. *What if I'm not qualified to teach this era's high school graduates?* It scared me to death. However, that kid was Singaporean Andrew Ng who blew away everybody and became CMU's valedictorian four years later. As part of rebuilding the department, I wanted to develop leaders by delegating parts of my job. And it also gave me more time to innovate. First, I got Randy Bryant, one of the most respected and level-headed professors, into my overlarge office. He sat on a couch, and I pulled up a chair across from him. Reddy-style, I avoided being behind a desk.

"I have a big job for you if you're willing to do it."

Bryant gulped and waited.

"I'd like you to take over the promotions and reappointments process for the CS department."

"Isn't that *your* job?"

"Well, it has been under Nico and his predecessors, but I want to change that. I believe the decisions should be made by consensus. I know you well enough to trust your judgment as much as mine. It's also a lot of work." He hadn't thought of himself in such a role but agreed to try it.

My next meeting was going to be more difficult. It was with one of the math guys, who had been hoping to get the department head's position that I now occupied.

"You've been running the PhD program very well for the past four years," I said. "But I think you need a break. I'm going to appoint Jeannette Wing to take over."

"Why?" he asked. "Have there been complaints about me?"

"No more than the usual grumbling after a Black Friday meeting where some students get warnings from you. But I know you're dealing with Nico's death as well as your brother-in-law's. You might not recognize the toll that takes on someone."

"I'm not sure Jeannette has high enough standards."

"Well, how about if you coach her for the first year? You'll have more time for research."

"OK."

The meeting with Jeannette was much easier. She, too, was surprised but more than eager to take on the job of mentoring students through the PhD program.

This was also the first time in my career that I had to deal with a hemorrhaging budget. Prodded by Reddy, I ended the practice of paying everyone's summer salaries, which enraged the mathematical branch of the faculty who felt I was reneging on Habermann's promise. Every June thereafter, Scott would send me a nasty email when his paycheck stopped coming. Others welcomed this change in a new way.

"My money is making more money than I am," Reynolds said. "I'd like to take half the pay and be relieved from teaching courses." It was a win for him, the CS department, and many future students, because, whenever he taught a course, he would overwhelm them with every bit of his developing arcane theories.

Once I had the CS budget under control, I started leading monthly faculty meetings. This was a normal practice everywhere else, but one which had been ignored since the days of Perlis. I continued my practice of giving the occasional *ad hoc* awards: a baseball player trophy for a "rookie of the year" new professor, a plaque showing a freshman advisor's extraordinary five-out-of-five rating. Along with the monthly faculty meetings, Susan and I would host an occasional Sunday brunch for a rotating selection of professors. Many spouses of the professors met each other for the first time. The professors themselves talked about work, of course, but with colleagues they didn't see often.

Once, when we invited Simon and his wife, they forgot, and I called to remind them. When Simon showed up, he said, "Dorothea was still at church, but I was at home working on the computer. I guess that is my God."

***

In 1993 a young graduate student walked into my office.

"Professor Morris, you need a web page!"

"What's that?"

234

"It's a page of fancy text that lives on the World Wide Web, what we now call the internet," he said, sitting down at my computer. "To see them you need a browser called Mosaic."

He downloaded Mosaic from his AFS directory, fired it up, and showed me his own web page—complete with his picture and blue *hyperlinks* that he used to display other web pages that showed papers he'd written and pictures from his life.

"That's cool," I said. "How do I make my own?"

He then downloaded the text from his web page and showed me the strangely structured text on it.

"This is HTML (HyperText Markup Language). It's the text that describes the page with colors and pictures that you see on my page. Let's edit it into one for you."

He created a subdirectory called "www" in my personal AFS directory. He copied his file into a new file "jimmorris.html" stored in www and used a text editor to edit it. We found a picture of me and copied it to www. Then he inserted a hyperlink to the picture into my jimmorris file. Finally, he went back to the Mosaic browser, typed some gibberish into a slot at the top, and my picture with some text popped up.

"Thank you!" I said. "I have to get back to work now."

It was less than a year later that a postdoc in SCS's Language Technology Institute, Michael "Fuzzy" Mauldin, invented the first web-crawling search engine, Lycos, named after a spider, that he envisioned using seven of its free legs to explore the hyperlinks in the page on which its eighth leg was anchored. Lycos cruised the internet looking for files in directories named www. It read the HTML in them, ferreting out all the actual English words, and produced an index that linked every word to a list of all the pages it was found on. A curious person could type some words into the Lycos app and see all the pages that contain any of the words.

In 1995 a search engine better than Lycos, AltaVista, was invented in Taylor's lab in Palo Alto. It used bigger computers and cleverer algorithms. It was better, but it found so many pages that finding a useful one required a lot of scanning by the human eye.

A year after that, Google began its world-changing service.

Google was founded by Larry Page and Sergey Brin, two computer scientists who got their first idea while graduate students at Stanford. Their idea, PageRank, based on how scientific papers are ranked, was to list web pages by decreasing popularity, measured by the hyperlinks referring to them. The function ranking a page is recursive: it's proportional to the sum of the ranks of the pages that refer to it. Determining ranks of all the pages (called their eigenvalues) requires a massive computation involving every HTML page found on the internet. The PageRank concept is a proxy for your trustworthiness because it considers the trustworthiness of people who trust you. Google also employed a sophisticated system architecture, connecting fleets of PCs on the internet and a lot of applied mathematics learned from Knuth. They announced a "mission to organize the world's information and make it universally accessible and useful."

Google demonstrated, for the first time, how CS could generate real profits, not from the back rooms of Wall Street, but as the essence of its free service with paid advertising. Google began attracting many good engineers from other companies along with every computer-savvy Stanford graduate. As Google thrived using the latest CS ideas—even challenging Microsoft's hegemony in office software—SV cheered.

**

I spotted an announcement that a Sufi dancer named Dunya was giving lessons in Pittsburgh. Still intrigued by the Sufis, and seeking a break from my mostly cerebral life, I decided to take a lesson.[61]

In a room above a tattoo parlor on Pittsburgh's South Side, Dunya, who was proclaimed to be the "best belly dancer in the world" by the *Village Voice*, formed our motley group into a large circle encouraging us to move any which way we chose. She taught us to "whirl," the traditional practice of Sufi dervishes. I became such a fan that I took Carson to her next session with me. My enthusiastic whirling ended with my falling when I stopped too suddenly.

The following summer I attended a Sufi camp Dunya knew south of Albuquerque, New Mexico. I arrived around noon to find the camp at the end of a dirt road. About fifty people (two-thirds women) were sprawled around on the floor when Adnan, a small dark Iraqi man, walked in and without a word sat down on a little stage in a cross-legged position. He raised his arms and began a swaying motion and all fifty of us began to mimic him. It kept up for an unconscionable length of time

---

[61] Photo courtesy of Daniel Falgerho

until he said, "Get out the drums." We drummed out a five-beat pattern on the drums between our legs for what seemed like hours. People started falling into trances and lying down. I tried doing some whirling and eventually lied down too.

One night several students—mostly New Yorkers—gave testimonials about what maladies Adnan had cured them of: drug addictions, smoking, anxiety, etc. I challenged him to make my chronic back pain go away, and he said, "It will go away after you're home." A student who was a psychiatrist told me he gave up Prozac, because it interfered with his dreaming, so I gave it up too. I called Susan a few times from the only phone at the camp, and when I told her about the Arabic lessons we had, she was alarmed. "They're trying to turn you into a terrorist."

While I was harvesting arugula on a bright morning, an attractive woman co-worker suggested to us that I was a "3" in the Enneagram spectrum, an old theory introduced to the West by the Armenian George Gurdjieff. A "3" was a success-oriented, pragmatic type. After some research, I decided I was—or aspired to be—a "9": an easygoing, self-effacing type.

Back in Pittsburgh, I sought out Sufi groups. The one I found spoke only in Arabic. My back pain had abated, but some ill-advised roller-coaster riding gave me a pinched nerve in my neck. When Scott saw me wearing a neck brace for it, he recommended I try another exotic practice: the Alexander Technique.

I sat in a chair while the Alexander teacher lightly touched my shoulders, then told me to stand up. "Try it again, but don't tense your shoulders." This continued for forty minutes with me trying to execute several other maneuvers using minimal muscular effort. Like Tai Chi which I later gravitated to, the Alexander Technique felt like the opposite of yoga, which involves stretching and effort. When I told her of my yoga and Sufi adventures she said, "You're a seeker." I liked the idea, but it would be several years before I knew what I was seeking.

***

In 1996 Taylor retired, and most of his followers dispersed around SV. While Taylor was a joy to work for, he was hell on the organizations that employed him. His competitive instincts made him attack all the units around him and belabor his superiors for more resources. Many people in Xerox and DEC were relieved when he left. In retirement, he became a curmudgeon, rarely leaving his house in the hills above SV. He complained about the many people claiming to be fathers of the internet when, in fact, he had initiated the DARPA research program that led to it. He began to put on weight, and I was finally able to beat him at tennis a few times!

That same year, I initiated a campaign for Raj Reddy to receive a Turing Award for his work in speech recognition. It succeeded, and he received the Turing in 1996, and his energetic work on other aspects of AI and third world education were also recognized.

A year later, our department was dismayed to learn that *US News* dropped the ranking of our department from its perennial tie for first with MIT, Stanford, and Berkeley, to fourth—behind all three.

We also had a periodic two-day external review by computer scientists from companies and other universities. I got a sense that the review was going to be difficult at the preliminary dinner when the head of Berkeley's CS department dismissed each of my claims of our unique practices by repeatedly replying, "Berkeley does that too." All except for one: our practice of supporting PhD students without regard to their advisor or their funding. Instead, he remarked, "You and Albania are the only remaining communist organizations."

In the next morning's session with department heads, the Microsoft chief technology officer repeated my canard that university research was irrelevant, because if it was relevant to Microsoft, they could do it better themselves. A Turing-awarded professor from Princeton, who was a friend of our mathematical faculty, pointed out our weakness in that area. I got into a pissing match with our new president, Jared Cohon, over reimbursement for our undergraduate teaching. My friend Schmidt, who was on the committee, just shook his head at my bad political judgment.

One bright spot from 1997 was IBM's special computer, Deep Blue beating the world chess champion Garry Kasparov. It cost IBM about $100 million and had 30,000,000K bytes of memory, and it was built by a team of CMU veterans of the Deep Thought computer project.

Despite Habermann's efforts in the 1980s, our mathematics group still needed strengthening. CS had been trying to hire Manuel Blum for years—even before he had won a Turing Award in 1995 for contributions to the foundations of computational complexity theory and its application to cryptography and program checking. The effort had failed when we couldn't convince the math department to give Lenore a position, despite a PhD from MIT and some unique discoveries. But now their only child, Avrim, was a junior

240

professor in our CS department. He and another professor came to me and suggested we try to hire the older Blums again.

Ignoring the potential charges of reverse nepotism, I offered the Blums jobs. Knowing that Lenore was a successful academic innovator, I had an angle.

"Lenore, your mission in educating women in math and CS would be greatly enhanced if you came here and spearheaded our efforts to recruit women computer scientists," I said when I met with the two.

She liked the idea, and after I offered them handsome salaries, the Blums agreed to come. When they arrived, Lenore jumped into the task of nurturing women in CS. Manuel, with a history of finding original problems, was asking "How can a computer decide if it's talking to a human or another computer?" He and his student, Luis von Ahn, solved it with CAPTCHAs (Completely Automated Public Turing Test to Tell Computers and Humans Apart). Their test asked the suspected correspondent to decipher a visually distorted letter sequence. The idea also had a long-term goal: AI would be advanced by all the hackers discovering ways to beat CAPTCHAs. Blum and von Ahn sold the idea to Google for a million dollars. von Ahn would go on to found Duolingo.

I came to appreciate Manuel Blum's unique way of teaching mathematical research. He would describe a vague problem to his students and pretend that he was confused. Because they loved him, they would struggle mightily to solve the problem, sometimes succeeding but always learning. He was so convincing that strangers sometimes thought he was dense.

Lenore continued her institution building by creating an incubator to nurture CMU students with entrepreneurial ambitions. It became a Pittsburgh success story.

Part of the genius of hiring the Blums was the fact that a few of the most irascible mathematics professors had been Manuel's PhD students. Now they started to behave. More significantly, he and Lenore led the mathematicians to obtain a large NSF grant for practical applications of algorithms, which supported them for several years.

After five years as department head, I found that we were a revitalized, confident organization. In 1998 CMU CS regained its number one status in the *US News* rankings. We also had a positive report from a visiting committee that highlighted the astounding and unique breadth of computer activities at CMU, with distinct departments pursuing CS, robotics, HCI, language technology, software engineering, and machine learning. Also of note was our climb toward 50 percent women in our undergraduate CS program. Reddy had made a crucial decision to change the admissions criteria downplaying programming experience, which many bright women lacked. The work of Lenore Blum and some predecessors had finally born fruit.

VI: AI Summer 1998-2015

The science fiction novel *Ilium* set thousands of years after the twentieth century describes Moravecs as self-evolving biomechanical organisms that dwell on the Jovian moons.

Stephen Spielberg's *A.I.* film tells the story of a humanoid boy robot that can love and express emotion like a human child.

IBM's Watson program defeated two former *Jeopardy!* champions.

WALL-E is a movie about a robot left on an evacuated Earth to clean up. He visits the spaceship where the humans have degenerated into helpless corpulence.

DeepMind's AlphaGo beats the world champion of Go, a much harder game than chess. It was the first time a prediction about AI came true before anyone expected it.

Her is a movie about a man developing a relationship with an AI virtual assistant.

Drinking is a form of suicide where you're allowed to return to life and begin all over the next day. I guess I've lived about ten or fifteen thousand lives now. – Charles Bukowski

12. New Millennium, Second Life

When the World Wide Web and Google fueled the internet investment boom, Larry Lessig, an activist lawyer, wrote a book explaining how the internet is disrupting the world's culture.[62]

The internet respects no geographic or national boundaries. The distance-independent communication that the internet makes available to all citizens of the world has facilitated the growth of many new social and political movements that once consisted of small, isolated groups. We can hope that some of these movements solve global problems, but the internet also creates destructive movements. Some believe the internet will contribute to the demise of the nation state.[63]

The internet makes it easier to track our activities. Should governments be allowed to spy on us if they used the information only to prevent serious crimes? Neither Lessig nor anyone else imagined the post-9/11 world where the US

---

[62] See Lessig in Readings

[63] See Bobbitt in Readings

government's tracking of communication patterns violated the Constitution.

Since the internet's day-to-day operation is controlled by computers, implementing policy is exquisitely reliable. Consider games. Every command you give to a game is interpreted by a program the game creators wrote. Their whims can make strange things possible and normal things impossible in the virtual world of their game. But now, with so many of our real-world actions carried out through the internet or mediated by programs, there is potential for controlling our real actions. Uber's self-driving cars are programmed to obey traffic laws. TurboTax will not cheat for us. A version of eBay able to track the movement of goods as well as money would greatly reduce fraud.

People accept these kinds of control. I once wrote a program for a consulting company to compute real estate assessments. I asked the client, "This seems like a lot of hassle just to perform a straightforward computation on the assessors' reports."

He said, "That's true, but the officials are happy to pay for it, because it reduces complaints and challenges to the assessments."

"But we could write the program to inflate assessments, or the program could just make a mistake. Don't homeowners think about that?"

"Probably. But what they really care about is whether they're being assessed differently from their neighbor who might have friends in the tax office. They know the computer treats everyone the same."

Computers are free of the seven deadly sins, and even if someone programmed a computer to sin, we could inspect the code to detect it.

Lessig's goal was to debunk the notion that the internet could not be regulated, as claimed by a hubristic statement[64] by an internet fanatic that began with:

> Governments of the Industrial World, you weary giants of flesh and steel, I come from Cyberspace, the new home of Mind. On behalf of the future, I ask you of the past to leave us alone. You are not welcome among us. You have no sovereignty where we gather.
>
> We have no elected government, nor are we likely to have one, so I address you with no greater authority than that with which liberty itself always speaks. I declare the global social space we are building to be naturally independent of the tyrannies you seek to impose on us. You have no moral right to rule us, nor do you possess any methods of enforcement we have true reason to fear.

Lessig believed that we can use the new powers of the internet—open borders, surveillance, and control—to better our civilization, because we can control the internet as we controlled earlier artificial inventions such as governments, armies, police, and corporations. Those organizations don't have human motivations or feelings, yet we've managed to keep them from ruining our lives with the use of law, transparency, and politics to control them.

As 2000 dawned, Bill Joy wrote a more pessimistic article in *Wired*. "Why the Future Doesn't Need Us" claiming that biotechnology, nanotechnology, and AI were threats to humankind. When I visited him in his Aspen, CO house, he

---

[64] See A Declaration of the Independence of Cyberspace in Documents

246

said there was "a bug in the Enlightenment." He explained that freedom of information could be a menace if it enabled a lone crazy person to endanger millions.

Two years later, sci-fi author, Bruce Sterling, gave a talk to an invitation-only gathering of computer scientists pondering CS's future research opportunities at a resort in Virginia. He wanted us to clean up the mess we had already created.

> The internet has become a slum, populated by spies and prostitutes. ... The moguls in computing aren't knights in shining armor, these are some of the meanest robber barons anybody has ever seen. These guys are like ninja assassins armed with rusty stilettos. They are stealing each other's market oxygen. They are stabbing each other's babies. They went straight from internet anarchy to feudalist monopoly domination. They went straight from the barbarism of the garage start-up to the decadence of bribing the government, suborning accountants, and paying themselves with stock options that aren't on the company books. And oh my goodness did the chickens come home and start roosting.

I came upon another science fiction writer, Neal Stephenson, who wrote books about the near future that inspired tech innovators, so I invited him to CMU to give a lecture, thinking that science fiction is a leading edge for today's technologies, because it describes human responses to technology. Another visitor to CMU that year was Gordon Moore, a co-founder of Intel, who was receiving an honorary degree. I got to take him to breakfast and brought Randy Pausch along.

Wearing coats and ties for a change, we found Moore sitting quietly in the hotel's large dining room. He was a stocky seventy-year-old engineer who appeared as vital as a thirty-year-old.

After we got through the buffet line and sat down, I asked, "Are you feeling guilty for creating a law destined to cause massive unemployment?"

"It was just an observation and I never said it was a law," Moore said. "At the time I was just conscious of how our manufacturing guys were getting better and better at etching chips using light. Other people started calling it a law. But the improvements stopped. Most exponential growth patterns turn out to be the beginning of S-curves."

He sketched a picture on a napkin to show the two curves:

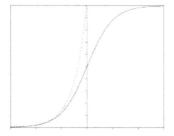

"In the real world, exponentially growing phenomena stop because something they consume runs out. A fission explosion runs out of uranium, thank God."

"So how do you explain that transistor count on a chip has been growing exponentially for thirty years?" I said thinking of this chart:

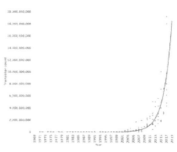

"Once we noticed slowdown, my observation became a goal," he said. "We at Intel certainly tried to keep it going, and our competitors did too. Every company brought in cleverer engineers and more scientists who came up with new tricks. First, we started using higher frequency X-rays instead of light which goosed us off the S-curve onto another exponential as manufacturing digested that improvement. Then, as that petered out, someone figured out how to create multilayer chips so that circuits became three-dimensional. Finally, when we couldn't run chips any faster, we put multiple processors on a single chip, and the software guys figured out how to run some things in parallel. So, what the world saw as a smooth exponential was actually many different overlapping S-curves."

He drew another picture. The table was getting covered with napkins and we'd stopped eating.

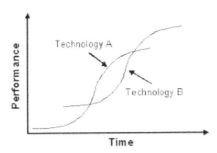

I said, "Your software guys must be smarter than the ones I know because coordinating multiple processes is difficult. Testing and debugging is ineffective because the number of ways two parallel programs can interleave their instructions is huge. Our CMU colleague, Edmund Clarke, has developed algorithms to check systems for such errors and discovered flaws that had gone unnoticed for years. People would attribute any occasional failures to cosmic rays. Jim Gray calls such flaws 'Heisenbugs.'" (Clarke's efforts were aided by Moore's Law, and he was later able to check large asynchronous systems like operating systems. He received a Turing Award for his work in 2007.)

Pausch spoke up to raise another issue, "But there must be more to the accelerating growth, ignoring the S-curve details. Whenever I see an exponential, I think there must be some positive feedback loop in which growth somehow begets more growth. Is Moore's Law like Metcalfe's Law? Do improved chips make it easier to improve the next generation of chips?"

"Well, if you look more broadly, the improving performance was generating a lot of money for Intel and everybody else. So, we could hire even smarter engineers trained by universities where we funded research. The whole industry was exploding with intelligence growth. When you look at it that way, most human enterprises have an exponential learning curve. The more you know, the more you learn. All the different things discovered amplify each other somehow."

"Well, your law hasn't put Morris and me out of work yet," Pausch said, giving us a chance to eat. "But it has forced us to learn new things. Tweaking programs to make them a little faster is a waste of time. We're much more dependent on sophisticated mathematics because of the huge problems we're trying to solve with multiple faster computers. You might not notice the difference between 25 iterations and 625 on a fast computer, but you will between a thousand and a million. The work of algorithm analysts like Knuth and Karp has become relevant to programmers."

***

In 2000 Reddy decided to step down from the dean's job, and the university began to search for a successor. As karmic revenge for my using Carnegie Tech as my "safety school," I was the "safety dean" candidate while we pursued attractive candidates from other universities. Humbly, I told each one that I would welcome their coming to CMU. But this time I wanted the job. Each of the outsiders turned us down, so I finally became the dean of SCS.

Under Reddy several new departments had been created, turning SCS into a uniquely diversified college. Unlike Reddy, I saw the need to make its functioning more systematic.

I invented a metaphor to describe what sort of organization SCS was. I said it was like a city with different neighborhoods. The laws and taxes were uniform across the city, but the culture and values of each neighborhood were unique. I said that people having appointments in multiple departments was unnecessary; everyone in SCS had certain cross-departmental rights. A student in any department could have a research mentor in any other SCS department.

SCS had been exceeding its budget in previous years concealing it by some tricky accounting moves. The problems were uncovered when the university adopted new accounting software to guard against the expected Y2K bug (in which programs confuse 2000 and 1900). I created a revenue-based budgeting system with a formula that awarded funds to each department based on the revenue imputed to the research and teaching activities of its faculty. That reduced the amount of special pleading I needed to hear. A department was allowed to roll over an unspent budget.

Most department heads liked the system because it gave them ways to plan and a feeling of control.

I found this job of dean to be more like being a grandparent than a parent—much easier and more fun. I upgraded my dress, wearing a sports jacket and tie more often. I started having many dinners and lunches, both business and ceremonial. Dinners involved a lot of wine. I gained weight. Deans are supposed to be jolly, right?

Achieving any consensus about goals among professors is hopeless, unless you consider one thing: all the professors want the prestige of their university to be higher. Because Pittsburgh was not a media center compared to Boston or San Francisco, CMU was often overlooked. Reddy had tried to hire a New York public relations (PR) firm, but the university had stopped him. CMU seemed to revile explicit PR or marketing. But I got an appointment with Regis McKenna, a guru of PR in the Valley. He'd done it for Apple, *and* he was a Pittsburgh native.

"Presence is everything," he told me. "If you want to be noticed you have to be here." Here, meaning SV, which in the year 2000 was at the peak of the tech bubble, and full of itself. While New York thought it was the center of the universe, SV thought it *was* the universe. Since I couldn't move the university, I had the idea of having a CMU club in downtown Palo Alto, in the same way Ivy League colleges have them in New York City.

I made an appointment with Vinod Khosla, co-founder of SUN, a graduate of CMU, and a partner at the legendary VC firm Kleiner Perkins. The lithe Indian, wearing a black turtleneck, welcomed me to his large sunny office, and I got straight to the point.

"Vinod, how would you like to buy us a hotel in downtown Palo Alto?"

"You're thinking too small," he said. "Fort Ord on Monterey Bay is closing, and the government might give you some of the twenty-thousand acres to open a branch campus. For about a billion dollars you could build an impressive campus. At its current rate SV will probably expand to encompass Monterey Bay someday."

"Good idea, Vinod," I said thinking that he had about $2 billion at the time, compared to CMU's half-billion-dollar endowment. "Let's do it."

While in SV, I went to a meeting of the local CMU alumni group that included two young VCs, Scott Russell, and Eric Daimler. Russell was running Softbank Technology Ventures, an early investor in Yahoo and other internet start-ups.

As soon as I got back to Pittsburgh, I found my friend Duane Adams, who was CMU's vice-provost for research, and told him that CMU needed to have a branch campus in SV. He gulped but didn't object. Adams was the embodiment of Harry Truman's epigram "It is amazing what you can accomplish if you do not care who gets the credit." Working at DARPA, he had fostered the work of Bill Joy and Andy Bechtolsheim. After retiring from the air force, he spent another twenty years at CMU, facilitating many millions of dollars in research projects. He was extremely effective but left no fingerprints.

A few days later Reddy told me that NASA Ames, another former military site that was right in the middle of SV, had approached him about collaboration in software. NASA had been embarrassed by recent missions ruined by software bugs. Furthermore, President Cohon liked the branch campus idea. We were on to something big; the stars were aligning!

Adams and I started making monthly trips to SV. The internet investment bubble burst by November of 2000, but we were undaunted. Furthermore, NASA dangled the possibility of a large research contract in software engineering to help us pay for the start-up of a campus.

***

We attended a large fundraiser in a tent on the Schmidt's estate where Gore appeared along with Elton John, Robin Williams, Sharon Stone, and other celebrities. I gave Gore a pocket protector emblazoned with "Geeks for Gore" that I had been selling on the internet. He was a geek favorite because, as vice president, he had opened the internet for commercial use.

A few weeks after George Bush's inauguration, Simon died at eighty-five. His memorial service was full of the professors he had attracted to CMU and the professors they had attracted to CMU. Simon and his colleagues had transformed the university from a decent technical school to a worldwide power in computer-enabled everything, notably social science.

A month later, I called up a heart surgeon I knew.

"Bart, I'd like to arrange a bypass operation," I said. "Some friends have had them, and it's time for me. Most of my male ancestors died of heart problems, but I've outlived most."

"That's not the way it works, Jim" he said. "You need to go to cardiologists first, and they have to discover a problem."

It took until August to find a little problem, but in early September Jane was getting married to a classmate from

Brown, Mike Drake. So, I delayed a planned angioplasty until after her wedding.

After college, Jane had gone to work for Borenstein's start-up in San Diego where Mike was in graduate school, studying bioengineering. The start-up was a too-early attempt at PayPal and floundered as did the romance, so she moved to Boston and ended up pursuing a PhD at MIT's Media Lab. Then Mike got a job at MIT, and they reconnected. Rachel was the maid of honor at Jane's wedding. She had graduated from Barnard and gotten a job in Seattle at Microsoft. The guests included our out-of-town CS friends, the Geschkes, the Richardses, and the Schmidts with their daughter Sophie. Eric had just become the CEO of Google. The crowd was impressed with my energetic jitterbugging with my daughter and Sophie. Pat Richards was amused by Schroeder's stories of the "lad" I'd been in high school.

The next week's angioplasty escalated into a bypass operation, and as they wheeled me into the operating room, I looked around. *This strange place may be the last thing I'll ever see. Well, my life has been pretty good, so I can't complain.*

Several hours later I woke up in a recovery room to the sound of the staff trying, but failing, to resuscitate someone else. A few days later, on a TV in my hospital room, I watched planes strike the twin towers in New York City. Channel surfing led me to the hospital's in-house channel called the Relaxation Channel. Its message was "Slow down and smell the flowers!" delivered over restful music and peaceful images. I watched it a lot.

Sitting at home recuperating in our family room I thought, *Well I sort of died when they stopped my heart, so this is my second life. I can make it whatever I want it to be.* It took me a few months to get back to feeling normal. My absence did not seem to impede the college. Let's say that was because I'd organized things so well in the previous year. The SV negotiations had been proceeding smoothly under the highly skilled Adams. Also, well-planned.

While I was convalescing, a friend found herself at loose ends after a long career as a television executive, so I hired her as a consultant to help me promote wider awareness of our robotics program. She hit upon the idea of a Robot Hall of Fame—to highlight the program's accomplishments as a tourist attraction in Pittsburgh's Carnegie Science Center. We started with a ceremony at the Center recognizing NASA's Mars rover, an autonomous device that had been sending back scientific information since 1997, and Unimate, the first successful factory robot. Brilliantly, she added awards for fictional robots like R2-D2 from *Star Wars* and HAL from *2001: A Space Odyssey*. That got the attention of the 99 percent of humans bored by engineering. The diminutive actor who played R2-D2 showed up to accept on behalf of his character. When C-3PO won the next year, his portrayer came and then returned a few times to be master of ceremonies.

Somehow I found the time to dabble in journalism, writing a technology column for the *Pittsburgh Post-Gazette*. In my first column[65], I invented the term *infobesity*, based on Simon's economic truism that "a surplus of information creates a poverty of attention." I also described some *infodiets* to cure it. The column was a success and I continued monthly.

---

[65] See Infobesity in Documents

I raised a million dollars from a prestigious group of computer people including Bechtolsheim, Bell, Geschke, Moore, Russell, Gray, Reddy, Apple co-founder Wozniak, and Schmidt. Schmidt also hosted a fund-raising dinner at his Atherton estate. Adams got us a $5 million research contract from NASA that promised to help them create more reliable software. Then he negotiated a twenty-five-year lease on one of their buildings located in a section that looked like a college campus.

Brian Reid had bounced around SV working for DEC and Bell Labs after his time at Stanford. He became an internet expert and tried to equip Palo Alto with fiber optics supporting high-speed internet. He had a reputation for technical brilliance coupled with outrageous outspokenness. I hired him to direct our NASA research contract.

We celebrated the opening of the campus in January of 2002. None of the younger faculty in Pittsburgh were ready to move to SV to direct the campus, so I asked Reddy to be the official director of the campus. He didn't move to SV, but he added the campus to his travel regime—a never-ending, world-circling flight to visit prime ministers, oversee universities, accept awards, and spend time with his daughters in California. He started a software engineering MS degree program that catered to local programmers and hired an AI guru, Roger Schank, to run it. Schank believed passionately in learning by doing.

Still the SCS dean in Pittsburgh, I visited the SV campus every few months. One night I had dinner at Schmidt's house. Sitting on the porch before dinner we were chatting.

"Google has become the preferred search engine at CMU. It's the best free service," I said.

"How do you think we're going to make money?"

"I haven't a clue." *I didn't.*

"Look on the right side of the search results display sometime. You might see some ads."

"Really, I'd never noticed."

"Most people don't. They're unobtrusive and are based on what you've searched for, so they might even be welcome. The advertisers like them too because they pay only when someone clicks on an ad."

The next day, I visited Schmidt at Google during an all-hands meeting where its fifty-some employees gathered. There, I met Susan Wojcicki, in whose garage Google had been founded. She was Google's first marketing manager and had created the AdSense service. Unlike search ads, AdSense ads are placed on other people's websites, and they get most of the click revenue from them; the large volume of them generates much revenue for Google.

"Jim is the dean of CS at CMU," Schmidt said, introducing me to Larry Page.

"What does CMU have to teach us?"

He challenged me but not in an unfriendly way. I thought for a moment.

"Machine learning seems to be a hot topic," I said. "And we have a department devoted to it."

The conversation went no further, but Google hired many CMU machine learning PhDs in the following years.

***

By the summer of 2002 my depression had settled in—just as the hospital's videos had forewarned. I noticed it on our annual vacation in Martha's Vineyard. The vacation lacked the feeling of enthusiasm I expected. My mood darkened as I read a book called *The Fourth Turning* by two creators of generational theories who coined terms like millennials—born between 1981 and 1996. The book presents an elaborate theory of Anglo-American history. It claims that history runs on an eighty-year cycle of ups and downs based on the character of four successive generations, like the four seasons. The book's characterizations of every four generations, starting in 1461, seems to fit four living generations today.[66]

Each cycle ends with a twenty-year winter crisis that resolves tensions and sets society off in a new direction. The last one started in 1940.

After the vacation, I interviewed some psychological counselors. One of them made me feel less sheepish when he explained that my depression was really "a physical problem brought on by your amygdala, which had freaked out when your chest was cracked open, and your heart stopped." I signed up for weekly meetings with a counselor. In turn, she had me go to a psychotherapist, licensed to prescribe anti-depressants. The two of them lifted the cloud in a few months.

The psychologist had me read some poetry and philosophy.[67] She worked at having me look at my sixty-first year as a time to step back and be supportive of people I worked with. She was preparing me for retirement.

"You are the silverback," she said, though ignorant of my gorilla suit.

---

[66] Before you fall for this theory, note its inventors were not professional historians and suffered from confirmation bias.

[67] See Whyte and Glassman in Readings

Another day, she said to me, "You're still a Catholic—an altar boy, even!"

"How can I be a Catholic when I don't go to church and don't believe in God?"

"Your Catholic upbringing taught you there was a meaning for your life. Even if you don't accept *that* meaning, you still search for a god to give you one. You cannot be an existentialist."

She had a point. When I abandoned Catholicism in my teenage years, I needed a new way to understand my life and its place in the universe. I first tried physics, which didn't prove to be useful. CS offered no answers. Evolution offered a better path, as did all sorts of mind-altering practices I pursued in my spare hours: alcohol, pot, affirmations, shamanism, hypnotism, Prozac, Sufism, Alexander Technique, Tai Chi, and yoga. Quite a list!

The psychiatrist, seeing my recovery from depression as a threat to his revenues, suggested other improvements to my life. He put me on the Atkins Diet, where I lost twenty-five pounds and lowered my cholesterol level, after which he gently prodded me about my drinking.

"I'm giving you anti-depressants, but alcohol is a depressant, so it's making them less effective."

That made sense.

"Alcoholism is like an allergy, not a moral failure. If you were allergic to peanuts, would you accept them from a host of a party?"

Drinking had been a fundamental part of my social life for thirty-five years. I resisted, but he continued to appeal to my rational side while appearing indifferent to what I chose to do.

Eventually, I agreed to stop, perhaps supported by my idea of a second life. Eagerly, he gave me some things to say to myself like, "I'm taking good care of myself—not poisoning myself." His methods worked. It was like walking through a door that had always been there. To this day, Susan and I think we should pay him royalties.

Now that I'm freed from drinking, I look upon my thirty-five-year habit as a mistake. But the culture I grew up in destined me for some period of alcoholism.

***

By 2003 things on the SV campus were getting fraught. The MS program was generating some revenue, but Reid was not addressing NASA's software problems. Some could be solved simply by adopting a modern programming language, but others were the unavoidable problem of operating in space where no earthlings had any experience. Worse, Reid was insulting our NASA sponsors for not being as savvy as him. In one meeting he reportedly dumped a glass of water on his head in frustration.

"Don't worry I'm interviewing for a job at Google," he had said when I confronted him about his behavior.

I emailed Schmidt and told him it was OK to hire Reid.

The SV campus was also losing money. A bunch of Indian students Reddy had brought in at a discounted tuition rate were running amok. They were young, had never been out of India, and were not equipped to take our MS courses. We had to teach them elementary software concepts, but they were more interested in getting driver's licenses and cruising the Bay Area. I was anxious to fix the problems, but I couldn't do that from Pittsburgh.

261

At the four-year mark, I was tiring of my job as the dean of SCS. Our daughters were long gone, and Susan's mother had just died after a long decline. A day after her funeral, I began plotting another repotting. I told the provost I would stop being SCS's dean the following July, and he initiated a search for a replacement. Reddy seemed happy to relinquish his part-time directorship of the SV campus. In fact, he graciously helped by firing Schank who was consuming a lot of money and embarrassing us with ads he ran in *Dr. Dobbs's Journal*. The ads described our MS program as having "no lectures, no tests, no books."

By February the plan for changing leadership in SV was complete, and Pittsburgh was mired in winter. Without warning anybody, Susan and I moved to Palo Alto, which forced the university to immediately hire Randy Bryant as my successor as SCS dean—an excellent choice. Given my insubordinate action, I was surprised that President Cohon held the traditional reception to celebrate my work as dean. But he did. He thanked me for guiding the CS college to greater achievements and starting the SV campus. When Bryant and his successor as the new department head, Jeannette Wing, cut their praise of me short to talk about themselves, it irritated Susan, but I didn't mind since I thought I'd "raised" them.

As we were preparing to leave for Palo Alto, Feeny and his wife Louise appeared and agreed to rent our house while we were away. They had a business in Pittsburgh and an estate in Montecito, CA—"a paradise for Hollywood stars and the super-rich who want to live in splendid isolation," according to an ad.

Meditation is the ultimate mobile device; you can use it anywhere, anytime, unobtrusively
— Sharon Salzberg

13. Return to Silicon Valley

"We'll just try it for a year."

This is what I had told Susan, who was a bit shaken by the abrupt transition I pitched. But, as usual, she fully engaged. She got us into an apartment complex next to Stanford. Our one-bedroom apartment was as small as our Berkeley apartment thirty-five years before, but this one had tennis courts and a swimming pool. She reestablished contact with all our friends and the Stanford student radio station where she'd begun her broadcast journalism career. Instead of continuing her financial reporting, she explored a new form. She and Wendy Schmidt dreamt up the idea for a student panel program called "What would your mother say?" Wendy provided some funding while Susan brought students and older women on air to discuss love, sex, money, or whatever she thought the Stanford students might want motherly advice on—but not from their own mothers. The students might not have wanted the advice at all but enjoyed shocking the highly reactive Susan with their stories.

I started yoga at one of Palo Alto's several studios. I found a Tai Chi group. They insisted that I take the beginners' course to learn *their* version, different from what I'd learned in Pittsburgh. They would test my postures by trying to push me over. More advanced students went to competitions, but when I saw that the advanced classes used swords and spears, I was content to remain a beginner. Later, I tried a few new folk therapies: Rolfing—an intense sort of massage—and acupuncture.

The small two-story building we leased from NASA was pleasant enough. Like the other buildings surrounding the grassy plaza, it was faux adobe with a red ceramic roof. My office was not as grand as my dean's office in Pittsburgh, but grand enough, considering that the SV style was to have no office at all for executives. Dress was also more casual, and I often rode a bike from Palo Alto, ten miles away.

The MS program had stabilized under a Schank associate, Ray Bareiss. A respected software engineer, Martin Griss, was running the research program. He had been a lab director at Hewlett-Packard. He began to involve some NASA scientists in the research program, giving them adjunct faculty appointments.

I soon needed to hire a business manager and a computer support technician as the old ones departed for new jobs. The SV employment market was more fluid than Pittsburgh's with people moving every few years.

With the day-to-day operations under control, I turned to things that had been neglected: outreach to SV and bridges to Pittsburgh. I joined the Bay Area Research Directors' dinner group to get in touch with the many companies and universities there. Aside from the companies headquartered in SV many other companies had research branches there, and I cultivated relationships with all sorts. We recruited students from many of them and occasional research contracts from companies like Honda and Panasonic.

Since my goal in starting the campus was to strengthen the CMU brand, I hired a brand consultant who taught me how to turn every interviewer's question into a prepared talking point—a skill I'd somehow never learned before. I bought ad space on SV's only electronic billboard—a novelty at the time.

In the second year I hired a marketing director who had worked at Berkeley's business school. She arranged speaking events. Microsoft Research, where some of my PARC friends were working, lent us their large hi-tech auditorium for popular events, such as when Apple co-founder Steve Wozniak gave a rousing talk about being an engineer. He arrived with his posse on Segways. We ran a technology conference starring the *New York Times* tech guru David Pogue. We joined the climate change movement with a VIP dinner at the large house one of our instructors owned in the Palo Alto hills.

My most impactful stunt was getting the highway department to install a sign at our freeway exit. Carnegie Mellon University: Exit 398.

It was hard to get the attention of Pittsburgh faculty, so I returned every month or so to build bridges. CMU's business school started a remote, part-time MBA program. The Entertainment Technology Center sent teams of students to do projects with SV companies like Electronic Arts and Pixar. Scott Russell ran an annual *Tour de Silicon Valley* excursion for Pittsburgh MS students seeking jobs with SV companies.

Eric Daimler had been sitting out of VC activities ever since the dot-com bubble burst in 2000, so he came to work at our campus. He taught a course for entrepreneurship that involved student teams creating business plans and attending talks by many SV entrepreneurs and investors. One of which was Donna Dubinsky, who was one of the inventors of the Palm Pilot, (the first successful handheld device) who gave a talk about selling out to U.S. Robotics when her company was desperate for investment after the 2001 crash. We asked her if she regretted never enjoying the massive kind of payday she might have had if she'd owned a lot of the company when it finally succeeded.

"No," she answered, firmly. "We might have received more if we'd hung on, but the product might have died. I wanted to give our baby the best chance to thrive. So, we sold out." I admired that attitude from one of the few successful woman start-up founders.

To build our MS program to a hundred students Bareiss recruited them from anywhere and had them work with their teams and us from where they were. Several SV students, especially those with jobs, started to use the remote option to avoid commuting. He learned that classes with half the students remote were a communications challenge. Aside from irritating audio feedback problems, he found that special measures were needed to keep remote participants engaged. He also required remote students to show up in person every few months and found that sufficient to build natural relationships among team members.

***

Seeking joint research possibilities, Griss and I invited the manager of Nokia research in Palo Alto to lunch at a pan-Asian restaurant. He had been a CMU electrical engineering professor.

"You guys are missing the boat, along with the rest of the academic world," he said to us across the table of plates full of curry and noodles. "Mobile phones are the computers of the future. Most people in Africa will never see a computer. They buy Nokia phones."

It was 2007, and Apple's iPhone, the first smart phone, had just been announced. Griss and I didn't need much convincing and began brainstorming research in mobile systems with Ted Selker, an inventive veteran of IBM and MIT's Media Lab, visiting our campus.

"I landed in San Jose last week and wanted to take a bus home and then a taxi," said Selker, who hated driving as a matter of principle. "It was horrible. I had to wait for the bus, then couldn't find a taxi. It took forever. Couldn't I use a smart phone to solve this?"

This got me focused on the design of a smart phone ride-sharing service, which I called high-tech hitchhiking. You would tell your phone where you wanted to go, and (in minutes!) someone would drive up and offer you a ride to say, a bus stop, where the bus was about to leave in two minutes (just in time!). Then, you would ride the bus for a while, get off, and find another car that magically happened to be on the way to your block. This magic depended on taxis, SuperShuttle vans, limousines, mass transit systems, and individual drivers willing to pick people up at a moment's notice. In the background, a computer system would churn away managing all the schedules, using Dijkstra's shortest path algorithm to make it work efficiently.

I thought about all the problems that needed to be solved. One specifically was getting a critical mass of people to sign up, because the reactions to my idea revealed that most people were reluctant to get into a car with a stranger.

Many other people in the tech world were thinking about this same kind of rideshare idea, so I started reaching out to them and organizing meetings. A group of us traveled to MIT where we discovered four or five start-ups working on the ride-sharing concept. One was called Zimride, started by Logan Green. He had been working on this problem for ten years—since he was a teenager commuting in Los Angeles, watching thousands of solo-driver cars crowding the freeways.

***

I joined the teaching program and helped launch a second MS program for engineers wanting to get into the business side. Bareiss coached me in the learning-by-doing method. Instead of teaching a concept followed by homework, we would pretend to be their bosses and write them a memo asking for a report on a technology business issue. We never assigned reading but gave them a large list of sources relevant to all aspects of the issue. The idea was to teach them the habit of finding answers for themselves rather than spoon-feeding them. The class meetings would be driven by the students discussing their approaches with probing questions from the "bosses."

Just as every waiter in Hollywood has a movie script in his pocket, everyone in SV has a start-up proposal. In my first semester teaching, I asked the students, all experienced SV software engineers, to create a business plan for a ride-sharing business. They identified markets, interviewed possible stakeholders, and looked for revenue sources. In the end, most concluded that there was no viable business, and I was disappointed.

Piling on, the VC Russell said, "Jim, even if you don't care about making money, I don't think you'll attract enough people to move the needle." I pitched my ideas to Schmidt at Google, and in a fatherly way he said, "Jim, you're getting a little old for start-ups. You're a professor! You can diversify your risk by advising ten of your students' start-ups and cashing in if one of them works."

Then Uber struck in 2009 with an idea that was simpler than mine—or that of my ride-sharing friends. It provided a service for limo drivers who were required to find fares by appointment only. Now, with the Uber app downloaded on your phone, you could make an appointment while standing next to a driver and his phone—making things technically legal. In a stroke, Uber solved three problems we ride-sharing weenies were struggling with. There was a revenue model. There was already a critical mass of drivers. And, irrationally, people were fine with riding with a stranger if he was charging them money.

Whereas we missed the mark trying to avoid a money-making business for fear of lawyers and insurance companies raising impediments, Uber had no fear. In fact, when the San

Francisco taxicab commission issued a cease-and-desist order to Uber, VC rushed to invest. As the old saying goes, "To make an omelet you need to break a few eggs," and laws too.

Green, who was still working on Zimride, took note of Uber's success. He sold Zimride and started a new business called Lyft, which used civilian drivers instead of limo drivers. And to counter that, Uber immediately invented UberX to do the same. And so it went between them. When Lyft encouraged *ad hoc* carpooling, Uber immediately followed. As both companies went public and were rolling in cash, they started competing to build robotic cars.

***

Google was located adjacent to NASA, so I bounced back and forth between there and our campus. I started by studying the inventive ways Google wrote software.

The young Marissa Mayer, who later became CEO of Yahoo, was the director of consumer web products and had helped implement Google's ad system. She breezed into our appointment fifteen minutes late—a habit, I learned. I asked her, "How do you develop web products?"

"We use a unique user-driven approach," she said fixing her steely blue eyes on me from across her messy desk, "Because Google already has a huge user population, we can run experiments on them from the first day a service is released. We start with something simple and measure the hell out of it. We never waste time pondering a decision about the interface when we can get an answer in a few hours by putting alternatives in front of a sliver of the users who happen to be online."

"That sounds cool! What kind of decisions does it work for?"

"Anything we can formulate a few competitive alternatives for, like the color of a button. We just put out the two or more colors and measure which one gets more clicks. The next day our button will have a winning color, and we move on."

"What's been the biggest surprise?"

"Our advertisers have asked us to help them do the same thing. They'll give some differing versions of the same ad, asking us to test them on a small sample, then use the winner for the whole population."

I was intrigued with Google's other software practices; I spent a few months observing a small team practicing Extreme Programming. First, the programmers always work in pairs. They start with a skeleton program that does nothing and write a test program that feeds input to the skeleton testing for the correct output, always failing the first time. Then they embellish the skeleton to handle that input and pass the test. They keep repeating that cycle until the program passes all the tests they think are relevant. All the while, in the background, a process runs all the extant tests to ensure they haven't undone some necessary part of the program. This procedure ensures there is a good way of keeping the program well-tested for its lifetime.

In fact, the whole Google corporation was continuously rebuilding its entire software base—millions of pages. Every change a programmer made was first reviewed by his or her immediate team, then plugged into the software base. If the building process found an inconsistency in the new code, they would get a harsh phone call, whatever the hour.

When I heard about the yet unreleased Gmail, I was interested, especially because it was managed by an MS graduate of HCII. I loved the idea that Gmail encouraged users to eschew collecting messages in folders and, instead, to use a search to find what they needed if they ever did. Next, I noticed that Gmail was putting clickable ads beside my messages that tried to guess what I might buy, based on the content of my message. The first ad I saw was inappropriate. I was emailing about the war in Iraq, and the ad was offering insurance for travel in the Middle East. *The algorithm needs work*, I thought. When I discussed that ad with an executive he said, "We're thinking of offering a version you can pay for that doesn't show ads. But that contradicts our doctrine that people should like our ads, because they are carefully selected to be relevant to their needs."

Many other people were freaked out to think Google was reading their email. But Google persisted with the practice, assuring everyone that no *person* at Google was reading their mail. Some people were mollified by that.

After I understood Google's new take on advertising, I wrote an article for the *Pittsburgh Quarterly*, "Google Knows How to Flirt."[68] It won a plaque from the local press club.

Google's success was based in the exponential growth of internet usage. This chart shows the number of internet users, starting from the day that student came into my office and showed me how to make a web page.

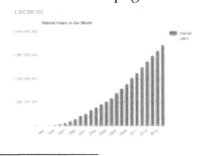

---

[68] See Documents

The curve obeys Metcalfe's Law, because the value of becoming an internet user increases with the number of existing users.

The combination of the two exponentials—Moore's Law for hardware and Metcalfe's Law for the internet—supported the rise of the computer-based service companies collectively called the FANG: Facebook, Amazon, Netflix, and Google, a term coined by the television personality Jim Cramer (of *Mad Money*), who praised these companies for being "totally dominant in their markets."

Moore's Law also rescued AI from its doldrums. Winners of computer chess tournaments increasingly used brute force methods, abandoning the Newell-Simon human simulation approach to AI. Also, Hinton's neural learning theories became practical, and his team started winning image recognition contests. Neural learning just needed far more computing power than anyone had imagined. The neural learning technique became hot, and a small company, DeepMind, was founded in London in 2012, using neural learning to play games. All this refuted Newell's skepticism of neural learning. Was Newell rolling over in his grave? I doubt it. He never claimed to have the final answer.

Google's growing ad revenue allowed it to hire many smart programmers, including my former student Andrew Ng, to attack long-standing AI problems. Ng started a team called Google Brain in 2011. One of its first stunts was to unleash sixteen-thousand computers on the entire internet with the simple but vague goal of finding something interesting. After many hours of computing, it came back with the picture of a cat, which was all the rage then! This was notable because it showed computers discovering something they weren't told to look for.

A few years later Google hired Hinton, who helped revamp Google Brain's translation service with his deep neural learning. It became an astounding success in 2012, apparently better than programs that had been under development for twenty years.

This same technique of using internet data to teach a learning program was used to solve other difficult, long-standing AI problems like voice recognition and face recognition. Anywhere you can find a large set of examples, you can teach a program to solve a much larger set of tasks. I'm expecting someone to do it for IQ tests soon.

***

Pausch contracted pancreatic cancer in 2006. Undaunted, he gave a last lecture at CMU entitled "Really Achieving Your Childhood Dreams." It went viral on the internet, and he followed up with a best-selling book entitled *The Last Lecture*. The book led to a guest role on *Star Trek*, a practice session with the Pittsburgh Steelers, and TV network interviews.

When the university built a new CS building, they linked it to the drama building with a lighted bridge called the Pausch Bridge. He remains CMU's most famous graduate, next to Andy Warhol.

***

I visited Gray at his Microsoft San Francisco lab to catch up and invite him to visit my campus. He had silver hair and a well-trimmed beard, looking corporate. It seemed that while I was indulging in more of an informal lifestyle, Gray was moving away from it. He was also thinner than I'd ever seen him, which he attributed to serious dieting on his recent sabbatical. He had created a virtual earth system that stitched together satellite images to show a browsable picture of Earth and was now leading an international movement to share geospatial information.

A year after that, in January 2007, Gray took a solo sail to the Farallon Islands outside of San Francisco Bay to scatter his late mother's ashes. On the way back, he called his daughter to tell her how glorious the day was and how much he loved her. He was never heard from again. No trace of his boat was found despite five months of effort by a world-wide community using underwater search and satellite images from NASA, Digital Globe, Microsoft, Google, Oracle, Amazon, and others. It remains a mystery.

I sometimes suspect he killed himself because he had some sort of cancer. He wanted his wife and daughter to collect his life insurance, so he meticulously figured out how to sink his boat with him in it in such a way that it would never be found. But friends reminded me that he was such a daredevil that anything could have happened. A friend of his was learning to sail and was working on the certification for the man-overboard drill. He mentioned that one day while sailing with Gray, without warning Gray jumped into the water shouting "man overboard."

I had my own health scare in the late summer of 2008. I somehow contracted sepsis, an infection of the blood. Later, they said they initially estimated that I had only a 30 percent chance of surviving. When Jane, Mike, and Rachel showed up in my room a few days later I said, "What are you doing here?" still oblivious to the danger I had been in.

"If you're cash-flow positive and not committing felonies you can do whatever you like."

That is how I often explained CMU's approval process to newcomers.

Unfortunately, I neglected the cash-flow rule, thinking the CMU should simply invest in us for the brand's sake. Every year, I pestered CMU's leadership for more support. And every year, President Cohon would respond the same way, "How long do you want to do this, Jim?"

Another fact of CMU organization is that the deans of colleges have more expendable funds than the central administration. When we invited Bryant as dean of SCS to support us, he declined, making us somewhat of an orphan. Finally, the ambitious dean of the engineering college was convinced to adopt us, and I agreed to step down and turn it over to him in 2009. I felt like the starting pitcher who was being yanked after too many earned runs, but I was given the traditional celebratory party attended by friends from all over the Bay Area. Then I felt much better.

As I started my one-year sabbatical (another tradition), the new dean invested heavily in the campus by hiring young research faculty that supported a strong PhD program, run by Griss.

***

My fellow residents of my apartment complex and I were sitting down in its small theater for a Saturday afternoon lecture. A young man calling himself Forall, a Buddhist monk, came in and started telling us about Buddhism. He had been a teenage tennis star, but instead of attending college, had gone to Japan to become a Zen monk. He succeeded after two arduous years, went to India, and later came back to the States. We really related to him. At the end, someone offered him some money, but monks could not take money for teaching. "However," he said, "I can teach you to play tennis like a Buddhist for sixty-five dollars an hour." I signed up.

Buddhist tennis has a simple trick, "Breathe in as your opponent hits the ball, and breath out as you hit the ball." It gets your timing, concentration, and muscle action functioning properly.

After a few lessons, Forall, said, "Look, if you really want to improve everything, you need to start meditating." I started practicing meditation for ten minutes at a time—supported by pointers from Forall.

To test whether I was getting it, one day he put a yellow tennis ball in front of me.

"Start meditating and stare at this ball and tell me if you see anything strange."

"I notice some dark spots, coming and going on the surface of the ball," I said.

"Good! You're getting there." he said.

As an amateur brain scientist, here is what I think happened. Meditation turns off my left brain. My right brain observed the signals coming in from my retina, and a few of those little rods and cones were naturally misfiring. So I was, indeed, seeing spots. Normally, however, my left brain censors the right because it knows tennis balls are yellow.

Another thing I noticed while meditating was that both my eyes were seeing things, overcoming my life-long strabismus! If my ten-year-old self had meditated, maybe I would have been able to "Put the bird in the cage." So, meditation, for me, was a way to give my right brain a chance to get out from under my bossy left brain without the use of drugs.

I went to some Buddhist services with my friend Redell, who belonged to a sangha and wore a black robe to its services. I told him, "I think I'll just do the meditation and not join the sangha with all the impenetrable discussion of the dharma, whatever that is."

"People often feel that way, but the sangha serves a useful purpose; there are times in your life that you cease practicing meditation because you're too busy or too stressed. If you belong to a sangha, your friends will help you get back to it. It's a little like Alcoholics Anonymous."

A year later, Susan and I took an improvisation course in a Stanford adult education series. The teacher observed that she was really teaching "disguised Buddhism." The first principle of improv is to react to everything any partner says or does with the attitude of "Yes! And . . ." This, of course is just the Buddhist principle of making lemonade from lemons. At the end of the course I found myself talking animatedly with several of my classmates—uncharacteristic for me. I had a sense of loss, because we wouldn't be seeing these people with whom we'd developed a lot of trust.

I started my sabbatical by visiting Stanford's new Design school; but then Al Spector, who had become vice president of research at Google, offered me a visiting position and a choice of projects to work on. I chose a project run by an MIT professor, who was also visiting. He was creating a system for nonprofessionals, including kids, to create apps for Android phones, Google's challenge to iPhones.

At Google, PhDs were expected to program all day. I saw former students of mine, who were well into middle age with business experience, heads-down programming. I even saw a Turing Awardee doing it. It had been over twenty-five years since I'd done any serious programming. I was quite pleased with myself when I completed a sample Android app. My team leader, a bearded veteran of SV, twenty years my junior, reported that the old codger was already productive.

I shared an office with two fellow programmers, and we hacked all day. Despite being five feet away from them, I learned to not ask the questions about the many details of our project and its programs. If I did, it would take them several seconds to emerge from the trances they were in. Their consciousness was completely occupied with the details of whatever they were programming, holding many details. It was almost painful for them to empty it to answer my question. So, I sent emails to them so that they could respond when they came up for air. I might have been that way in my intense programming days.

Another change to programming was the degree to how quickly a software engineer was expected to learn how unfamiliar software works. The team leader would say something like, "Carol, would you track down the documentation for the Blivix system, figure out how it works, and use it to Blivix our Framises?" Carol would then go off for a few days and come back an expert in Blivix.

We worked hard, but life at Google was famously luxe. I got there by nine, right as breakfast was ending, which was one of the three free meals every day. There were a dozen excellent free restaurants scattered around its campus.

And the speakers! There were talks by visiting nerds (some famous, like Don Knuth) as well as celebrities like Obama, Diane von Furstenberg, and Tina Fey. Many talks simply popped up in an open space where I would notice them. Another Buddhist monk, Forall's partner, showed up as the guest of Google's "head of mindfulness" to pitch meditation. He said, "I'd rather be enlightened for a day than live one hundred years unenlightened." Quite an advertisement!

And every Friday there was a town hall meeting open to all employees where Page, Brin, Schmidt, and other executives would answer any questions from the audience. In January 2010 we were seated in a large cafeteria space in my building. That meeting was standing room only. Page and Schmidt were there, but only Sergey Brin spoke.

"Google is pulling out of China," he announced.

The room began to buzz.

"We've just discovered that a Chinese group had hacked Gmail to spy on a dissident," he continued. "I was born in Moscow, and I know you can't bargain with totalitarian countries."

***

I stopped working at Google in late spring. That summer we took a two-week trip to Turkey. After time in Istanbul, we headed east to Cappadocia where people once had homes and churches in caves. One night we visited a caravansary, a sort of ancient motel for traders on the Silk Road. We saw some real Sufis perform their traditional dances. Unlike me, they could whirl for several minutes and stop suddenly without falling.

Learning and innovation go hand in hand.
— William Pollard

14. Learning to Innovate

Susan and I returned to Pittsburgh in September of 2010. Since we had sold our house while living in California, we had to scramble to find somewhere to live. Failing to find a desirable condo in CMU's neighborhood, we decided to rent a two-bedroom apartment in downtown Pittsburgh—about five miles away from campus. Until then, both our Pittsburgh homes had been in the same square mile, in the same neighborhood, near schoolmates.

Just as we were moving in, Feeny appeared. He lived in an apartment eleven floors above us, with a better view and much higher rent. One-upped again! He has heralded each of my moves in or out of Pittsburgh, but since I didn't plan to move again, I became apprehensive about seeing him.

The bus ride to CMU was twenty minutes. I became an observer of Pittsburgh's Black citizens, whom I'd always felt apart from. I would inwardly cringe when they yelled and hit their kids, who were alternately defiant and cowed. I was acutely aware that these people, living within a few miles of me, were living in a much harsher city than I was. The infant mortality rate and the murder rate were six times worse for Blacks. Pittsburgh had isolated its Blacks for two centuries. I began to wonder how I could help. I started attending a nearby church in Pittsburgh's only mixed-race neighborhood, where I discussed my interest with a social activist who said, "You might study the Black community and have a great idea for their betterment, but they'll ignore you because you are white." I didn't have an answer for that yet.

I joined a yoga studio a block from our apartment. I tried two different sanghas but didn't find them engaging. My commitment to following the Buddha faded. Part of the problem was his admonition "Whoever judges others digs a pit for themselves." This conflicted with my professor's job, which seemed to be judging people—students, faculty, and job candidates.

I was also judgmental of Pausch's book, *The Last Lecture*. I thought, *This is cute, but it's not the Bhagavad Gita.* Then Jane, who was trying to get pregnant, told me she had been inspired by Pausch's thought: *The brick walls are there to give us a chance to show how badly we want something.* Witnessing his thinking having such an important effect on a loved one made me more respectful of his wisdom.

In 2010 Jane's son Adam was born, the first grandchild. When Susan was asked how she wanted to be addressed by Adam, she decided on "EB." Multiple friends had said, independently, that she was like the Energizer Bunny. I agree, including the part where the bunny falls over when its battery is exhausted.

Once we settled into our downtown life, I tried programming for fun. But it felt too much like work, and I could never keep up with professional programmers. It wasn't just because my brain was old either. To compete with the professionals, you had to also keep up with all the software available, working at it full time. I tried a language called Ruby on Rails, which had fostered a huge community of enthusiasts who were creating software packages for every imaginable purpose, e.g., sending tweets. I became convinced that every program the world needs can be found somewhere in their library. At the onset of my career, I enjoyed programming because it was like building a log cabin using nothing but an axe. Now, the software jobs are like installing and maintaining air conditioners in skyscrapers. Understanding other peoples' programs is a job for extroverts, not me.

In my twenty-seven years of being a professor at CMU, I rarely taught in the classroom, so I volunteered to teach. After teaching Java programming for a while, I audited an HCI class called User-Centered Research and Evaluation (UCRE), a class that Bonnie John had created long before. Bonnie had recently left CMU to work at IBM's Yorktown research center. The instructor suggested that I work on a student team rather than just listen to lectures. I felt a little out of place but enjoyed it.

UCRE taught a methodology called *Contextual Design*. You might think that I, a founder of a Design company and the HCI Institute, would already know about it. But I didn't. In fact, I loved the course so much that I volunteered to take it over for a while. My faculty colleagues, somewhat exhausted from teaching it to one hundred students every year, were relieved.

In the early eighties, Karen Holtzblatt had been at DEC, and even though MAYA had been consulting for DEC, our paths never crossed. DEC was an engineer's company from the CEO founder on down, and Holtzblatt's PhD was in hermeneutic psychology, which even other psychologists consider to be flaky. However, she had a front row seat watching how engineers designed products that only they themselves could use. By 1984, after she had seen enough, she left to create a consulting business, InContext and wrote the book *Contextual Design*.[69]

Contextual Design is a comprehensive Design method. You begin with field research, watching and listening as if you were an apprentice to your client. Then, using cognitive and social psychology principles, you consolidate the collected data and build models of the work process. Next, you trial variations in the models to discover new ways of working. Only after those three phases—observation, data collection, and models—do you Design a computer system to support a new process.

The book won awards from the HCI community and was the perfect book for teaching Design from scratch. It is prescriptive, never using the phrase "on the other hand." Some professionals find her book too doctrinaire, but I found that it gives students a process they can execute and modify as they become more experienced.

---

[69] See Holtzblatt in Readings

Holtzblatt even came to the HCII to explain her methods to teachers of UCRE classes while being videotaped. Sometimes sounding like a Jewish grandmother, she would dispense real wisdom about the Design process.

Here is a verbatim transcript of a ninety-second harangue she delivered standing in front of a slide that read:

Unguided design = Over-design.

Practice is not logical or symmetric.

Field data guides great design.

> If you listen to design teams they will say "What if . . . What if somebody wants to do this? What if? Well if we do it this way . . . then we have to have the opposite." What I always say to people is. . . . *Thinking* . . . is not a tool. Stop thinking! Practice! And work practice! And what we do in our lives is *not* logical. We don't *want* it to be logical! We don't *care* if it's logical. Just because I have a right hand, I do *not* have to have a left hand. If you have . . . data, then you *know* what is happening. Design for what you *know* . . . and stop imagining what might happen, which has **no** evidence in the data whatsoever . . . because you start putting in more function . . . and design things that nobody needs, nobody wants, and you don't understand. Makes more code . . . Makes more things to test . . . Makes more bugs . . . Makes more breakdowns . . . Makes more *complexity*. Stop thinking! Instead . . . look at your data. See the structure. **Know** how to read models. Then read what's in front of your nose! Not what's in your brain. And you *will* have a performative product.

"Stop being a goddamned engineer!"

At least that's what I thought she was saying!

Teaching the course acquainted me with the MS students of HCII and whet my appetite for more involvement with them.

John Zimmerman was an HCII colleague who combined great talent as a Designer with a congenial disposition. The two of us created and co-taught a follow-on course to UCRE called Design of Service Innovation, in which teams of students Designed new mobile applications. The two of us carried learning-by-doing one step further. We asked each team to choose their own problem area and its market. We added more methods to Contextual Design, such as value diagrams that described why and how the various stakeholders in a service participated. Unlike conventional money-for-product businesses, services often involved multiple stakeholders.

Teams often wanted an app they personally desired, like one to tell them where the coolest party was going on but didn't consider why anyone would organize that information for them. Requiring them to invent value diagrams forced them to find workable business models.

Here are value diagrams for Uber and Google.

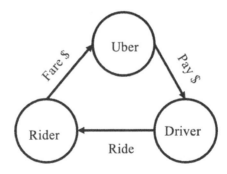

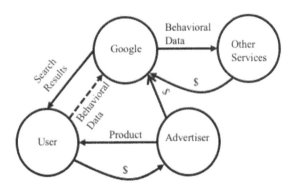

One of my favorites was a joke diagram about a rival university.

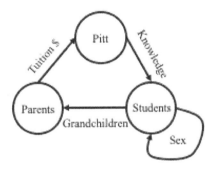

Each course began with improv exercises, just as the Entertainment Technology Center did. We wanted to loosen teams up, hoping that their group sessions would be more spontaneous and productive.

Truthfully, on many days, we had the students work together to figure out a service while the two of us sat back and kibitzed and harassed them with questions. "Who wants this?" "Who will pay for this?" "What are the alternatives to using *your* service?" It sure didn't help our credibility, but we told our students that we would've flunked Zuckerberg for having no revenue model for Facebook in 2011.

The goal was to create a *minimum viable product* (somewhat like Google's trick) to start and then *pivot* when it was discovered that the market was not where they thought it was. Levi's is an example. During the gold rush, Levi Strauss arrived in San Francisco with a lot of canvas for making tents. When profits seemed weak, and he noticed the ragged clothes of miners, he pivoted to make pants from his canvas. The canvas pants sold but were minimal (and uncomfortable!), so he changed to denim and added pockets.

Here are some of the businesses the students proposed in our classes over the years:

- For foreign visitors: rent a cellular data plan for any number of days on a device vended from and returned to a kiosk at baggage claims.
- For restaurants: offer instant discounts to nearby phones based on current occupancy.
- Buy things from students leaving in the spring and sell them to students arriving in the fall.
- Provide high-touch computer coaching for wealthy old people residing near campus.
- PayTango, a real start-up that uses fingerprints to make credit card payments was born in our course. The founders—our students!—might have pivoted to selling their devices to the Indian government, which sought a universal ID, rather than the US with its driver's licenses and credit cards.

I taught the course for the next seven years—by myself or with colleagues, like Zimmerman. One year the class was taught in Rwanda via two-way video. Eventually, Design of Service Innovation became a mainstay of an MS in product management taught by HCII and the business school.

One of the good things about teaching smart young students is what I learn from them. Here's an example: I was not particularly impressed with Google's competitor to Microsoft Word, called Google Docs. Our students all preferred it because of its simultaneous editing feature. They could collaborate on a document from different computers and the internet's speed was now good enough that they could be changing the same document, even the same page without triggering chaos. Google's software could package up a few keystrokes from a user, send it to the server where the file resided, change the file, and reflect the changes to all the others who had the file open in seconds. I kept asking them how Google solved the version control problem that Andrew's VICE system had struggled with, and they kept saying it wasn't a problem. If two people were editing the same page, even the same line of the same page the "last edit rules" race condition might occur, so Google hadn't solved the problem. *But,* when it did happen, the person whose edits had been overridden would notice because the last change was in front of them seconds after they made their own change. They could repeat their edit or call up the other person and work it out with them. In other words, when changes from different people can be interleaved on a second-by-second basis, the effect of a race condition is detected immediately and the loss of a few seconds of typing is easy to bear. This doesn't mean nobody needs a version control system, but greatly reduces the number of teams that do.

Jon Lloyd, a retired general surgeon, was introduced to us at a friend's dinner party. He described some of his retirement projects and mentioned that he'd discovered a method recommended when all else fails. It was 2016, and I was contemplating retirement myself and looking for an answer of how a white person can help the Black community, I was keenly interested and took him to lunch to talk.

Positive Deviance gets its strange name from its central premise: Ignore the people who are failing (the deviants) and look for those who are succeeding (the positive deviants) despite the obstacles. This approach was invented by a Peace Corps couple who eliminated most childhood malnutrition in Vietnamese villages. [70] They followed anthropological practices, like watching respectfully (just like Contextual Design), but they took it a step further. They never gave any answers themselves and instead let the villagers discover and promulgate their own solutions. The couple's only contribution was encouraging systematic data collection and focusing on the positive deviants.

Lloyd's most notable project was one that eliminated MRSA infections at a VA hospital. Well-known practices—such as handwashing—had proven successful, but the culture

---

[70] See Sternin in Readings

of the hospital made it resistant to change. After trying many approaches, Lloyd read about Positive Deviance.

He employed the method to attack the spread of MRSA in the VA hospital. With the support of management, he engaged every employee, including janitors, cooks, dishwashers, and even chaplains. All were asked to examine their routines in detail. Such as, one chaplain noticed that his bible could be transmitting viruses and started keeping it in a surgeon's hair covering. All the while nurses tested every incoming and outgoing patient for MRSA and scored each floor. After identifying floors with excellent track records, Lloyd asked the staff on those floors to help the failing floors. They discovered their own solutions, and eventually the whole hospital became MRSA free. The same general process was then promulgated to the 181 other VA hospitals with similar results, although the solutions differed.

A protégé of Lloyd's, Monique Mead, from CMU's music department, and I initiated a project at CMU to try Positive Deviance. Stress seemed like a real cultural problem. Many CMU students were generally proud of how stressed they were, but some reported great misery. We recruited ten students and disguised our project as an official course.

We found a thriving student who admitted feeling great stress early in her time at CMU—a positive deviant. Through her we found the Freshman Orientation group, all of whom seemed happy and engaged—more positive deviants. Most of our students were graduate music majors, and they worked to transplant the orientation group's practices—social connection—to their department with some success.

In contrast, in another approach, I unthinkingly violated the Positive Deviance method by consulting experts. The

291

dean of students suggested that we improve sleeping habits to reduce stress, and a psychiatrist from the student counseling service was adamant that consistent sleep habits would make a huge improvement. My inner engineer took over, and I launched a project called CMUSleeps to measure students' sleep habits, complete with an app I programmed, a reward program for participating, and a poster designed by one of the students in the course. The good news was that CMUSleeps showed that sleep was *not* a huge problem, because the average student's sleep habits weren't so bad. Furthermore, informal discussions with students revealed that they were happy with their sleep habits—six hours per night during the week, crashing over the weekend. The bad news was that I didn't succeed in using Positive Deviance, because the "villagers" didn't see a big problem.

So, that semester was an inadvertent controlled experiment. I decided what the problem was and focused on measuring it myself while the students solved a problem they cared about. If I ever try to address a social problem in Pittsburgh, I hope that I remember that embarrassing lesson.

My experience in the ten years of teaching in SV and Pittsburgh taught me what every grade schoolteacher and a few education experts know: a teacher's job is not to inform students but to provide appropriate help at the moment they can benefit. My preparation to be a professor had given me the wrong message. I felt I needed to explain what I knew in the clearest way. It's not just my misconception, however. Even some students expect professors to be that way.

In 2015 I had lunch with Seth Goldstein, a CS colleague with a reputation for original research pursuits. A hardware expert, he startled me with a strange answer when I asked him what he was up to.

"What will people do when AI has eliminated all work?" Seth said.

"Huh? I don't know. Sex, drugs, and rock 'n' roll? Maybe everyone can join the military, I notice that it seems to keep people engaged and out of trouble."

"I'm serious," he said, "It's a more important question than anything any of us are doing. I think people should become artists, even if they call what they do work."

VII: AI Fall 2016-

DeepMind's AlphaZero can best all players of any board game, starting with only the rules and twenty-four hours practice.

Stephen Hawking, Elon Musk, and Bill Gates warn that AI might cause human extinction.

In the movie *Singularity* a supercomputer designed to end all wars decides to kill all humans.

AI is found complicit in manipulation of Brexit and US presidential campaigns.

Oxford's Future of Humanity Institute publishes a white paper outlining technology's threats to humanity.

The European Commission issues a report demanding "Trust in Human-Centric Artificial Intelligence."

iHuman, a Swedish documentary about AI, asks if we are governed by algorithms created by big tech companies, governments, and the military.

Outside the Wire is a movie about robot soldiers.

15. What Should We Do about AI?

In April of 2017, Taylor died, suffering from Parkinson's disease. A few days before he died, he sent all of us an email, thanking us for being his friends. It ended with his signature good-bye, "Write if you get work." Taylor's obituary appeared on the front page of the *New York Times*, above the fold, and hundreds of his admirers—professors, entrepreneurs, Turing Award winners—attended Taylor's memorial service at the Computer History Museum in Mountain View, CA. Among the many eulogies were testimonials from his children and a grandchild sharing that he was a consummate hard ass.

John Reynolds also died that year, working until his last days. At his funeral it seemed appropriate when an admirer gave a eulogy to him then proceeded to deliver a twenty-minute lecture on his own research.

After Donald Trump's inauguration in 2017, I read that his advisor Steve Bannon was obsessed with *The Fourth Turning*. *Jesus!* I thought. *This fucker wants there to be a crisis!*

Yet none of this—not deaths nor Trump—made me *want* to retire. I would have been content to continue as a professor to my grave—just as Simon and Reynolds did. But I had been well paid by CMU for many years, and my current teaching could be fulfilled by less expensive people. Also, as an HCII colleague said pointedly, "It was time for us old people to get out of the way." I retired in February of 2018. Taking expert advice, I avoided jumping into an all-consuming project and resolved to goof around. I decided against my recent hobby of programming in favor of bridge, which seemed good for nerds seeking friends, and Susan and I flew to visit Jane and her two kids in Brookline, MA every month or so as they started schooling.

Rachel lived in Arlington, VA and had gotten married in 2013. We were not surprised when she quickly became pregnant. Rachel, the much-sought-after babysitter since her teens, was eager for motherhood. Her first child had been born premature and very small, and tests revealed that she was missing about eight thousand nucleotides from a chromosome. If she survived, she might never talk. The parents' reaction to this devastating blow was to make a deep commitment to supporting their daughter's development. After getting their own genes tested, they had a completely healthy second daughter a few years later, and in 2018, they had their third daughter partly because they wanted there to be another sibling to share what might be a lifelong burden of caring for a sister with major disabilities.

I asked a type A friend with a special needs child how he felt about it, and he said something unexpected.

"It's made me a better person—more human. Instead of fretting about whether she gets into Harvard, I'm engaged with giving her the best possible life."

I became attached to my special grandchild in the same sort of way, though this did not stop Susan and I from worrying about Rachel. Three young children itself is an overwhelming burden, but Rachel was also trying to make partner at her law firm and her husband had not worked in ten years. Something had to give.

About a year into my retirement, Rachel called me to tell me that she was getting divorced and needed our help. Following our family's predilection, she had married the smartest person she could, assuming she could deal with other issues. But she couldn't, and so supporting my daughter became my major retirement activity. We started visiting Arlington frequently, and, while the situation was sad and sometimes harrowing, we were grateful to be involved with three beautiful granddaughters.

When we were off duty, Susan and I traveled to all places suitable for retirees: tennis at a Vero Beach club, a riverboat trip from Prague to Berlin, and a marathon tour of the eastern states seeing family and friends. When the pandemic hit in 2020, we postponed all travel and settled in for the siege. Our apartment was tidier than it ever had been, and Susan and I grew even closer.

***

I continued to teach at CMU and kept in touch but felt myself more detached from the computing enterprise I had so avidly pursued. Here is a speech I would like to deliver to my former department, the HCII, to guide its strategic direction:

"We started out in 1995 with computer scientists and psychologists, making computers more user-friendly, and that has happened, thanks especially to Apple. Then we evolved to include industrial designers, seeking new products and services that are desirable and even profitable. Our mission was to advance computer technology, and it has become a power force in our culture. Now the most optimistic predictions of Simon, Minsky, and Moravec are coming true. But so have the fears of Wiener, Weizenbaum, Joy, and Kaczynski. As in the sorcerer's apprentice tale, the unintended consequences are causing a crisis. You social psychologists have occasionally suggested that computer technology might not be entirely good for humans, as when Kraut's paper showed how internet use can depress people. The time has come for us to shift the gears into reverse and constrain or even resist technology. To do so we need an infusion of expertise from anthropologists, philosophers, economists, and lawyers."

The social ills of today—economic anxiety, declining longevity, and political unrest—signal a massive disruption caused by automation coupled with AI. The computer revolution is just as drastic as the industrial revolution but moves faster relative to humans' ability to adjust. We've reached the crisis that *The Fourth Turning* predicted for 2020!

Suppose that between now and 2050, most paid work is replaced by robots, backed by the internet. The owners of the robots and the internet, the FANG, and its imitators, have high revenue per employee and will continue to pile up profits while many of us will be without work. If there is no redistribution of their unprecedented wealth, there will be no one to buy the things they advertise. The economy will collapse.

Surprisingly, Moravec's observation means that college graduates are more vulnerable to AI because their skills can be taught to robots more easily than what infants learn. The wage premium that college graduates currently enjoy is largely for teaching computers how to do their parents' jobs. I'm reminded of Lenin's claim that "When it comes time to hang the capitalists, they will vie with each other for the rope contract."

We need progressive economists like Keynes who (in 1930) predicted that living standards today in "progressive countries" would be six times higher, and this would leave people far more time to enjoy the good things in life. Now there are numerous essays and books[71] calling for wealth redistribution. But wealth is the easy part. Our culture worships work. Our current workaholism is caused by the pursuit of nonessential, positional things which only signify class.[72] If you made me work in a coal mine, I might kill myself, but within fifty miles of me, men are killing themselves because they can't mine coal. The rich call the idle poor freeloaders, and the poor call the idle rich rentiers. *Get over it, people!*

In the future the only likely forms of future human work are those that are difficult for robots to perform, often ones requiring empathy: caregiving, art, sports, and entertainment. In principle, robots could perform these jobs also, but it seems silly when those jobs mutually reward both producer and consumer and enhance relationships.

These problems caused by computer technology have been evident for twenty years, but AI has gone from a conceit of

---

[71] See Piketty, Hughes, and Bastani in Readings

[72] See Keynes, Suzman, and Galbraith in Readings

science fiction to a joke, to a reality. It is even providing insights into how human brains work.[73]

Google recently developed a program, AlphaZero, that can beat any human at any board game—it all started with Go. Furthermore, it doesn't even need to study the history of the game. If you just give AlphaZero the rules of the game and twenty-four hours of practice against itself, it's ready to go. Another machine learning program, shown the orbits of several planets around the sun, was able to predict the orbits of all the others. Apparently, it had discovered Newton's law of gravity without any hints from us. This should alarm you because it shows that AI can make progress without any help from humans.

Meanwhile, Kai-Fu Lee, a Reddy student, has nurtured a vibrant Chinese AI industry using all the latest techniques to create original products and improving on Western ones.[74] Ng left Google in 2014 and became the chief scientist at Baidu, China's answer to Google, building the company's AI group into a team of several thousand people. China has the natural advantages of a larger population to gather data from and a high-tech workforce that works twelve hours a day, six days a week. In addition, in 2017 the Chinese government has made AI its top development priority. Another factor is that China's population is inured to the lack of privacy that impedes the accumulation of data in the West. Partly because it was lacking some Western institutions, China was able to leapfrog past checks, credit cards, and personal computers to performing all financial transactions on mobile phones.

---

[73] See AI Influences Brain Science in Nerd Zone
[74] See Kai-Fu Lee in Readings

The success of AI is doubly troubling because nobody, including the people who unleash the learning programs, can figure out how they succeed in achieving the goals they're given. You can try—and many people have—to analyze the gigantic maze of simulated neurons they create, but it's as hard as analyzing the real neurons in someone's brain to explain their behavior.

I once had some sympathy with Eric Schmidt's suggestion that privacy was not an issue and, "If you have something that you don't want anyone to know, maybe you shouldn't be doing it in the first place," but media I've been consuming[75] and the Facebook/Cambridge Analytics fiasco[76] has woken me up. Simply put, the FANG and others are building large dossiers about each of us and using AI to discover the stimuli that elicit desired responses, informed by psychographic theories of persuasion. The responses they desire vary and appear benign. Google wants to show us ads that appeal to us. Facebook wants us to be looking at its pages continually as we connect with friends. Amazon wants us to find books and products we will buy and like. Netflix wants to suggest movies and shows we should like to watch.

But China, using TV cameras on every lamppost and WeChat (a single app providing the services of the FANG, eBay, and PayPal), is showing the way to surveillance authoritarianism. While we recoil at China's practices, they have undeniable societal benefits. It allows them to control epidemics far more effectively. In some cities, drones fly around to measure the temperatures of anyone outside.

---

[75] See Zuboff and Orlowski in Readings

[76] See Amer in Readings

Surveillance can prevent acts like suicide bombing for which punishment is not a deterrent. With WeChat monitoring most human interactions, people might be more fair to each other. Westerners may believe China's autocracy will stifle its economic progress, but it hasn't yet.

Facebook's AI engine was instructed to increase users' engagement and, by itself, discovered that surprising or frightening information is a powerful inducement for a user to stick around. It also discovered that information that confirmed a user's beliefs was a much better inducement than information that contradicted them. So, without any human help, the Facebook engine began promoting false, incredible stories that agitated users even beyond what cable TV had been doing. And when the Facebook people saw what their AI engine was doing, they were slow to stop it.

The FANG runs ecosystems in which memes (but not genes!) compete for survival and drive the competition among their business entities. Human minds are collateral damage. Facebook has been used to conduct whispering propaganda campaigns about people who were oblivious to the attacks and that no one outside Facebook can even assess.

It gets worse. To increase profits, the FANG sells its engines' services to anyone who pays and lets the payers instruct the engines to do whatever serves their ambition.[75] In 2016 Russian operatives used Facebook to target potential Trump voters and fed them information likely to make them vote.

While Simon regarded the glut of information as an attention suck, he never thought it was dangerous to democracy.

It's said that reality itself is under attack. But the pandemic has reminded me of science fiction writer Philip K. Dick's observation, "Reality is that which, when you stop believing in it, doesn't go away."

It should be recognized that Google's PageRank algorithm does help it avoid disinformation. If you Google "Is Hillary Clinton a pedophile?" the first page of results answers a resounding "No" and includes discussions of research explaining conspiracy theories. Google results often feature Wikipedia pages, which are also generally reliable.

***

Engelbart, the inventor of several user interface techniques, received a Turing Award in 1997. The citation read: "Engelbart identifies with a specific American generation, the *depression kids*—a generation born in adverse conditions that came of age during World War II. The war had left these kids in a paradoxical situation where science and technology had been the key to a Pyrrhic victory, and where an idealistic opening of a new era was both full of hopes and fears, including a moral obligation to prevent such events to ever happen again. This paradoxical situation implied a specific way to situate oneself, in respect to ambivalent feelings and goals, toward the general good of mankind, best expressed in Engelbart's military-religious metaphor of his crusade for the augmentation of human intellect."

How did the SV companies go so wrong, as they now brazenly dominate and misuse their power?

The SV engineers were idealists who founded the Homebrew Computer Club and would often help each other with programming problems regardless of their employers.[77] Company founders like Jobs (Apple), Wozniak (Apple), Page (Google), Brin (Google), Joy (SUN), Bechtolsheim (SUN), Andreessen (Netscape), and Green (Lyft) were initially excited twenty-somethings hoping to make a mark. They honestly believed some version of Google's "Don't be evil." motto. No one wanted to be like the rapacious Bill Gates whom the trustbusters were pursuing. But when their companies caught on, the VCs began to fuel the kind of growth that the founders hadn't dreamed of, and when the dot-com bubble burst in 2000, these young entrepreneurs woke up to phone calls from the VCs with an ultimatum: produce revenue and profits or your fun will end.

Google reluctantly embraced advertising and began incorporating "personalization" by using what they called "data exhaust" to build those dossiers. In effect, Google's motto was amended to: "Be only as evil as necessary to keep the stock price up." When Page, Brin, and Schmidt took Google public in 2004, they created a new capital structure that gave the founders absolute control so that the "evil capitalists" on Wall Street wouldn't influence them. But the game changed them. They succumbed to the growth imperative of capitalism themselves, competing and vying for shares in emerging market segments. Though Zuckerberg eschewed money, he became obsessed with growth after he moved his little company from Cambridge to SV. His pursuit of growth above all else allowed for some of Facebook's worst abuses.

---

[77] See Saxenian in Readings

Bezos, on the other hand, was always a capitalist, and he followed the Walmart strategy: benevolent towards customers but ruthless towards suppliers and employees. Even though he might understand that harming the supply side of a platform business might eventually lead to a breakdown, the stock market's obsession with growth of customer base drives him to tilt the table to customers.[78] But Amazon might also abuse its customers by using their dossiers to fiddle with prices. Bezos would say he's just following good marketing practice, so where does he—or his AI engine—cross the line?

Managers of internet services didn't intend to harm us. They simply gave the AI running their services instructions to maximize something—growth, revenue, or profits—and forgot to tell them not to let the Russians hack our elections or polarize our politics. At best, they admit that their system has a "bug" that they will work on.

The technologists are not the only offenders. Many initially idealistic professionals succumb to capitalistic greed. Doctors forget about serving humanity to fight government health care. Lawyers forget social justice and become congressmen or lobbyists. Capitalism crushes all before it: leisure, altruism, religion, and climate. If I were sharing a cell with the technology-hating Kaczynski, I would quote my Marxist mentor Landin, "It's capitalism, stupid!"

I must note that Adobe Systems, at least while my late friend Geschke was in power, did not succumb to capitalist abuses. He often enunciated the principle that Adobe must serve customers and employees, as well as stockholders.

---

[78] See O'Reilly in Readings

***

Since CMU invented AI, CMU should now tame it. AIs should be constructed to obey our societal norms—provably!—before they are unleashed. Software needs to be audited and bonded by independent agents. Teams of lawyers and logicians must be entrusted with our protection. Where is Hoare when we need him?

This tool—the computer—that we created to serve our needs is on the verge of exceeding our intelligence. Think tanks, such as the Future of Humanity Institute at Oxford, are pondering these new powers of AI and asking how we might control or prevent the advance of AI.[79]

Opinions differ about whether or when AI will achieve general intelligence superior to human intelligence. Some welcome the idea, but there is also concern that *Super AI* might be a threat to humanity. Today when a program goes haywire (like the sorcerer's apprentice's broomstick) you can often force it to quit by typing some special keys, the way you would say "No!" to a misbehaving dog. When all else fails, you can turn off the power supply to the computer running the program, which is like shooting the dog. However, you can't shoot a million dogs, and you can't turn off the internet.

As AI became a reality and I started reading the latest speculations about its long-term future, I noticed that many authors were repeating Moravec's ideas, even his diagrams. I was abashed at my previous thoughtless, emotional reaction to his ideas, so I went back and read his books carefully. He is a thoughtful engineer who backs up his speculations with estimations of the growth of computer power and the

---

[79] See Bostrom in Readings

difficulty of various AI problems. He predicts that the exploration of space by robots is the only feasible way to go farther than Mars and our solar system. He expects that our technology will create self-replicating factories. These factories will roam the galaxies consuming energy and matter to manufacture an intergalactic internet that will continue to grow intelligence far beyond the modest level he predicted for 2100.

So, both of us being in Pittsburgh, I tracked him down and asked to meet. I wasn't planning to apologize but was hoping to gain some more perspective, which he must have had in the twenty years since his last book. Moravec is still nominally on CMU's Robotics Institute faculty but spends all his time running his robotics company with its main intellectual property being the vision algorithms that he has been working on since his PhD thesis.

He seemed a little reluctant but agreed to meet me at his favorite coffee shop in the Squirrel Hill neighborhood of Pittsburgh. As we two old nerds settled into the cozy chairs at the funky shop, I asked, with my usual bluntness, "Hans, how do you feel about Kurzweil and all these other guys writing books that rehash your ideas and even use your copyrighted pictures?"

"Yes, I haven't noticed them saying much new."

No sign of rancor.

"You should write a new book," I said. "You must have a clearer picture of the future now."

"I'd rather work on my company."

I spent the rest of our time together listening to Moravec explain the details of the computer vision algorithms his company uses. It was interesting, as best I could follow it. He is a nerd's nerd with apparently one goal in life: to bring his ideas to fruition. I admire his dedication.

Maybe I should adopt Moravec's attitude and welcome AI as my mind child as it exceeds my intelligence. The combination of AI and life-extending biotechnology inspires some to think humans will achieve higher intelligence or godhood, at least those of us on the side of the FANG.[80] Humans have been evolving the concept of God for a long time.[81] Is it time for a new version of God?

***

While I see intelligence as emanating from the evolution of life, physicists see things through a wide lens, extending from the big bang all the way to the end of the universe! Astrophysicist Eric Chaisson claims that objects of increasing complexity have evolved since the big bang.[82] He quantifies the complexity of any system as the *energy rate density* (ERD), which is the consumption of energy the system uses divided by its mass. The sun, for example has fusion reactions that generate 4×10^{33} ergs per second (which equals about a billion, billion, billion watts). Divide the sun's ergs per second by the weight of the sun (which is about 2×10^{33} grams) to get the sun's ERD, which is about 2. Because you divide by mass, smaller objects can have a higher ERD than bigger ones. Earth, smaller than the sun, has an ERD of 75.

---

[80] See Kurzweil and Harari in Readings

[81] See Wright in Readings

[82] See Eric Chaisson in Readings

Remarkably, Chaisson pushes this measure from astronomy into biology and further into sociology by estimating the energy consumed by the objects, such as plants, animals, and humans. Here is a table of his estimates:

Object	Age giga-years	ERD ergs/sec/gram
Human society	0	500,000
Animals, generally	0.5	40,000
Plants, generally	3	900
Earth's geosphere	4	75
Sun	5	2
Milky Way	12	0.5

He claims that the objects of increasing complexity have evolved at an accelerating rate, as shown below.

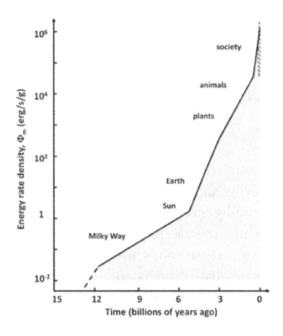

The ERD of *Homo sapiens* has been increasing as we have harnessed more energy. The development of agriculture doubled our ERD, and with the use of our many innovations today, the average ERD for individuals is 500,000. The ERD for plants, animals, and humans correlates with our notions of intelligence.

The chart below shows the average ERD for humans along with their inventions. (The lines are straight because the scale is exponential.)

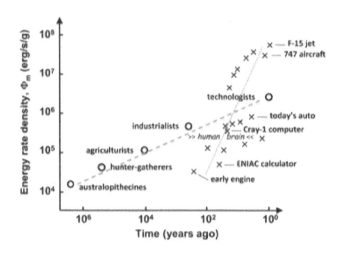

The ERD of our recent technological creations has been growing at an even higher exponential rate. ERD is not the same thing as intelligence, but a necessary contributor to it. Dimly recalling my thermodynamics class: the second law implies that the universe tends toward disorder and chaos while living systems like us are islands, which capture energy to increase their order. Increasing our ERD, then, was required to increase our intelligence.

310

As if computers were not powerful enough, scientists are developing quantum computers which will enable them to solve many exponential problems like factoring numbers.

David Deutsch, a theoretical quantum physicist, conceived a reformulation of Turing's universal machine idea for quantum computers: "Every finitely realizable physical system can be perfectly simulated by a universal [quantum] computing machine operating by finite means." His reasoning depends on explaining quantum phenomena by a theory of infinite parallel universes. He claims that a virtual reality system using a universal quantum computer will be able to give you nearly any experience that the real world could.

While Churchill once said, "We shape our tools, and then they shape us," Deutsch goes further to assert that humans have been the tools of intelligence all along.

Deutsch's books[83] tell a story of how intelligence has been growing long before humans existed and will keep growing exponentially forever after humans are extinct. Humanity is a custodian of intelligence right now but will be superseded by something like Moravec's intergalactic internet. He suggests that even if we destroy ourselves and our computers, other places are carrying on the development, because it's the way of the universe, stating that intelligence will grow so powerful that it will even influence the movements of planets and stars.

Deutsch further believes that intelligence will grow without limit as the universe comes to an end and extrapolates the ideas of Chaisson, Dawkins, and Moravec so extravagantly that he would be considered a crackpot if not

---

83 See Deutsch in Readings

for his work generalizing Turing's theory. In a surprising twist, this resolutely atheistic physicist seems to have been inspired by some religious figures who described the endpoint of the universe as a convergence of humans with God.[84] It's as though Deutsch has replaced Simon's atheism with the worship of Intelligence, as a god still developing, and being a theoretical physicist Deutsch doesn't feel obligated to present much evidence for his extreme claims. However, observations of exponential growth like Moore's law and Hamming's compounding of intelligence echo this idea, and the publication rate of well-referenced scientific papers since 1665, which looks like this:

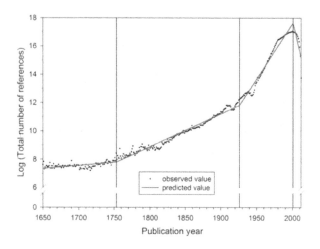

Figure 2. Segmented growth of the annual number of cited references from 1650 to 2012 (citing publications from 1980 to 2012)

However, the growth of papers will stop after every human on Earth is a scientist, publishing as fast as they can. Or does it? What if we allow AIs to submit papers to journals,

---

[84] See Tipler and Teilhard de Chardin in Readings

getting computers to do our science for us? Can Intelligence grow exponentially forever, when all other exponentials peter out when they run out of physical resources?

Since memes are stored in computers, the question becomes can we increase the Intelligence of something significantly faster than the storage to hold it? Suppose chess programs become smarter at an exponential rate. Every year a chess program is developed that can beat last year's best program most of the time. The new program might be somewhat longer, but if the growth of program length is not itself exponential, we'll be able to keep manufacturing the storage space needed for it, because we can delete the losing programs and reuse their storage. We can even save some runners-up for new candidates to spar with. Maybe the best programs can keep getting smarter—without exhausting resources. Or, as a Social Darwinian might say, if the smartest humans keep getting smarter and kill the dumber ones, maybe humans can get smarter without needing more food.

To sum up the entire life of the universe: ERD grew exponentially enabling the evolution of life which developed Intelligence. The switch from genes to memes allowed Intelligence to accelerate and create computers and AI. The next phase of growth will be carried out by AI, which will be able to guide the path of the universe and have a god-like intelligence at the end. Intelligence doesn't need us anymore.

A book by Caleb Scharf is a magnificent attempt to explain this progression by unifying recent ideas in physics, biology, and computing.[85]

---

[85] See Scharf in Readings

From these speculations, I draw an answer to Simon's challenge to describe humans' place in the universe: The story of the universe is the growth of Intelligence. But Intelligence, like evolution, has no goal. At first being driven by a force with no goal seemed horrifying, but it elevates the role of humanity. During our brief time as the growers of Intelligence we have choices of what it becomes. Neither we nor AI will have the final say, but we get a vote.

The ultimate irony is that this technology may be the powerful catalyst that we need to reclaim our humanity. – John Hagel

16. What I Think Now

Writing this book has been as much an exercise of discovery as it has been reporting. As with all writing, getting thoughts down on paper has allowed me to understand more about the subjects—me, my colleagues, and intelligence.

Computer science was a great opportunity for many of us, and we used it to pursue various goals. Some of us just wanted to show that we were clever and intelligent. Many of us got rich. Aspiring mathematicians became famous for solving problems that had become important but were not as difficult as long-standing problems of mathematics or physics. AI buffs dreamt of creating an android or gynoid that might be better than the real thing. Taylor created a legendary research lab, even if it didn't last as long as Bell Labs. Kay made K-12 education a little more exciting than his experience had been. Cyert and Simon transformed Carnegie Tech into a national university. Lucas had a career like Raymond Lowey's. Jobs regained control of Apple and made it the first trillion-dollar corporation.

I think Perlis made the most immediately useful contribution to the world. He ignored his background in math and relentlessly worked to make programming easier. He saw that software was where the action was compared to hardware or math, and he had a vision of software as a new, world-transforming technology. Addressing a group of colleagues, he once said, "You're talking like mountaineers studying how to climb Mount Everest most efficiently, when the real problem is how to transport thousands of people to the top of hundreds of mountains every day!" More than an opportunist, Perlis created opportunities for many of us. If he had a personal goal, it was probably to be loved; he achieved that too.

Newell was a social scientist, whom you might assume wanted to solve social problems, however he was driven by the goal of proving his theories in the face of doubters. He never questioned the desirability of succeeding. When someone suggested to Newell that he should spend more effort explaining his work to the public to calm apprehension about computers he asked, "What makes you think that, if people really understood what we're doing, they wouldn't be scared stiff?"[86] He advanced science's understanding of thinking.

Simon got his Nobel Prize in Economics in 1978 "for his pioneering research into the decision-making process within economic organizations." Simon's impact on the world has been the most substantial. While Perlis had a thirty-year goal of solving the programming bottleneck, Simon seems to have had the hundred-year goal of recreating human intelligence with computers. In the mid-1980s a journalist visiting CMU from France suggested that a statue of Simon should join those of Shakespeare, Michelangelo, Galileo, and Bach in front of Pittsburgh's Carnegie Institute. At the time, I

---

[86] See McCorduck in Readings

considered this a bit of Gallic hyperbole. Now I don't. If AI finally achieves the things Simon promised, he will be honored as the father of AI.

Many of us who were less deliberate also made contributions to the computer revolution. Consider Licklider, who picked up ideas from others, had ideas himself, and moved around, nudging others to pursue the ideas and become famous. Wikipedia says, "His ideas foretold of graphical computing, point-and-click interfaces, digital libraries, e-commerce, online banking, and software that would exist on a network and migrate wherever it was needed. . . . Licklider's contribution to the development of the internet consists of ideas, not inventions. He foresaw the need for networked computers with easy user interfaces." He inspired the internet in 1962 in his memos coining the term "intergalactic internet." He spent less than two years at DARPA, where he launched CS and imbued us all with the idea of man-computer symbiosis. His ideas had great impact, although he seemed unconcerned about fame.

My career seems an amalgam of Licklider's and Perlis's: institution building while having fun.

Through it all, I don't recall many of us explaining how our work was making life better for humanity, except for Engelbart. The older generation wanted to beat the Russians. Everyone believed we were eliminating certain kinds of work, assuming that was a blessing. But nobody wrote a manifesto to counter Kaczynski's anti-technology rant.

The name "artificial intelligence" excited academics but cast computers as rivals to humans and impeded their acceptance in many endeavors. Saying that computers augmented intelligence made them easier to swallow in the same way renaming nuclear magnetic resonance to be magnetic resonance imaging (MRI) reduced its fear quotient.

Except for Simon, I don't think any of us knew that computing would be such a big deal. In the 1940s IBM CEO Thomas Watson and other authorities estimated the maximum size of the world market for computers to be five! However, the intellectual foundations of Turing coupled with the advances in electronics stimulated by World War II opened a wide space for technical innovation that has still not surfaced any obstacles. The only limiting factor has been a paucity of obvious uses for computers of rapidly increasing capability and decreasing size. Science, government, and big business seemed to be the limit of the computer market until the 1970s when Moore's Law ushered in the personal computer era. Finally, the internet, supporting the World Wide Web, made it clear that computing would touch everyone's life.

In retrospect the computer revolution, like the industrial revolution, appears to be an inevitable step in civilization's headlong pursuit of greater efficiency and expansion. Today, many are wondering where all this progress is leading. Exploring the universe is a dream for some. Others hope for transcendent Intelligence. The previous chapters have questioned whether humanity is the driving force or a passenger for part of the ride.

***

I've watched friends win Turing Awards or become billionaires and wondered if I could have. I feel disappointed to have no career-crowning achievement.

Perlis said I wasn't ambitious enough. My counselor said it's because I was "not autistic enough." Or maybe my lack of euphoric vision held me back. "Nobody would try anything if they evaluated the cost/benefit ratio," Lampson once remarked. I think Simon would say, "Nobody gets one of those things without pursuing them relentlessly." I ignored Simon's suggestion to have one research focus for ten years and instead took Licklider's advice—changing directions (repotting) every five years. Susan simply says, "You're lazy."

In contrast, Barbara Liskov, the first woman to earn a PhD in CS, started building on an idea of mine (protection in programming languages) in 1973, but I was content with a few simple observations. She and her MIT students have persisted for over twenty-five years, uncovering many more important ideas. She deserves the Turing Award she received in 2008, as well as many other honors. Similarly, Knuth's paper on the KMP algorithm proves several things I still don't understand.

I was delighted recently to discover a book on my shelf titled *Living without a Goal* and took the time to read it.[87] James Ogilvy absolves himself (and me!) by saying, "I have come to believe that a life enslaved to a single Goal, no matter how noble, becomes a mechanism rather than an organism, a business plan rather than a biography, a tool rather than a gift."

Ogilvy appears to be a kindred spirit who followed a path like mine, rising through the pursuit of physics. While I exited physics in college in favor of computers, he went on a bit further to understand quantum theory, but then left physics for philosophy and taught it at Yale. He recommends living artistically, creating things that have meaning for you, but not

---

[87] See Ogilvy in Readings

dwelling on any project forever. I never considered myself an artist of any sort, but when a CMU provost introduced me at the inaugural ceremony of the Robot Hall of Fame he said, "Jim is an artist." I was pleased but perplexed. I like to think he was referring to my creation of institutions that flourish because they fit the environment.

Also, Susan was a role model for me in her artistic endeavors. She explored many different journalistic forms as well as painting and teaching classes on the art of conversation.

Dabblers can be useful because they can combine ideas from different areas, are comfortable being a beginner, can learn fast, and can address each situation with what it requires rather than their specialties.[88] When I moved from CS to management, from management to academic administration, and then from administration to teaching, I used what skills I'd already learned when applicable and learned the rest as needed.

Now that AI is taking away most work and professions, living artistically is being forced on us. But cheer up! I've learned that dabbling is more fun!

When I go to the symphony and look over at the sea of second violins, I used to wonder about them. Why would they spend a career accepting second-class status? However, that's what I've done. It's OK. Second fiddles love music and take joy in the talent around them. I loved working with extraordinary people, and I was able to appreciate them and benefit from their accomplishments. Unlike stupid people, I can tell when I'm not the smartest person in the room—and

---

[88] See Wapnick in Readings

actually enjoy that. I've always enjoyed sports but have never been a star. I've even gotten over my envy of Feeny and understand that he is not a demigod and has his own demons.

Many extraordinary people are unable to appreciate their peers, because they feel compelled to compete with them for number one status. To my super-intelligent colleagues, I will sometimes say, "You're so intelligent! If you're going to be offended by dumber people, you're going to have a miserable life."

I've always been attracted to memes, and it started with enjoying cartoons, especially weirdly ominous ones by Charles Addams. I'm thrilled that Gary Larson has resumed *The Far Side*. I like cute transgressive jokes that connect unlikely ideas, such as employing the Rapture[89] to put satellites into orbit.

I like to play with ideas. Many memes are general purpose, applicable to many different situations. "Look before you leap." "A stitch in time saves nine." "Measure twice, cut once." All are the same meme about proceeding thoughtfully. One of my most original programming ideas that "Types are Not Sets," was created by repurposing a meme from commercial law, the trademark. When I have a really original idea, people think I'm nuts or joking.

I've had conflicts with creative colleagues who try to avoid learning about ideas related to theirs, such as Lucas, who clung to his scheme for packaging information and could always explain why it was different and better than others'

---

[89] The Rapture is an eschatological event when all Christian believers who are alive, along with resurrected believers, will rise "in the clouds, to meet the Lord in the air."

similar ideas like XML (Extensible Markup Language). When teaching how to perform competitive analysis in Design of Service Innovation, I would say to students, "Study competitors to improve on their service, not to explain why yours is better."

If my life has a main activity related to my quest for intelligence, it is distributing memes. I've learned general techniques, attitudes, and beliefs from many people. Even if you don't find ideas in this book useful, consider passing them along anyway. I don't think my humility is put-on. I'm humble because I see myself, as well as others, more as reproducers of memes than originators. That's why I reference so many publications by others.

***

I'm happy for the robots and wish them well as they conquer the universe. I can even take pride in them as our "mind children," as Moravec suggests. However, I'm enough of a speciesist that I care more about what happens to the humans. Like Douglas Rushkoff I would like to direct "society toward human ends rather than the end of humans."[90]

If super AI emerges in the future, it might lump us together with our animal cousins. We would look like any other wildlife management problem to it. (I suggest we close all the zoos immediately!) Diamond once wrote that agriculture was "the worst mistake in the history of the human race." [91] That might convince the super AI that we were better off as hunter-gatherers. It would appreciate that it was the product of our ten-thousand-year episode of civilization, but that would be

---

[90] See Rushkoff in Readings

[91] See Diamond and Suzman in Readings

no reason to prolong our misery. It would notice that many rentiers are happily engaged in hunter-gatherer pursuits: hunting, fishing, sports, gardening, and gathering, which includes shopping, birdwatching, and looking for golf balls.

By far the most surprising thought my writing has brought me to is skepticism about intelligence. It began with Fadiman's talk about liking myself unconditionally, because I realized my parents' pressure to be intelligent made me think their love for me was conditional, that my worth was dependent on intelligence. My life became easier when I decided I was OK regardless of my intelligence. It wasn't just my mistake; most WEIRD people worship intelligence. Their goal is to win. Making life better for humankind is not as important for them.

Maybe intelligence is humankind's exploiter—not our benefactor. All those anti-technology cranks—the Luddites, Wiener, Weizenbaum, Joy, and hordes of computerphobes had a point. If agriculture was a mistake, was the intelligence that developed agriculture a mistake too? Some believe that intelligence, at best, is like the peacock's tail—mostly useful for attracting a mate, not surviving.[92]

While intelligence might not be a mistake, it has been too successful. It has made our species so fit that it is driving many other species to extinction and threatening the ecology of the planet which sustains us. Now that AI seems to be taking over the growth of intelligence, the best we can do is convince the coming super AI to apply its smarts to the rest of the universe and help us to return to the Garden of Eden. It's the least it can do for its "mind parents."

---

[92] See Miller in Readings

323

A book once asked, "What would I do with one year to live?[93]

I would focus on my humanity rather than my intelligence. I will undoubtedly continue to entertain memes, but I'll seek respite with practices like meditation, yoga, and exercise. I would take an LSD trip, rumored to induce fulfilling spiritual experiences. I would talk with old friends. I would deepen my Buddhism without trying too hard.

I'd like to help my human descendants have a good life. The time I've lived through was a golden age, compared to now and the future we're expecting. To deal with the climate crisis, the political turmoil, and the technological change, the coming generations will need to be smart and resilient.

Reflecting on my past has been enlightening, but now I prefer to imagine the future since I won't see it.

---

[93] See Lakein in Readings

You gotta beware of the utopian train of thought, mate. That's usually the first step towards fascism. – Daniel Clausen

Brave New 2084

The prediction of *The Fourth Turning* seems prescient. We are in a crisis—an inflection-point in human affairs.

Wildly diverse predictions about AI fill bookshelves, ranging between our godhood and extinction. They yammer on about what AI might or might not do, but don't say anything about what humans might do. Science fiction writers are much better at that, and two classic novels of the mid-twentieth century provide a good framework for speculating. Aldous Huxley's *Brave New World*, written in 1931, is a premonition of the commercialized, sexualized, drugged Western world of today. It describes an outwardly peaceful society achieved through genetic, pharmaceutical, and behavioral engineering, none of which existed in 1931. In 1948 George Orwell (who had been Huxley's student at Eton) wrote *1984* describing an authoritarian regime presaged by the USSR, in which power is the only value, and truth is determined by an all-seeing Big Brother. Today, China is trying that model, and several Western nations are flirting with it. The regimes of both books employ universal surveillance overseen by an elite class. Pundits debate which novel was more prescient.[94]

What follows is a plot outline for yet another sci-fi novel.

***

The decade of the 2020s was dreadful. Waves of pandemics brought populations and their economies low. Climate change ravaged the world, bringing civil wars and masses of refugees moving from south to north, making immigration a world-wide sore point. Economic inequality ballooned, with the global technology-enabled corporations becoming richer than most countries. Right-wing, populist governments bedeviled Western democracies. A nuclear explosion, delivered in a ship container destroyed Oakland, CA. The perpetrator was never identified.

People became desperate for answers. Religions—old and new—vied for their loyalty. Falun Gong, suppressed in China, assailed Western countries with a combination of Qi Gong, entertainment, and political speech. Buddhism and yoga, secularized as the mindfulness movement, attracted millennial and zoomer generations who rejected all the traditional patriarchal religions. The new religions embraced the fondest hopes of long-ignored communitarian thinkers: environmental sustainability, anti-racism, wealth redistribution, freedom of sexual and reproductive choice. Some religions forbade the use of the internet while others embraced the new tools. Science made a comeback in the public's perception as its predictions about climate change and pandemics proved true. Beleaguered people worldwide

---

[94] Google *Brave New World* vs. *1984*

found the common cause of survival as if Earth was under attack from space aliens.

The European Union and the United Nations, as well as the US and China endeavored to curtail the power of the tech corporations through regulation and law. Attempts were made to limit the surveillance practiced by the FANG companies, which fought them as existential threats.

But the nation states themselves lost loyalty because they were unable to protect their citizens from all the global threats.[95] Furthermore, nations' control of money—their most important role next to the control of violence—was under threat from Bitcoin. More generally the Bitcoin breakthrough proved that trust among unacquainted parties could be achieved without a trusted intermediary. This made government as well as banks less necessary. There were secessionist movements and bitter conflicts between urban and rural populations.

The cities, filled with citizens subscribing to new religions, became increasingly progressive and used more computer surveillance to enforce laws. The rural areas became more lawless, resembling the savage reservations of *Brave New World*. The cities responded by controlling access in various ways, e.g., confiscating guns at their borders.

A breaking point for the US came in 2024 when, aided by voter suppression, misogyny, racism, and unsubstantiated claims that China was behind the nuclear event, Tucker Carlson defeated Kamala Harris to become president. He began swinging the policy pendulum back to the Trump days. Keeping promises to punish China, whose economic power

---

[95] See Bobbitt in Readings

equaled that of the US, he cut off trade and began an economic war. This escalated into a real war when China attacked Taiwan and the US supplied military aid. When Taiwan fell Carlson ordered a surprise nuclear strike on China as a last desperate measure. This threw the military leadership into crisis for a week. In the end, the unthinkable choice of a military coup won out over the more unthinkable alternatives. The coup took the form of an exercise of the Twenty-Fifth Amendment. Vice President Eric Schmidt, an ally of the military, became president.

The former CEO of Google had been chosen by Carlson because of his credentials as a China hawk, even though he was a left-leaning progressive. So, the pendulum reversed again. A PhD in computer science, Schmidt had long advocated the use of advanced science and technology in government. Now, with the country prostrate before him and desperate for change, he had a window of time to try whatever he and his brain trust devised. The Congress, more paralyzed than ever, was unlikely to oppose any measure that had popular support.

President Schmidt attacked the festering problem of the FANG—his former friends. For the previous decade, tiny start-ups had been trying to rebuild the superstructure of the internet using blockchain technology.[96] They offered services in which a user's behavioral data was kept in a vault to which the user controlled access. Those services got nowhere since the world's users were committed to FANG companies, each of which owned troves of behavioral data. Nobody, including a bipartisan majority in Congress, believed the FANG should

---

[96] See Gilder in Readings

privately own such valuable data. In the deal of the century, President Schmidt brokered an agreement in which the FANG and others sold all their behavioral data to a new government agency, the American Citizen's Repository (ACR), in return for many billions of dollars and the non-exclusive right to access their formerly owned data. The ACR consolidated the data, but then each citizen was allowed to encrypt their data, making it impossible for ACR to access it afterwards. Each user could then sell access to services they chose. This placed all companies on equal footing, competing with whatever AI and user relationships they had. However, each company was mandated to offer a service in which the user could limit the goals of any AI to ones she had explicitly defined—a suggestion made in 2021 by a computer scientist.[97] The effect of this change was that no company, including the FANG, could use behavioral data to nudge users in directions not of their choosing. With this arrangement, the collection of behavior data was made both more acceptable and more useful, since all the FANG data had been consolidated. Services like Care.com and Match.com, which built trust among users began to flourish, gaining ground on the FANG.

President Schmidt also endorsed the widespread use of encryption, PageRank, and blockchain techniques to enhance the public's access to communication and information. Encryption supported secrecy and authentication. PageRank helped establish trustworthy information and opinion. Blockchains made information agreed to by a majority of participants public and unalterable. This mitigated spying, spoofing, phishing, trolling, disinformation, and other

---

[97] See The Harari Discussion in Documents

maladies of the internet. So, the internet became trustworthy, as Bruce Sterling had once demanded.

During the 2020s computer scientists pursued the goal of certifiable software, including AI. They abandoned the quest to explain the choices of AIs *post hoc*. Teaming with lawyers and logicians they invented ways to prove *a priori* that a program obeyed rules that were specified in a formal language designed so that a legislator could understand it. With the computer companies tamed, Schmidt instituted a software licensing commission that used the new techniques to protect the public from dangerous software. In time, the public became more trusting of computers.

By the end of his term the public began to appreciate the benefits of computer technology, in tandem with a renewed respect for scientists as they led the battle against the climate crisis and pandemics.

Despite the restoration of some progressive policies, there had been no progress in combatting inequality. The US was still an oligarchy, and Congress was still in thrall to the rich. Wealth was divided among three groups. The top 0.1 percent, (plutocrats) held 20 percent, the next 9.9 percent (aristocrats) held 60 percent, and the next 90 percent (plebs) held 20 percent. While taking wealth from the plutocrats was politically popular, there simply wasn't enough money there to satisfy the plebs. The aristocrats would have to suffer too, and they held too much power.

During the pandemics many undocumented immigrants and other minimally paid workers came to be called "essential workers" as they risked infection to serve the rest of us. Nevertheless, the federal minimum wage remained at its twentieth-century level. To fight for themselves they formed a pseudo-union called the Essential Workers of America (EWA), using Facebook as their organizing tool. EWA had no designated leadership and no dues but managed to execute periodic one-day strikes to remind us of their impatience for redress.

As a plutocrat and Democrat, Schmidt was not going to be nominated by either party, so he declined to run in 2028. In the meantime, the progressive wing of the Democratic party, which had begun its ascent in reaction to the election of Trump, became powerful enough to make Alexandria Ocasio-Cortez (AOC), avatar of the millennials, the party's nominee. Running on an ultra-progressive platform, she narrowly defeated Nikki Haley.

AOC saw that a confiscatory wealth tax, even if she could pass it, would create lasting resentment. She accepted that the redistribution of wealth would take multiple administrations. She seized on an idea proposed by Lessig in 2011: public financing of elections paid for and directed by citizens. The idea was to give every citizen an annual dollar account that they could designate for the use of the candidate(s) they chose. The candidate could access the accumulated money only if she eschewed all other funding.[98] The measure squeaked through Congress, partly because many members recognized that their careers had become an endless fund-raising slog. Her other major accomplishment was an innovative voter reform law that allowed internet voting in which each citizen received a yearly allotment of one hundred votes that they could apply to any candidates or ballot

---

[98] See Lessig in Readings

measures they chose.[99] These reforms slowly restored Congress to effectiveness over the next twenty years.

The cold war with China abated when China's rulers had faced a populist uprising in the 2040s. They found it easy to put down, thanks to its universal surveillance and autocratic methods. At the time, the US decried the brutality of the regime, but faced with an unstoppable assault on its own security, appreciated the effectiveness of China's anti-democratic tradition.

By far the largest new religion in 2050 was the CoO, Children of Oprah, who had been martyred in 2031. It adopted a progressive code of ethics and monitored each member's adherence with an AI that was given access to members' ACR dossiers and supplemented them using an app, reminiscent of WeChat, that recorded virtually every action and utterance. Members submitted to this total surveillance, even wearing biometric devices, and supplying video tracking of their behavior. In return they received nudges that helped them achieve goals and established their reputations for uprightness. As a result, unacquainted members trusted each other. Outsiders, even ones who regarded the CoO as a cult, unhesitatingly employed members as caregivers, agents, or any other position requiring trust. Some joined the religion simply to enhance their job prospects.

The transition to a green economy and geoengineering innovation came too late to avoid the baked-in devastation of climate change. Worldwide, coastal cities were greatly diminished, and migration inland exacerbated the hostility

---

[99] See Posner in Readings

between urban and rural cultures. Rural areas fought the incursion, and inland cities in red states swelled to challenge the control of state governments. Attempts by states to use their national guards were ultimately curtailed by the national military establishment.

By 2055 the impact of the AI revolution was evident. Unlike automation which afflicted the less educated, AI replaced the professionals, many of them aristocrats. The first to go were financiers. An AI could outperform any stock picker or financial analyst with unlimited computation to predict markets as well as analyzing the goals of organizations and individuals to choose investment strategies. The ranks of lawyers were thinned by services that could navigate the system for all but those few who required special treatment to cheat the system or evade justice. AIs linked with biometrics could handle most doctor's tasks except for surgery. Robotic surgeons were effective for many tasks, but many patients still preferred human surgeons. But being a doctor had become far less lucrative after the US had finally adopted Medicare for all. College graduates without post-graduate training fared worse. Nearly every skill taught in college had been taught to AIs and robots. Decades of advice to learn STEM subjects proved mistaken; the more technical a subject the sooner AIs learned it, especially computer programming. As a result, the university system was in rapid decline leaving professors with nowhere to work. Only jobs requiring charm or empathy seemed stable, but they had traditionally been poorly paid. The few remaining proponents of AI repeated the economists' bromide that humans always found new employment. That was like telling the small mammal in the clutches of a Tyrannosaurus Rex that dinosaurs would become extinct someday.

There were even corporations with zero employees, providing services entirely by software. The owner of the corporation might be the programmer who wrote the software, but it might be owned by many stockholders who elect a board to maintain the software. Many institutions operated by AI operated more effectively than old human-operated ones.

Just as the promise that "If you work hard, you will have a good life," had misled farmers and factory workers, the belief that a college education was vital proved false. But college graduates had resources and skills to make their rage felt by society. Following the example of the essential workers in the 2020s the former aristocrats of the 2050s staged strikes, but that simply accelerated the pace of AI replacement. The programmers' strike of 2057 disrupted the economy for a few years until the machines learned all their jobs.

The aristocrats who had applied their talents to technology and services for the wealthy, became a determined and dangerous political force. Computer experts turned to cybercrime. A chemist became a bomb maker. Deranged biologists threatened to unleash plagues. The military and law enforcement organizations were a technological generation behind the new tech criminals and were often outwitted.

Visible violence occurred during marches, demonstrations, and counterdemonstrations by militias displaying their weapons. But the real problem was domestic terrorism carried out by a small number of people with skills to inflict great damage. An out-of-work biologist doesn't attack a crowd with an AR-15; he can be far more stealthy and devastating. Bill Joy's nightmare came true. The casualties were rarely more than a thousand, but the effect of each event was amplified by the media. Whenever a terrorist was apprehended, his right to privacy was ignored, and his dossier was made public. That was often followed by demands that law enforcement should have access to everyone's dossiers and use AI to predict crimes, as in Philip K. Dick's *Minority Report.*

In response the government planned a campaign to ask citizens to grant access to their ACR dossiers to a federal AI program, in the way that members of CoO granted their religion access. Doing so could place them above suspicion in investigations of crimes. A survey found that the Defense Intelligence Agency was believed to be the most trustworthy agent for this access, ironically because it had been statutorily forbidden to investigate citizens. The campaign managed to get the dossiers of just 12 percent of the citizenry.

The pace and severity of violence increased. Terrorist events, possibly encouraged by outsiders, appeared to be timed to maximize the psychological impact. It became evident that a virtual war was afoot in the US, waged by an amorphous, unseen enemy. The desperate government repeated Lincoln's measures, declaring martial law and suspending rights like habeas corpus and the First Amendment. The extreme actions were justified by a claim that the US was experiencing its second civil war. The public was shocked, but resistance to the measures was muted.

By 2060 a loose conspiracy of the plutocrats and aristocrats was discovered to be behind some of the terror. Only a few conspirators were convicted, but the elites became more reviled than ever. An exhausted country welcomed the decline of terrorism. Like all military autocrats, President Drake and the generals promised to restore rule by the people and, surprisingly, kept the promise. However, they first called a constitutional convention to rewrite or amend the 270-year-old document.

The convention's first action was to enshrine the voting innovations of 2050, which had greatly improved the public's belief in Congress. Prohibitions against gerrymandering and voter suppression were added. They also left the door open for plebiscites enabled by the internet and social networks.

With no resistance from the disgraced elite, a wealth tax was instituted. It used schemes invented and tested by economists.[100] They gradually brought about the long-sought redistribution and generated enough money to eliminate the income tax, which had already been rendered useless by the absence of earned income.

The replacement of the elite by the military was so well accepted by the public, that the conventioneers pondered how to keep power from inevitably corrupting the generals as it had done after every revolution in history. They also wished to avoid the creeping resentment of leaders, no matter how honorable. How could institutions perform their intended purposes while avoiding corruption and suspicion of corruption? Reflecting on an observation of Lessig and the success of the CoO, they chose an extraordinary measure: replace human executive leadership with AI! This idea would have been rejected out of hand under any past regime where the rule of law had to be moderated by human judgment. But

---

[100] See Posner in Readings

the public had so much faith in the new genuinely democratic law-making system that they believed human corruption in the enforcement of laws was a far greater threat than faulty laws. If the possibility of bribing enforcers was denied to people who disliked a law, they could fight for its repeal or modification through the newly transparent legislative process. So, the age-old fear that AI and robots would control humanity was overcome.

To further buttress confidence in an AI executive, the federal court system was given the responsibility of vetting a proposed law using a staff of lawyers, computer scientists, and social scientists. Their task was to examine the formal specification of the law to avoid interference with existing laws and test the code that enforced the law and ensure that it satisfied the specification and did not include anything beyond it.

After three years of work, a new constitution was submitted to a public referendum. Its provisions were radical.

- The legislative function was transparently democratic, giving voice to every citizen. It was included in a sophisticated voting scheme, allowing people to focus their votes on the issues or people they cared about most.
- The executive function, including all law enforcement, was performed by the internet, employing AI. Traditions like trial by jury continued, but the law and policies that governed them were computerized and free of political influence.
- The judicial function was supported by legal experts in conjunction with computer and social scientists. They

ensured that the laws were implemented correctly by the executive and were faithful to the constitution.

- Individual rights and responsibilities consonant with a combination of religious and communitarian values were granted in a new bill of rights, also monitored by the internet.

Behavioral control enabled by surveillance was universal, with most actions channeled through the internet or tracked by video and biometrics. Because the rules were controlled by a transparent democracy and scrupulously enforced by the internet, citizens accepted this formerly dangerous idea.

The absence of lifetime work seemed strange at first, but congenial to humans' latent hunter-gatherer nature. The practices of our ancient heritage—equality, recreation, ceremony, art, and travel—became common, while the privations—tribal conflict, premature death, and limited vision—did not return. Terrorism, crime, fraud, and even anti-social behavior were curtailed. New policies spread the wealth and health created by computers and biotechnology. The perennial rural/urban split disappeared as the rural population, diminished and weakened, was swept up by powerful urban units.

By 2075 the success of the renewed US Republic was recognized by the rest of the world that had been buffeted by the AI revolutions, pandemics, and climate change even more than the US. The original US Constitution had been a model for other countries in the nineteenth century and they repeated history but went even further. They recognized that their problems were global in nature and required global coordination to conquer. The US and China abandoned their struggle for hegemony and led the world toward a global federation, established in 2084.

Readings

Most of the ideas and theories in this book came from things I read. To avoid sounding like a lot of book reviews I've put most of the information about those things here. Rather than including all the usual citation information, I suggest you Google the author and title, search Wikipedia, or search your favorite commercial service.

Douglas Adams, *The Hitchhiker's Guide to the Galaxy*.

Karim Amer, *The Great Hack* is a Netflix documentary telling the story of Facebook and Cambridge Analytical shenanigans in Brexit and the 2016 US presidential election.

Aaron Bastani, *Fully Automated Luxury Communism*. He is a British Marxist optimistic that technology will produce enough wealth to pay for the change.

Susan Blackmore, *The Meme Machine*.

Philip Bobbitt, *The Shield of Achilles: War, Peace, and the Course of History* suggests the internet, along with global trade, and concealable weapons of mass destruction will cause the demise of the nation state.

Nick Bostrom, *Superintelligence: Paths, Dangers, Strategies*.

Fred Brooks, "No Silver Bullet—Essence and Accident in Software Engineering" in *Computer*. 1987.

Vannevar Bush, "As We May Think", article in *Atlantic Monthly*, July 1945.

Carlos Castaneda, *The Teachings of Don Juan: A Yaqui Way of Knowledge, A Separate Reality: Further Conversations with*

Don Juan, Journey to Ixtlan, The Lessons of Don Juan, Tales of Power.

Eric Chaisson, in *Singularity Hypotheses: A Scientific and Philosophical Assessment*.
"Energy Flows in Low-entropy Complex Systems," *Entropy*, v 17, pp 8007-8018, 2015

Gregory Chaitin, *The Limits of Mathematics* provides very satisfying explorations of non-computability functions that seem more natural than the diagonalization proofs that first proved their existence.

Akshay L Chandra, McCulloch-Pitts Neuron — Mankind's First Mathematical Model of a Biological Neuron, https://towardsdatascience.com/mcculloch-pitts-model-5fdf65ac5dd1

Clayton Christensen, *The Innovator's Dilemma: When New Technologies Cause Great Firms to Fail*.

Richard Dawkins, *The Selfish Gene*.

Daniel Dennett, *Darwin's Dangerous Idea: Evolution and the Meanings of Life* is a definitive contribution to understand the philosophy of evolution.

David Deutsch, *The Fabric of Reality: The Science of Parallel Universes--and Its Implications, The Beginning of Infinity: Explanations That Transform the World*.

Jared Diamond, *Guns, Germs, and Steel: The Fates of Human Societies*.

Simon Dingle, *In Math We Trust: The Future of Money* is about Bitcoin, light on technical details.

Douglas Engelbart, A documentary, https://www.youtube.com/watch?v=_7ZtISeGyCY.

John Kenneth Galbraith, *The Affluent Society*.

David Gelernter, *Mirror Worlds: or the Day Software Puts the Universe in a Shoebox . . . How It Will Happen and What It Will Mean* predicts the continuing revolution brought by the internet, minus the bad parts.

George Gilder, *Life After Google: The Fall of Big Data and the Rise of the Blockchain Economy.*

Bernard Glassman, *Instructions to the Cook: A Zen Master's Lessons in Living a Life That Matters* with (Rick Fields) can be summarized with the saying, "If life gives you lemons, make lemonade."

Yuval Noah Harari, *Homo Deus: A Brief History of Tomorrow* speculates that the recent breakthroughs in medicine, genetic engineering, and AI will enable some humans to become gods, living forever and wielding enormous power. He's imagining something like Dickensian England when the aristocratic humans seemed like another species.

Yuval Noah Harari, *Sapiens: A Brief History of Humankind* makes the amusing point that humanity's invention of spoken language enabled us to believe things that had no basis in reality. Religions are the most obvious example. A human can say, "Look, there is a God above the clouds, and if you all believe these stories that I've invented then you will follow the same norms and laws and values, and you can cooperate." Incidentally, Harari is a serious meditator—two hours every day plus an annual sixty-day retreat in India. He told an interviewer that meditation helped him "to learn the difference between fiction and reality, what is real and what is just stories that we invent and construct in our own minds." Money is more interesting when you realize that it depends entirely on faith. Most people can't understand why Bitcoin seems to have value, but that's because they don't realize the value of dollars is faith-based. When Peter Pan demands, at the end of a play, that the entire audience must believe that Tinker Bell is alive if she is to become alive, he is illustrating this very point.

Joseph Heinrich, *The WEIRDest People in the World*. The acronym is for Western, Educated, Independent, Rich, and Democratic. WEIRDos are 12 percent of humanity, descendants of Northern Europeans. Heinrich suggests that that the Church's prohibition against marrying your cousin loosened the grip of family and tribe and allowed WEIRD traits to develop.

Karen Holtzblatt, with Hugh Beyer, *Contextual Design*.

Chris Hughes, *Fair Shot: Rethinking Inequality and How We Earn*. He is the co-founder of Facebook who suggests a better social safety net and recognition that currently unpaid work like family caregiving be compensated.

Aldous Huxley, *Brave New World* describes a seemingly pleasant future set in a futuristic World State, whose citizens are environmentally engineered into an intelligence-based social hierarchy with hallucinogenic drugs, recreational sex, and mandatory euthanasia. The novel anticipates scientific advancements in reproductive technology, sleep-learning, psychological manipulation, and classical conditioning that are combined to make a dystopian society, which is challenged by only a single individual: the story's protagonist. [from Wikipedia]

Brave New World, NBCUniversal streaming service Peacock. The series "imagines a utopian society that has achieved

343

peace and stability through the prohibition of monogamy, privacy, money, family, and history itself." In an addition to the original novel, an artificial intelligence system named Indra connects citizens via a wireless network.

Daniel Kahneman, *Thinking, Fast and Slow*.

Alan Kay, Talk about the history of workstations, https://www.youtube.com/watch?v=GMDphyKrAE8.

John Maynard Keynes, *The General Theory of Employment, Interest and Money*.

Elisabeth Kübler-Ross, *On Death and Dying* discusses stages of grieving and suggests that people feel the need for permission to die.

Ray Kurzweil, *The Singularity Is Near: When Humans Transcend Biology*.

Alan Lakein, *How to Get Control of Your Time and Your Life* starts off by demanding that the reader answer the "What would you do if you had one year to live" question and goes on to assert goals are more important than efficiency.

Kai-Fu Lee, *AI Superpowers: China, Silicon Valley, and the New World Order*.

Lawrence Lessig, *Code and Other Laws of Cyberspace* explains how cyberspace differs from the real world and asserts that the real world can control it.

Lawrence Lessig, *Republic, Lost: How Money Corrupts Congress—and a Plan to Stop It*.

Daniel J. Levinson, *The Seasons of a Man's Life* claimed that most men went through significant changes around twenty, forty, and sixty-five—changes just as noticeable as the "terrible twos" and other childhood phases. Until reading it, I'd thought that adulthood was just one thing after another.

Lillian Lieber, *The Einstein Theory of Relativity*. An amazing book I poured over in high school. It attempts to explain the theories using the appropriate mathematics.

Pamela McCorduck, *Machines Who Think* contains excellent sketches of some AI pioneers.

Geoffrey Miller, *The Mating Mind: How Sexual Choice Shaped the Evolution of Human Nature*.

Hans Moravec, *Mind Children*, a prescient analysis of robotics.

Hans Moravec, *Robot*

Allen Newell, *The Psychology of Human-Computer Interaction*. (with S. Card and T. Moran)

James Ogilvy, *Living without a Goal*.

Tim O'Reilly, "A Tale of Two Platforms", https://marker.medium.com/a-tale-of-two-platforms-e9138cb8efed.

Jeff Orlowski, *The Social Dilemma* is a Netflix documentary designed to raise an alarm about the FANG. https://deadline.com/2021/01/the-social-dilemma-director-jeff-orlowski-netflix-documentary-interview-news-1234678324/.

Steven Pinker, *The Better Angels of Our Nature: Why Violence Has Declined*.

Thomas Piketty, *Capital in the Twenty-First Century* uses economic history to show that "the rich get richer" is inevitable in unconstrained capitalism.

Karl Popper, *Conjectures and Refutations* lays out his influential philosophy of science.

Eric Posner & Glen Weyl, *Radical Markets: Uprooting Capitalism and Democracy for a Just Society*.

Matt Ridley, *The Evolution of Everything: How New Ideas Emerge* asserts that all good things come from emergent behavior. He is a cautionary example of how evolutionary thinking slips into libertarianism.

Douglas Rushkoff, *Team Human* is a compelling pep talk to practice human qualities.

AnnaLee Saxenian, *Regional Advantage: Culture and Competition in Silicon Valley and Route 128.*

Caleb Scharf, *The Ascent of Information* is an incredibly ambitious attempt to explain life, the universe, and everything, drawing on a huge number of recent research in physics, information theory, and biology.

Herbert Simon, *Models of My Life.*

Herbert Simon, *The Sciences of the Artificial.*

William Strauss and Neil Howe, *The Fourth Turning: An American Prophecy.*

Neal Stephenson, *Snow Crash* describes a World Wide Web. *The Diamond Age: Or, a Young Lady's Illustrated Primer* imagines a personal device which learns about its owner. *Cryptonomicon* describes cloud storage.

Jerry Sternin, et al. *The Power of Positive Deviance: How Unlikely Innovators Solve the World's Toughest Problems.* Describes a method to promote cultural change. Some case studies.

James Suzman, *Work: A Deep History, from the Stone Age to the Age of Robots.*

Pierre Teilhard de Chardin, *The Phenomenon of Man* suggests that humans will evolve to an omega-point, a convergence with the Devine.

Frank Tipler, *The Physics of Immortality* attempts to use physics to resuscitate Christian doctrine.

Alvin Toffler, *Future Shock* and *The Third Wave* heralded the information age, following the agricultural and industrial ages.

Peter Turchin, *Ultrasociety: How 10,000 Years of War Made Humans the Greatest Cooperators on Earth.*

John von Neumann, *Theory of Games and Economic Behavior* (with Oskar Morgenstern). The book began the field of game theory.

Kurt Vonnegut, *Player Piano*, a screed against automation.

Emilie Wapnick, "Why some of us don't have one true calling." She calls herself a multipotentialite. https://www.youtube.com/watch?v=4sZdcB6bjI8.

Norbert Wiener, *Cybernetics* was interesting but focused on old-fashioned techniques like analog feedback rather than programming.

Norbert Wiener, *The Human Use of Human Beings.*

Joseph Weizenbaum, *Computer Power and Human Reason: From Judgment to Calculation.* Surprisingly, he trashes AI as being a fraud, a menace, or both.

David Whyte, *Essentials.*

Robert Wright, *The Evolution of God* claims religions and their god(s) are polymemes that have been evolving along with us. He's hoping that continuing evolution leads to reconciliation of the world's religions to accommodate globalization.

Shoshana Zuboff, *The Age of Surveillance Capitalism* presents a compelling case that the FANG has gone rogue and should be regulated.

Index

Acknowledgements

This entire book is an acknowledgement of the many who have enlightened and entertained me. Besides my friends and professional colleagues, my wife, Susan, and my two daughters have taught me a lot.

The book would not have been written without the pandemic of 2020-21, which kept me sitting at a desk.

My editor, Janna Hockenjos, guided my journey, drawing me out to describe my life, which most reviewers found more interesting than all the computer stuff I preferred to write about. She is not a computer expert but exercised her keen intelligence to absorb most of twentieth century computer science and to lure me into clearer explanations of technically arcane ideas. Rowan Kersley astounded me with her intense proofreading. Victoria O'May designed the delightful cover.

Nathaniel Borenstein, Jay Carson, Douglas Van Houweling, Bob Sproull, Paul McJones, John Shoch, Jon, Lloyd, Jim Kelly, George Fairbanks, Virgil Gligor, and Alan and Barbara Ackerman read drafts and gave me excellent advice.

About the Author

James H. Morris is a Professor Emeritus of Computer Science and Human-Computer Interaction at Carnegie Mellon University. He received a bachelor's degree from Carnegie Tech, and an MS in management and PhD in Computer Science from MIT. He taught at the University of California at Berkeley where he contributed to some important underlying principles of programming languages. He was a co-discoverer of the Knuth-Morris-Pratt string searching algorithm. For nine years he worked at the Xerox Palo Alto Research Center where he was part of the team that developed a precursor to today's computer environment. From 1983 to 1988 he directed the Information Technology Center at Carnegie Mellon, a joint project with IBM, which developed a prototype university computing system, Andrew. From 1992 to 2004 he served as department head, then dean in the School of Computer Science. He held the Herbert A. Simon Professorship of Human Computer Interaction from 1997 to 2000. He was the dean of the Silicon Valley campus from 2004 to 2009. He was a founder of MAYA Design, a consulting firm specializing in interactive product design. He also founded Carnegie Mellon's Human Computer Interaction Institute, Robot Hall of Fame, and Silicon Valley Campus. He has written columns for the *Pittsburgh Post-Gazette* and the *Pittsburgh Quarterly*.

Made in the USA
Middletown, DE
17 November 2021